Levine's Guide to SPSS for Analysis of Variance

2nd Edition

Melanie C. Page
Oklahoma State University

Sanford L. Braver
Arizona State University

David P. MacKinnon
Arizona State University

Levine's Guide to SPSS for Analysis of Variance

2nd Edition

Melanie C. Page
Oklahoma State University

Sanford L. Braver
Arizona State University

David P. MacKinnon
Arizona State University

Routledge
Taylor & Francis Group
New York London

Routledge is an imprint of the
Taylor & Francis Group, an informa business

Cover design by Kathryn Houghtaling Lacey

Library of Congress Cataloging-in-Publication Data

Page, Melanie C.-
    Levine's guide to SPSS for analysis of variance / Melanie C. Page, Sanford L. Braver,
David P. Mackinnon.— 2nd ed.
        p. cm.
    Rev. ed. of: A guide to SPSS for analysis of variance. 1991.
    Includes bibliographical references and index.
    ISBN 0-8058-3095-2 (cloth : alk. paper) — ISBN 0-8058-3096-0 (pbk. : alk. paper)
    1. SPSS (Computer file) 2. Analysis of variance— Computer programs. I. Page, Melanie
C. II. Braver, Sanford L. III. Mackinnon, David Peter, 1957– IV. Title.

HA31.35 L48 2003
519.5'0285'5369— dc21   2003040883
                                                             CIP

In addition to the sources cited in the text for the data set used, several additional data sets are included on the
CD-Rom and are from the following sources:

From *The analysis of covariance and alternatives*. (p. 225), by B. E. Huitema, 1980, New York, John Wiley & Sons.
Copyright 1980 by John Wiley & Sons, Inc. This material is used by permission of John Wiley & Sons, Inc.

From *Design and Analysis: A Researcher's Handbook* (p. 161), by G. Keppel, 1991, Upper Saddle River, NJ, Pearson Education.
Copyright 1991 by Pearson Education, Inc. Reprinted with permission.

J. P. Stevens (1999). *Intermediate statistics: A modern approach* (2nd ed.), p. 174.
Copyright by Lawrence Erlbaum Associates. Reprinted with permission.

J. P. Stevens (1999). *Intermediate statistics: A modern approach* (2nd ed.), p. 358.
Copyright by Lawrence Erlbaum Associates. Reprinted with permission.

From *Computer-assisted research deign and analysis* (p.417), B. G. Tabachnick & L. S. Fidell, 2001, Needham Heights, MA, Allyn & Bacon.
Copyright 2001 by Pearson Education, Inc. Reprinted/adapted by permission of the publisher.

From *Statistical principles in experimental design* (3rd ed.) (p.853), B. J. Winer, D. R. Brown, & K. M. Michels, 1991, New York, McGraw-
Hill. Copyright 1991 by The McGraw Hill Companies, Inc.

Books published by Lawrence Erlbaum Associates are printed on acid-free paper,
and their bindings are chosen for strength and durability.

10 9 8 7 6 5 4 3

Contents

Preface

In the decade since the publication of the first edition of this guide (Levine, 1991), and despite the development of several more specialized statistical techniques, analysis of variance (ANOVA) continues to be the workhorse for many behavioral science researchers. This guide provides instructions and examples for running analyses of variance, as well as several other related statistical tests of significance, with the popular and powerful SPSS statistical software package (SPSS, 2001). Although other computer manuals exist describing the use of SPSS, none of them offer the program statements required for the more advanced tests in analysis of variance, placing these needed programs out of reach. This manual remedies this situation by providing the needed program statements, thus offering more complete utilization of the computational power of SPSS. All of the programs in this book can be run using any version of SPSS, including the recently released Version 11. (SPSS is currently available for a variety of computer system platforms, including mainframe, Windows, and Macintosh versions.)

SPSS for Windows has two methods by which analyses can be conducted: either through the pull-down menu method, in which you point with and then click the mouse (which is henceforth referred to as point-and-click or PAC), or by writing programs. These programs are called *syntax* and include the commands and subcommands that tell SPSS what to do. Mainframe applications only use syntax. The personal computer packages for SPSS use both syntax and PAC (the exception being the student version for Windows, which lacks many advanced analyses and does not use syntax). To be able to describe the full spectrum of available analyses and address the needs of the widest number of users, we focus more heavily on syntax, while still including examples for PAC. An additional reason for stressing syntax rather than PAC is that mistakes in the former are more easily recognized and corrected, assuring the user of the validity of the analysis being performed. The principle motive, however, is that there are useful analyses that cannot be performed through current PAC menus (e.g., simple effects).

PAC methods, however, are not slighted. Generally, these too are fully described (albeit comparatively briefly, as befits their lesser capabilities), typically at the end of each chapter. (An exception is chap. 2, where including PAC methods at the ends of the various subsections, e.g., data entry, data importation, saving data, and printing data, made more sense.) Those users intending to use only PAC methods may choose to go directly to those sections.

There are a number of separate programs included within SPSS that are available for ANOVA analyses. These include the ONEWAY, UNIANOVA, GLM, and MANOVA programs. Although portions of the text cover each of these programs (where appropriate), we chose the MANOVA program for primary explication throughout the book, because we find it maximizes the joint criteria of flexibility, power, and ease of use. We find, for example, that there are no analyses of variance tests that cannot be conducted one way or another by MANOVA, whereas the same is not true for the other programs. A seeming disadvantage of the MANOVA procedure, however, is that it is the only one currently unavailable through PAC. Because we feel that PAC methods are useful only for the simplest of analyses, this is not viewed as a shortcoming.

USING THIS BOOK

Readers will generally find complete sets of commands that can be directly applied to their desired analyses, with only the variable names or number of levels of factors having to be changed. The required syntax modifications for making these changes are discussed and illustrated in detail. In addition, methods of combining program syntax for performing several analyses in the same program are presented.

This book will be very useful to readers who already have or who are in the process of acquiring a substantial background and knowledge of the basic concepts of the ANOVA technique. Thus, the intended audience includes practicing researchers and data analysts, as well as advanced undergraduate and graduate students who are learning analysis of variance, for whom the book can readily serve as a supplement to their primary textbook. The authors believe that, before relying on any computer program, you should thoroughly understand what the computer is (or should be) doing with the data. This basic knowledge is essential for properly applying the data to test the desired effect, for understanding the output, and for confirming that the output is plausible and rational. Although this book provides cursory explanations of most ANOVA concepts, such as planned contrasts, interactions, power, and so forth, we do not attempt to provide thorough coverage of these ideas. A full explication of these concepts may be found instead in standard statistics textbooks describing ANOVA. Such textbooks almost always also feature complete coverage of the computational steps you would follow if you wished to conduct an ANOVA or any specific variant with calculations using a hand calculator or spreadsheet program. Thus, the book is profitably used simultaneously with coverage of an ANOVA textbook, which typically provides little on computer applications.

Alternatively, the book can be used as a reference work or handbook for those users with a working knowledge of ANOVA who need specific instructions in conducting specialized analyses, such as interaction contrasts in mixed two-factor designs. To facilitate this use, Table P1 indicates where each type of analysis (e.g., simple comparisons) can be found for each type of design (e.g., mixed two-factor design).

WHAT'S NEW

The first edition of this book was the first to offer the needed syntax for such analyses as interactions of contrasts, simple contrasts in multifactor designs, and other advanced tests people are likely to use in multifactor designs. However, some of that syntax is now out of date. In this second edition we have updated the old syntax to keep this material available. The authors acknowledge their debt to Gustav Levine for working out the syntax for the first edition (Levine, 1991).

In addition, the second edition of the book has been completely reorganized to provide all analyses related to one design type within the same chapter. Moreover, more examples of output and how to interpret that output are provided. We have also expanded the coverage of several topics, including analysis of covariance and mixed designs. Furthermore, we have added chapters on designs with random factors and multivariate designs. We have also included a CD-ROM with all of the data sets used in the book, as well as data sets to be used with the exercises found on the CD-ROM. Finally, we have made the simpler analyses easier to perform by explaining and illustrating the use of PAC SPSS, which offers a visually intuitive context for the less exhaustive analyses, as well as including a chapter detailing the syntax that PAC uses.

CONTENT

Chapter 1 introduces the guide and conventions used throughout the book. Chapter 2 is a basic chapter for people not already familiar with SPSS. It provides both the syntax and PAC sequences to read in data and perform simple data transformations (e.g., compute new variables). It is then possible to read or refer to the remaining chapters independently. Each of the next seven chapters (3

TABLE P1
Table of Topics

Chapter	Basic Analysis	(Main Effect) Contrasts	(Main Effect) Post Hocs (and Post Hocs on Marginals)	(Main Effect) Trends	Two-Factor Interaction	Simple Effects	Simple Comparisons (and Simple Post Hocs) (and Simple Trends)	Interaction Contrasts (and Trend Interactions)	Three-Way Interactions	Simple Two-Way	Simple Simple Effects	Simple Simple Comparisons	Simple Interaction Contrasts	Doubly Multivariate
3: One factor	20	25	28	32										
4: Two factor	42	49	50	50	45	51	52	53, 55						
5: Three or more factor	59					63	64	64	62	62	63	65	65	
6: One factor, within subjects	67	72	75	73										
7: Two or more factor, within subjects	81	84	92	84	84	88	89, 90	90, 92, 93	92	93	93	93	93	
8: Two-factor mixed	97	100	109	109	99	104	107	104						
9: Three or more, mixed	111	114				113	116	114	112	112	113	116	116	
10: ANCOVA	120, 125, 127	124	124											
11: Random factors	132													
12: Multivariate	145	149, 153	149						NA	NA	NA	NA	NA	150
13: UNIANOVA and GLM syntax	166, 177, 183	168, 171, 178, 180	171, 179	168, 178	171, 179	174, 181	176, 181	176, 180		NA	NA	NA		

Note. Numbers in table are the page numbers on which the topic may be found.

through 9) focuses on a particular type of ANOVA design and includes the commands for the types of tests that are available for that design. In these chapters, as with all chapters, most of the syntax programs presented are followed by annotated printout and information on how to interpret and report the output. Chapters 3 through 5 deal with between-subjects designs, where all the factors vary between the subjects. The three chapters deal with, respectively, one-factor, two-factor, and three or more factor between-subjects designs. Each chapter also discusses the kinds of specialized analyses (e.g., planned contrasts, trend analyses, simple effects) appropriate to that design. The next two chapters, 6 and 7, deal with within-subjects (or repeated measures) designs, where each participant receives exposure to more than one condition. Chapter 6 deals with one-factor within-subjects designs and two or more factors are covered in chapter 7. Chapter 8 deals with the two-factor mixed design, in which one factor is between subjects and the other is within subjects; chapter 9 considers three- or more factor mixed designs.

The remaining chapters deal with a number of topics related to ANOVA that are of special interest. Chapter 10 discusses analysis of covariance (ANCOVA) and chapter 11 explains designs containing random factors, including more information on within-subjects designs and ANCOVA using a specialized one-line-per-level approach. Chapter 12 introduces multiple true dependent variables and uses the multivariate capabilities of MANOVA and GLM. Finally, chapter 13 describes the syntax for the UNIANOVA and GLM programs, designed for those users who prefer them to MANOVA for their specialized analyses.

Although some later chapters make reference to concepts learned in earlier chapters, chapters 3 through 13 have largely been written with just enough redundancy so that it is not necessary to go through the entire book when dealing with a single design or a single type of test. Thus the guide is as readily used as a handbook or reference manual as it is as a textbook. Each chapter concludes with coverage of the PAC methods available from SPSS for Windows (Version 11).

ACKNOWLEDGMENTS

The authors would like to collectively thank all of those at Lawrence Erlbaum Associates who have been so helpful to us, including Debra Riegert, Jason Planer, Eileen Engel, and Art Lizza. We would also like to thank all of our students (undergraduate and graduate at Oklahoma State University and Arizona State University) and the reviewers for their useful suggestions: Richard G. Lomax, University of Alabama; George A. Morgan and Nancy L. Leach, Colorado State University; and Tenko Raykov, Fordham University. Individually, Melanie would like to thank her family, especially Darren and Jayden, for their patience and encouragement during this process and her department for their support. Sandy would like to thank his wife, Jodi M. Bernstein, and the PIRC staff. Dave would like to thank Kim, Lea, and Ross for their patience.

1 Using SPSS and Using This Book

This book explains how to perform numerous variants of a certain type of highly useful and common statistical analysis called *analysis of variance* (frequently shortened to ANOVA) using the SPSS computer software package, one of the most widely used and taught statistical software programs. As mentioned in the Preface, SPSS is available for several different platforms, including Windows, mainframe, and Macintosh versions, and knowledge of how SPSS is to be accessed is necessary and will not be provided here. It is assumed instead that the user will obtain the necessary information to access SPSS at the site where the program is to be run.

CONVENTIONS FOR SYNTAX PROGRAMS

The syntax programs provided in this book can be run on any of the previously mentioned computer platforms (except the student version of Windows, which does not allow syntax programming). The creation and editing of SPSS syntax programs depends on the platform and, for mainframe users, on the details of the installation and operating system. For Windows users, creation and editing of SPSS syntax programs is described near the end of the present chapter. Each syntax program presented is followed by an explanation of the different lines (or commands) in the program. The following conventions are used in this book when presenting syntax programs: The program commands and SPSS keywords are all presented in capital letters (however, they do not actually need to be typed as capital letters in order to operate properly).[1] The parts of any command or subcommand that are specific to a data set or analysis, in contrast, are all in lower case letters. It is assumed that a <RETURN> (or <ENTER>, depending upon the keyboard) will follow each command (i.e., program statement). These <RETURN>s are omitted in all figures in the book.

The numbers in the figures that precede each of the program statements are line numbers and are there only for reference within this text—**you should not type them in**. A lowercase *o* next to a line number indicates that that line is optional; if there is a lowercase *d* next to a line number, that line is also optional, but highly desirable.

A syntax program generally consists of both commands and subcommands and the specifications for each. In SPSS, any information that begins in the first column of a line begins a new command. Thus, any command that continues beyond one line must be indented (typically two or more indented spaces are apparent to the programmer). Subcommands always begin with a forward slash (/). They can follow on the same line as the command to which they refer or be put on separate lines

---

[1]For the sake of economy, the initial word of every command, subcommand, or keyword in SPSS can be safely abbreviated to the first four characters. Thus, a keyword introduced in the next chapter is "DIFFERENCE", which could be abbreviated as "DIFF". In this book, however, the full spelling is always used.

(as long as you indent on every new line). (Note that it is usually clearer to put subcommands on separate lines, as is the convention in this book.) SPSS commands and subcommands and their placement will become clearer as you see more examples in this book. In the programs presented here, SPSS commands end with a period; if a command is followed by a series of subcommands, the period is placed after the final subcommand. On some mainframe programs, this command terminator is not used. Check with your local mainframe staff about this. SPSS for Windows commands must end with a period.

Within the text descriptions of the programs, when we refer to a specific command or subcommand keyword, we capitalize and put it in double quotes. An exception is when we refer to something the programs do (e.g., MANOVA) rather than referring to them as a command: In the former case we simply capitalize. We also put any wording that is a direct quote from the output in double quotes (using the same combination of cases seen in the output). We use single quotes when we are referring to specifications for a command (or subcommand) that refers to some specific variable(s) in your data set. When we refer to commands in PAC, we use the exact combination of cases that is seen on the screen.

CREATING SYNTAX PROGRAMS IN WINDOWS

For Windows users, we describe how to create syntax programs here. First, open SPSS by clicking on its icon (and if necessary clicking cancel or the ⊠ at the top of the screen shown in Fig. 1.1).

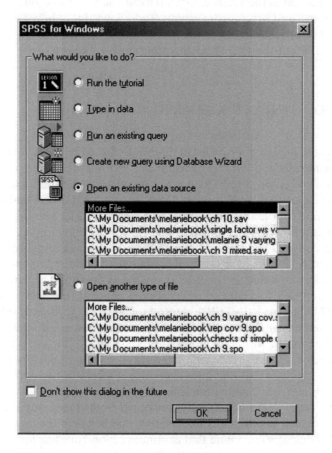

FIG. 1.1. Opening window when SPSS for Windows is accessed.

To begin writing syntax, click on File, then New, then Syntax (in future discussion, such click sequences will have a long dash between click options of the menus, as in File–New–Syntax), as seen in Fig. 1.2.

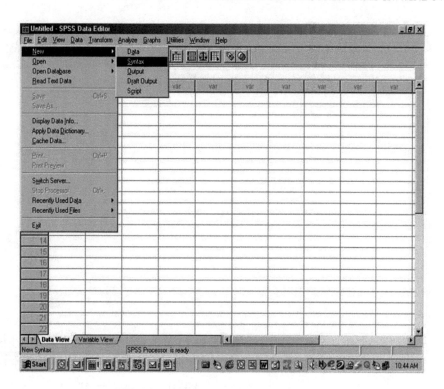

FIG. 1.2.   Opening a new Syntax window.

This will open up a new syntax window that looks like the one in Fig. 1.3.

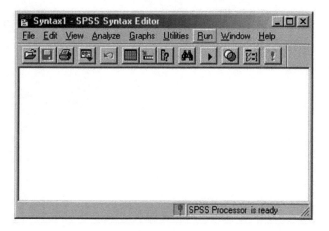

FIG. 1.3.   Blank Syntax window.

You may now begin typing in the commands and subcommands that comprise SPSS programs into the window, as described in the following chapters. Assume that the three lines seen in Fig. 1.4 were typed in by you, and constituted all that you wished to enter. You would then click on Run–All, as pictured in Fig. 1.4, to obtain the data analysis (you could also highlight all of the text and then click on the small arrow seen near the right side of the toolbar in Fig. 1.3).

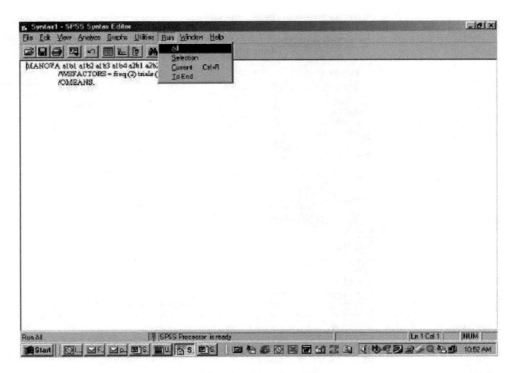

FIG. 1.4. Using Run–All.

The remaining chapters use these conventions and syntax to ready data for analysis and to conduct the analysis by ANOVA or related techniques.

2 Reading in and Transforming Variables for Analysis in SPSS

Before any data can be analyzed by SPSS with the technique termed *analysis of variance* (ANOVA), the data to be analyzed must be introduced to, or entered into, SPSS. Subsequent chapters explain how to perform the several variants of ANOVA presuming that the data are already entered. This chapter's focus is to provide information on how to get the variables into SPSS beforehand. Methods for reading in or directly entering the data are described, as well as those for performing simple data transformations (e.g., computing an average).

READING IN DATA WITH SYNTAX

Before examining the syntax in Fig. 2.1, the reader is strongly advised to reread the syntax conventions discussed in the previous chapter. For example, the line numbers are not to be typed in.

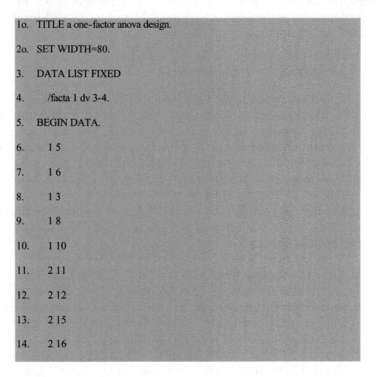

```
1o.   TITLE a one-factor anova design.

2o.   SET WIDTH=80.

3.    DATA LIST FIXED

4.       /facta 1 dv 3-4.

5.    BEGIN DATA.

6.       1 5

7.       1 6

8.       1 3

9.       1 8

10.      1 10

11.      2 11

12.      2 12

13.      2 15

14.      2 16
```

FIG. 2.1.   *(Continues)*

15.	2 9
16.	3 1
17.	3 9
18.	3 5
19.	3 8
20.	3 10
21.	END DATA.

FIG. 2.1.   Syntax commands to read in data.

The first statement in Fig. 2.1, "TITLE", is an optional command (i.e., it is perfectly acceptable to leave it off; note the *o* beside the line number) that allows the user to specify a title in the printout. You decide what the title should be. In this example, 'a one-factor anova design' was used. The title does not in any way affect the analysis. It will simply appear at the top of each page of the printout. The space between the command "TITLE" and the actual title is required. If you wish to use a long descriptive title, you may continue the title on the next line. To do this, simply indent the second line one space. However, SPSS will only repeat the first 60 letters of the title at the top of every page. Additional descriptive information can be added to the top of every page with the "SUBTITLE" command. The "SUBTITLE" command is placed on the line following the "TITLE" command, with the actual subtitle separated from the "SUBTITLE" command by a space as follows:

SUBTITLE example from chapter 2 of Page et al.

By default on many platforms, SPSS prints the results or output of your requested analyses on lines that are 132 characters wide. The optional command on line 2 reduces the size of the output to 80 columns, which will make it easier for you to see the entire output on your computer screen and, moreover, the output will fit on an 8.5- × 11-in. piece of paper. In SPSS for Windows, this control over output size is given on Edit–Options–Viewer (or Draft Viewer); then click the desired alternative on Text Output.

Entering Data with the "DATA LIST" Command

One of the most crucial steps in programming is telling the statistical package how to "read" your data file. There are several ways to do this, including, in Windows, typing values directly into the Data Editor Window, which is described later. The most general method, available to both nonWindows and Windows users, is through the use of syntax, specifically the "DATA LIST" command on line 3 in Fig. 2.1, which tells SPSS (a) where the data are and (b) what value to give each variable (or measure, or score) for each participant. If you have a very small data set, you may want to type the data within the SPSS program, as was done in the example of Fig. 2.1. If your data set is large, however, you may prefer to type the data in another file called an external file (a separate file of just data), which you will read into the program with the "DATA LIST" command, to be described later in this chapter.

The first example, however, assumes that the data are within the SPSS program, as in the example in Fig. 2.1. As seen in line 3, the command "DATA LIST" is followed by a keyword describing the type of format of the data, "FIXED" or "FREE" (more on this later). This line is followed by a subcommand (here in line 4; recall, however, that subcommands need not be on different lines) that provides the names you wish to give the variables and, for "FIXED" format, their column locations. Thus, this subcommand will tell SPSS which variables are in which columns for "FIXED" or in which order for "FREE". In this example of "FIXED", as will be explained in more detail later, line 4 specifies that the variable to be called 'facta' is in column 1 and the variable to be called 'dv' is in columns 3 and 4. Because, in this example, the data are included in the program, the "BEGIN

DATA" command on line 5 is used, followed by all of the data in lines 6 through 20 (in the columns or order specified on the "DATA LIST" command), followed by the "END DATA" command in line 21.

"FREE" or "FIXED" Data Format

The data format can be "FIXED" or "FREE". "FREE" format data indicates that each participant's score on each variable will be separated by one or more blank spaces. Furthermore, scores on a given variable may be located in different columns for different participants. However, the measures must be entered in the same order for all participants. Following is an example of a "DATA LIST" command for "FREE" format. To be particularly clear here, the blank spaces in the data are indicated with a "^":

DATA LIST FREE
   /id age m1 m2 m3.

So for the following data:

   142^48^4^^16^7
   78^^24^1^2^^33

SPSS will understand that, for the first participant (i.e., the first line of data just presented), the variable you wish to call 'id' is to have the value 142, the variable you want called 'age' is to have the value 48, that he or she is to get a 4 on the variable you want called 'm1' (perhaps shorthand for "Measure 1"), a 16 on 'm2', and a 7 on 'm3'. For the second participant (second line of data), the participant's 'id' is 78, his or her 'age' is 24, and he or she got a 1 on 'm1', a 2 on 'm2', and a 33 on 'm3'. (Note that there is inconsistently more than one space between scores; this is completely permissible with the "FREE" data format.)

Names you wish to give to variables can have no more than eight characters and they cannot begin with a number. Additionally, there are some sets of letters that can form keywords for some commands and, therefore, must be avoided as names. The sets of letters that you cannot use as variable names are the following: ALL, AND, BY, EQ, GE, GT, LT, LE, LT, NE, NOT, OR, TO, and WITH. Ideally, the variable names should also be mnemonic, easily recognized by you later. For example, if the first variable in the data file represents a participant's identification number, you might call that variable 'subjid' or 'id'. The program must be consistent in the use of the names in the "DATA LIST" and other later (e.g., "MANOVA") commands referring to the same variables.

"FIXED" is the other common data format. It is the default and thus the keyword "FIXED" does not actually have to be typed in if your data are in "FIXED" format. "FIXED" format means that the data are organized so that each variable is stored in a particular column (or columns). In this format, the subcommand contains an ordered list of the variable names you wish to use, each followed by the specific column or a successive series of columns where that variable is found. The columns containing a specific measure must be the same for all participants. Here is an example:

DATA LIST FIXED
   /id 1-3 age 4-5 m1 6 m2 7-8 m3 9-10.

Note that each variable is followed by a single digit or series of digits. The '6' following 'm1', for example, tells SPSS that 'm1' can always be found in column 6 for every participant. In contrast, 'id', 'age', 'm2', and 'm3' are more than single digit variables; the first number following each refers to the column containing the first digit of the variable and the final number refers to the column containing the last digit of the variable. These are separated by a dash ('-') in the subcommand. Thus, 'id' is in columns 1 through 3 and 'age' is in columns 4 through 5. Thus, for the following data:

   14248416^7
   ^78241^233

the first participant's ID number is 142 (first 3 columns), his or her 'age' is 48, and he or she got a 4 on 'm1', a 16 on 'm2', and a 7 on 'm3'. For the second participant (i.e., second line of data), the 'id' is 78, the 'age' is 24, and 'm1', 'm2', and 'm3' are 1, 2, and 33, respectively. Note that, when a variable is declared by the "DATA LIST" to have more than one column, but a certain participant has a value that requires less columns than specified, the columns to the left are blank. For example, whereas 'm2' has columns 7 through 8 devoted to it, the second participant's value is only one column long, the value 2. The initial column (i.e., 10's place) is therefore left blank (this process is called *right justifying*).

If a variable beginning in, say, the sixth column was called 'm1', the seventh column 'm2', and the eighth 'm3', you could refer to the column numbers just once, as with:

```
/m1 m2 m3 6-8.
```

or

```
/m1 TO m3 6-8.
```

If the variables took up more than one space, but all took up the same number of spaces, the same economy of space indication would be possible. For example:

```
/k1 k2 k3 10-15.
```

or

```
/k1 TO k3 10-15.
```

would mean that the variable 'k1' is in spaces 10 and 11, 'k2' is in 12 and 13, and 'k3' is in 14 and 15. The following three subcommand lines tell SPSS the same thing and are interchangeable:

```
/id 1-3 age 4-5 m1 6 m2 7 m3 8 iq 24-26.
/id 1-3 age 4-5 m1 m2 m3 6-8 iq 24-26.
/id 1-3 age 4-5 m1 TO m3 6-8 iq 24-26.
```

The "TO" shortcut is an excellent shortcut to enter a series of variables whose names differ only by the sequential number at the end. (In subsequent commands, the "TO" keyword can be used in a different way, as a shortcut to identify variables that were sequentially named on the "DATA LIST" or later created with transformations. For example, suppose the "DATA LIST" creates data in this order: q2, x, v3, iq, v4. Then 'q2 TO v4' can be used in later commands to refer to this set of successive variables.)

Look back at Fig. 2.1, beginning with line 6, and observe the succeeding rows. The first number in each row ranges between 1 and 3; that is because there are three values to the variable called 'facta'. The first five participants (each having a separate line) are in the first value or "level" of 'facta', the next five are in the second level or group, and so on. The second number for each participant refers to that participant's score on the dependent variable, called 'dv'.

Some Special Cases

You can leave blank spaces between the numbers in "FIXED" format; just be sure to skip the same columns each time and be sure to identify the correct starting columns for your variables. Occasionally, you might have a string (i.e., text, word, or alphabetic) variable, in which the value is not a number, but a letter or string of letters. For example, imagine that you have recorded gender in the data in column 7 as M or F, rather than, say, 1 or 2. In this case, you would follow its name in the subcommand with an "(a)", that is, 'gender (a) 7'.

Sometimes you may have a variable that inherently contains a decimal place but you have not actually typed the decimal place in the data. In this case, you may identify the number of decimal places you wish the variable to have in parentheses in the subcommand (e.g., 'gpa 8-10(2)'). This would tell SPSS that the variable 'gpa' is found in columns 8 through 10 and that columns 9 and 10 should be considered decimal places. For example, if you entered 347 for a participant in columns 8 through 10 and read it using the above format, the computer would read this as 3.47. Alternatively, you may choose to type the decimal place itself right into the data (e.g., type 3.47 into the set of data, rather than 347). Then, just allow an extra column for the "explicit" decimal place in the "DATA LIST" (e.g., 'gpa 8-11' instead of 'gpa 8-10'). This alternative allows different participants to have different numbers of decimal places.

Another possibility is that you have more than one line of data per participant. For example, if your data were in "FIXED" format but you had data for each participant on three successive lines, you would use:

```
DATA LIST FIXED RECORDS=3.
```

If this was the case, the "DATA LIST" command would be followed by multiple subcommands, each starting with a successive (line) number, telling the location of the variables for that line of data in the data file. For example, with 'RECORDS=3' you might have:

```
/1 facta 1 m1 to m6 2-7
/2 m7 1 m8 4-5 m9 6
/3 iq 1-3.
```

In this example, the participant's 'facta' is found in column 1 of the first line of the three lines of data each participant has. Variables 'm1' through 'm6' are found in columns 2, 3, 4, 5, 6, and 7, respectively, on the first line of data as well. On the second line of each participant's data, 'm7' is in column 1, 'm8' is in columns 4 through 5 (note that nothing useful for this program is found in columns 2 through 3) and 'm9' is in column 6. Then, on the final line of each participant's data, 'iq' is read in from columns 1 through 3. If you have only one line of data per participant, only one subcommand is used and you do not need the line number. Of course, if the multiple record data are in "FREE" format, no column numbers are necessary.

SYNTAX FOR USING EXTERNAL DATA

If the data are already stored on the computer in an external file, you have to identify your data file so that it can be retrieved and used by the program. To do this, add the "FILE" keyword to the "DATA LIST" command. (The specifications "FREE" or "FIXED", "RECORDS", and "FILE" can be in any order.)

```
DATA LIST FILE=exmp1
   /facta 1 dv 3-4.
```

In the example just presented, the name of the previously created data file to be analyzed is 'exmp1'. In this case, you would delete all the lines of Fig. 2.1 from "BEGIN DATA" through "END DATA". The exact form of the specification of "FILE" (here 'exmp1') varies depending on the platform. Some computer operating systems may require additional specifications for locating and retrieving the file from within the system; SPSS for Windows requires single quotes around the filename and the complete path specification. Such information for other platforms can be obtained at the local computer site.

DATA ENTRY FOR SPSS FOR WINDOWS USERS

Some additional methods of data entry are available to Windows users of SPSS. The most important involves the use of the Data Editor, which allows data to be entered directly. This Window can be seen in Fig 2.2.

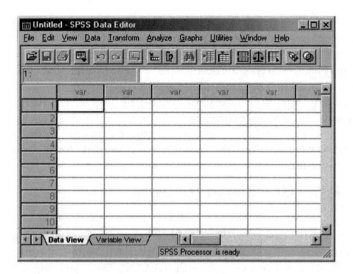

FIG. 2.2.   The Data Editor window in PAC.

As shown in Fig. 2.2, the main part of the screen is divided into columns (marked "var") and numbered rows or lines. Each line represents a participant and each column is a variable. If you ran the syntax in lines 3 through 21 of Fig. 2.1 (by clicking Run–All), the Data Editor would now look as in Fig. 2.3. As shown, the two columns are now called 'facta' and 'dv', respectively, and there are 15 rows of participant data.

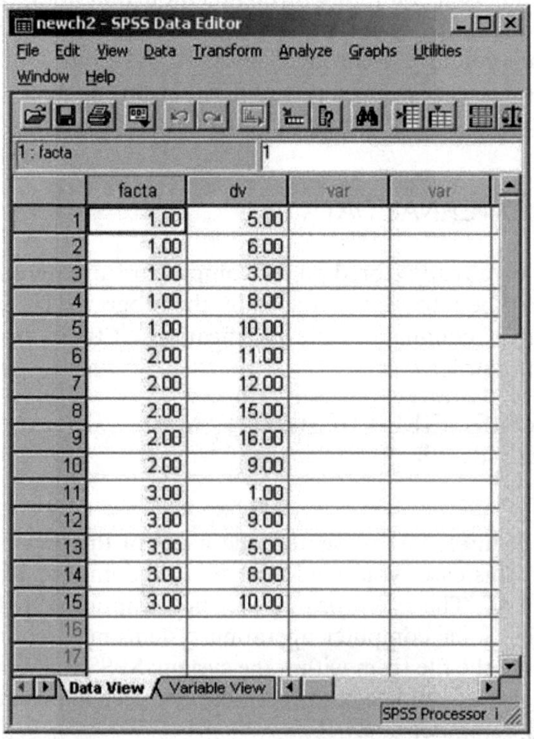

FIG. 2.3.   Data Editor window after running the syntax in Fig. 2.1.

You can also type data directly into a blank Data Editor window, navigating the cells with the keyboard's cursor keys or with the Tab and Return keys. When doing so, SPSS automatically assigns the variable names 'var00001' and 'var00002', respectively, to the data typed in, as shown in Fig. 2.4.

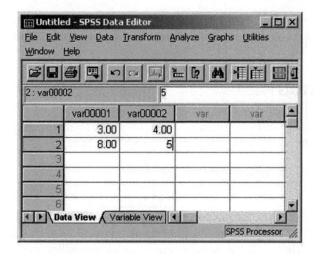

FIG. 2.4.   Data Editor window before variable names are assigned.

These variable names can be changed into more mnemonic names by clicking on the Variable View tab (this is available only on Windows versions beyond 9). When doing so, a new screen appears, which allows you to change variable names and specifications (see Fig. 2.5).

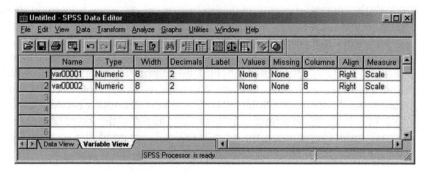

FIG. 2.5.   The Variable View window in the Data Editor.

By double clicking 'var00001', for example, you can then type in a preferred name for the first variable. You may return to the previous screen by clicking the Data View tab.

IMPORTING DATA

SPSS can also read many different types of file formats, often without loss of formatting information such as variable names. This makes opening data files as easy as opening a word processing document. SPSS for Windows' primary file type is the ".sav" file, which retains all variable names, values, and characteristics, all of which are restored automatically upon opening. To a lesser extent SPSS can also open standard spreadsheet files, usually retaining variable names. If you try to open an Excel file in PAC, you will receive the dialogue box shown in Fig. 2.6.

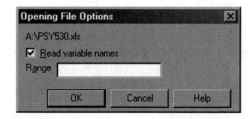

FIG. 2.6.   Dialogue box when opening an Excel file in PAC.

Be aware that earlier versions of SPSS are unable to open spreadsheets from versions of Excel beyond 4.0, so you may need to save your file as an earlier version before importing it into SPSS.

SAVING AND PRINTING FILES

After getting your data set into SPSS, you will probably wish to save it, so you can reanalyze it without reentering it. Syntax for saving SPSS data files is:

SAVE OUTFILE=filename.

The syntax for the file name depends on the platform or operating system. Windows users may also click on File–Save As, which will bring up a typical Windows Save window. Note that the extension is ".sav". There will also be occasions in which you will want to save more of your work than just the data set. Syntax commands can often become quite lengthy and complicated and you may want to save them as well. How you do this depends on your platform. From PAC, clicking File–Save from the syntax window will allow you to save your syntax. Syntax files have the ".sps" file extension. To save output, click File–Save from the output window. The format is a ".spo" file, but output may also be exported as HTML (".htm"), which works quite well, and as Rich Text Format (".rtf"), which works somewhat less well.

Both syntax and output may also be printed; as usual, how to do this depends on the platform. From Windows, when printing output you must select the items you want to include in the print job by highlighting or selecting them. There are two windows in the output viewer: the main window in which you see the actual output and a secondary window that lists the type of output in the main window (see Fig. 2.7). You can highlight items to print in either the main window or the secondary window. This tends to follow standard Windows methods: Hold <CTRL> and click on each item you want to add individually, hold <SHIFT> to add all content between click points, and so forth. Then click File–Print or the printer icon. Selecting Output at the top of the secondary window will allow you to easily print everything in the output viewer. It is a good idea to always use the Print Preview option (on the File menu) to verify that you are printing the output you desire in the format you wish.

OPENING PREVIOUSLY CREATED AND SAVED FILES

The syntax to load previously created and saved files into SPSS is:

GET FILE=filename.

From Windows, of course, an easy alternative is to click File–Open. This method can also be used to open syntax or output.

OUTPUT EXAMINATION

Once your analysis has been completed, output will be produced and should be examined. As usual, how you do this differs by platform. In Windows, an Output window is produced. Switching between the three windows (Data Editor, Syntax, and Output) is accomplished either by clicking the proper icon at the bottom of the screen or by clicking on Window at the top menu. Most of the output discussed in this book is produced by SPSS's MANOVA program. The SPSS output viewer sometimes shows only the first part of the MANOVA printout. See Fig. 2.7 for an example. The downward pointing (red) arrow at the lower left of the main (large) screen in Fig. 2.7 lets you know there is more printout that you cannot currently see. To view the whole printout document, after

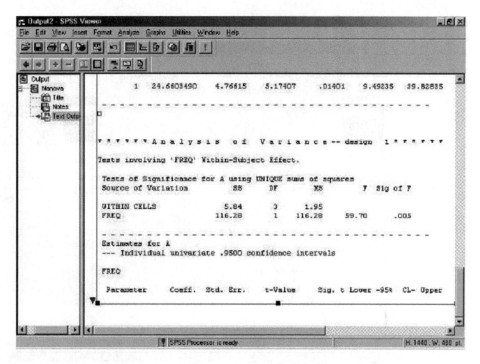

FIG. 2.7. Part of **MANOVA** printout initially visible in PAC; secondary window is on the left side of the screen.

clicking on the portion of printout you wish to expand, click Edit–SPSS Rtf Document Object, then Edit or Open, as shown in Fig. 2.8.

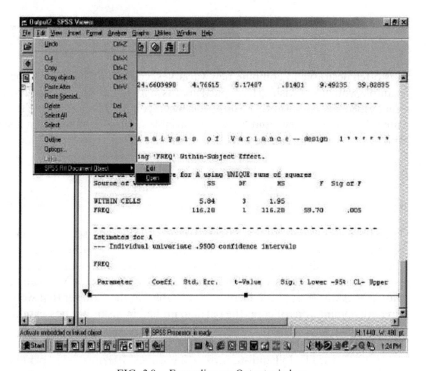

FIG. 2.8. Expanding an Output window.

An Output viewer will open that will allow you to examine (by moving the scroll bar) or print the entire output. You may also print only a portion of the output by highlighting what you wish to print with the cursor, then clicking File–Print, and clicking on Selection in the Print window, as shown in Fig. 2.9, before clicking OK.

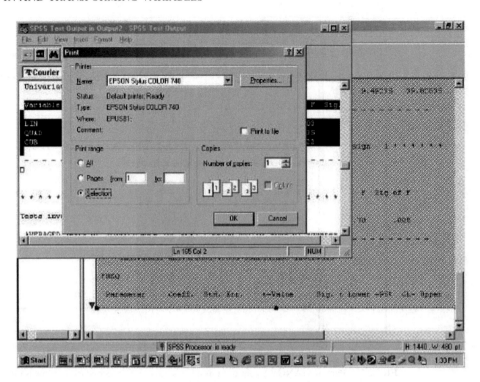

FIG. 2.9.   The Print window.

DATA TRANSFORMATIONS AND CASE SELECTION

"COMPUTE"

It is often desirable to compute new variables, commonly based in some way on existing ones. For example, you might wish to have participants' ages in months but you have their ages in years, which you termed 'ageyrs'. Another example is when you might want to find the sum of a set of scores. Assume that 'varx', 'vary', and 'varz' are variable names for items from a scale. Suppose you wish to find their sum. This can be done as follows:

1. COMPUTE agemnth=ageyrs*12.
2. COMPUTE sumxyz = varx + vary + varz.

The above commands add two new variables to the data set. Although any legal variable name is permitted for the new variables, to be mnemonic, the variable names 'agemnth' and 'sumxyz' were chosen. (The multiplication indicator is "*" and division is indicated by "/". Use parentheses, if necessary, to indicate the order of these arithmetic operations.) You can create any new variable this way. For example, suppose there were variables in the data set that were the numbers of all the different denominations of coins the participant had in his or her possession and you wanted to convert this to dollar equivalents:

3. COMPUTE dollequi=(quarters*25+dimes*10+nickels*5+pennies)/100.

The general syntax for such commands is the command "COMPUTE", followed by the new variable name, an equal sign, and then statements to create the new variable. There are also several special keywords that can be used in SPSS to simplify data transformations. The two most often used shortcuts are for calculating the mean (arithmetic average) or sum of a set of scores as follows:

```
4. COMPUTE meanxyz=MEAN(varx, vary, varz).
5. COMPUTE sumallq=SUM(q1 to q8).
```

Line 5 would add a new variable for each participant to the data set that was the sum of the variables 'q1' through 'q8' and give it the variable name 'sumallq'. Unlike the command on line 2 (or 1 or 3, for that matter), these procedures would give new scores for a participant even if the participant failed to respond to one or more of the items used to construct the score. In line 2, if a participant was missing one or more of the variables 'varx', 'vary', or 'varz', in contrast, 'sumxyz' would be missing. For the "SUM" and "MEAN" keywords, participants are assigned a missing value for a scale variable only if they failed to respond to all of the items on the scale. This may be undesirable; if so, the problem can be overcome by specifying a period and then a number after the word "MEAN" or "SUM" that tells SPSS to calculate the mean or sum if that person has data on at least that number of variables. For example, "MEAN.3" will calculate a mean for each person only if that person has data for at least three variables. Similarly, replacing "SUM" in line 5 with "SUM.7" would tell SPSS to calculate a sum only for participants who have data for at least seven of the eight variables that make up that sum.

"IF"

The "IF" command is used to analyze a logical statement or numerical expression. When the "IF" statement is true for a participant, SPSS follows a secondary command. When the statement is false, the secondary command is not followed. The secondary command is typically the equivalent of a "COMPUTE" statement without the word *compute*. For example, consider the following:

```
1. COMPUTE varp=2.
2. IF (varx=3) varp=1.
```

Line 1 would give every participant a score on 'varp' equal to 2. Then line 2 would change the value of 'varp' to 1 for anyone who had a 3 on 'varx'. Line 2 would not act on anyone who did not have a 3 on 'varx', so it would leave such participants' scores of 2 on 'varp' unchanged.

"RECODE"

The "RECODE" command is used most often for items in a scale that have been reverse keyed. For example, suppose you have items that measured sexist attitudes on a 1 to 7 scale in which 1 meant "strongly disagree" and 7 meant "strongly agree" with the sexist statement therein. You might have written some of your items (e.g., items 1, 5, and 8) to indicate low sexism, so that on these items 1 (strongly disagree) meant "high sexism" and 7 meant "low sexism". The keying on those items is opposite and must be reversed so that they reflect the way your scale is viewed. The following command accomplishes this:

```
RECODE var1 var5 var8 (1=7) (2=6) (3=5) (4=4) (5=3) (6=2) (7=1).
```

The form for this command is "RECODE", followed by the variable names of the variables to be recoded and then the way you want the values to be recoded in sets (in parentheses). The format is '(old value = new value)' and all values must be included. If you would like the recoded versions to have new variable names, include the keyword "INTO" after the last parenthesis, then give new variable names for each of the variables recoded. In the example just presented, three new variable names must be given. "INTO" enables the data set to contain both the old and the recoded (new) variables.

"SELECT IF"

There are many occasions in which you would want to run analyses on a subset of cases of participants from the total data. For example, you might wish to conduct an analysis only on women. The "SELECT IF" command can accomplish this. After the "SELECT IF", include a logical statement such as 'gender=1'. Unless the command "TEMPORARY" precedes a "SELECT IF", the excluded cases are permanently deleted from the active file (not from the saved version on disk, however). Note that the "TEMPORARY" selection is only in effect for the major command (e.g., "MANOVA") that follows it and if you wanted to run more than one analysis, you would have to reselect your subsample.

A variant on this is the "SPLIT FILE" command. This command allows you to split your file and run the analyses separately for each group. Thus, for example, if you split your file by gender, you would conduct the analyses on men and women separately. The syntax to do this is as follows:

> SORT CASES BY facta.
> SPLIT FILE SEPARATE BY facta.

This is a very basic overview of some of the commands that are necessary or useful in SPSS to read in or transform variables or select cases for analysis. The interested reader is referred to the SPSS manuals for additional transformation possibilities.

DATA TRANSFORMATIONS WITH PAC

Some Windows users may prefer PAC data transformations to syntax. Select Transform from the Data Editor window (see Fig. 2.10). You will see various options for transforming your data, some of which are familiar to you now.

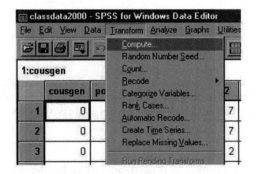

FIG. 2.10.   The Transform menu in the Data Editor.

Selecting Compute will bring up a screen that looks like the one seen in Fig. 2.11.

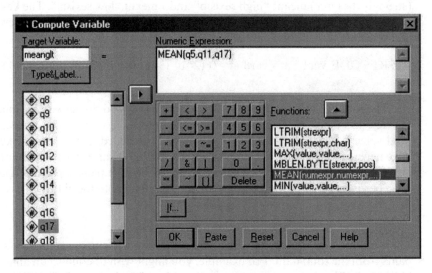

FIG. 2.11.   The Compute dialogue box.

You need to type a new variable name (here 'meanglt' was used) into the left top box. You will notice the right window with an extensive list of arithmetic functions that may be used to create new variables. Common ones include "SUM" and "MEAN" functions. A number pad and operator keys are also present to enter your own functions. In Fig. 2.10, clicking up (with the up arrow above the list of functions) the "MEAN" function then clicking over 'q5', 'q11', and 'q17' (with the right arrow near the list of variables) to create the new variable 'meanglt' is illustrated. Alternatively, 'MEAN(q5,q11,q17)' could simply have been typed into the Numeric Expression window rather than clicked over.

When recoding variables you can select to Recode into the same or a new variable, as shown in Fig. 2.12.

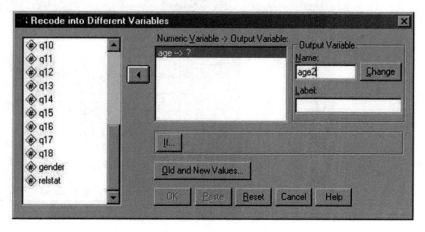

FIG. 2.12.   The Recode menu.

The Recode screen for recoding into different variables appears as in Fig. 2.13. In the example, after clicking the old variable 'age', 'age2' is typed into the Output Variable Name slot. Then Change must be clicked.

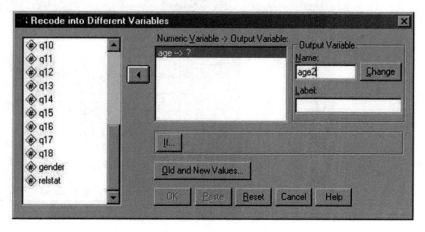

FIG. 2.13.   Recode dialogue box for recoding into Different Variables.

Values are selected next in a new window after clicking on the Old and New Values button (see Fig. 2.14).

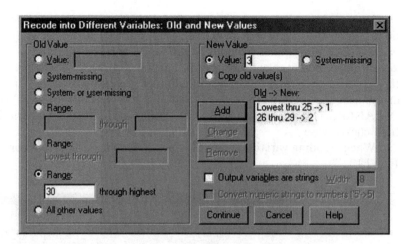

FIG. 2.14. Old and New Values dialogue box for recoding variables.

In the Old Value section you may specify a single value or an entire range. After selecting the old value to be recoded, you would then enter the new value for the variable. Once both an old and a new value have been specified, the Add button becomes available and is used to add that part of the recode process. You would proceed through the steps again until you finish recoding all the desired values. Then click Continue, then OK.

In this example, scores of 30 and above are about to be set to be equal to 3 in 'age2' (by clicking Add). In previous clicks, as indicated by the right window, the lowest value of 'age' up through 25 was set equal to a value of 1 and scores of 26 to 29 were set to 2. Clicking Continue, then OK completes the recode. Recoding an existing variable follows almost the exact same procedure, except that you will not be required to name a new variable.

The If routine is embedded within the Compute menu from the Transform menu (see Fig. 2.15).

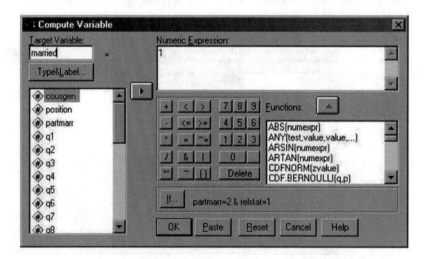

FIG. 2.15. The Compute dialogue box with the If button activated.

Once at this window you can build expressions to create your desired values. You must enter a separate If expression for each new value you want. An example is presented in Fig. 2.16.

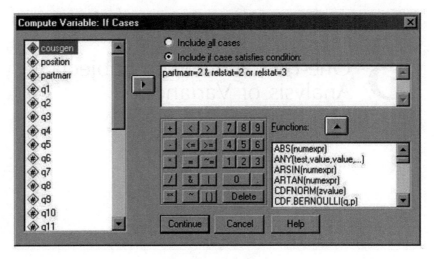

FIG. 2.16.   An example of an If routine.

In Fig. 2.16, the Compute (as specified on an unseen window) will be executed only if the variable 'partmarr' equals 2 and the variable 'relstat' equals either 2 or 3.

Selecting cases to analyze in Windows, if accomplished with drop-down menus, results in excluded cases being, by default, filtered out, rather than permanently deleted from the active data set. You can access the Select Cases menu from the Data menu in the Data Editor window (see Fig. 2.17).

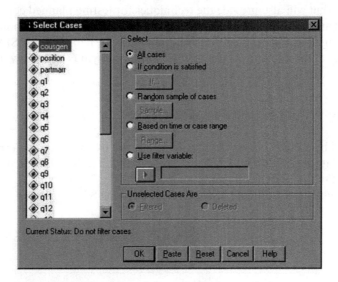

FIG. 2.17.   The Select Cases dialogue box.

Clicking "If condition is satisfied" darkens the If button, which, when clicked, brings up a new window which allows typing in a logical statement. Then click Continue, then OK. The PAC version allows you to choose whether to filter or delete cases. Deleted cases are removed from the data set and will be lost permanently if the working data file is saved with the same name. Filtered cases are merely turned off and can be used again later, by returning to this screen and clicking All cases.

3 One-Factor Between-Subjects Analysis of Variance

In chapter 2 you learned how to read in and transform data. In this chapter you will learn commands to analyze the simplest analysis of variance (ANOVA) design, the one-factor completely randomized design, often called simply *one-way* or *one-factor ANOVA*. This is the appropriate analysis when participants are assigned to or belong to one of two or more groups, each participant has a score on the dependent variable, and you wish to compare the means of the various groups on this dependent variable. This chapter will not only include the commands for the overall (or "omnibus") *F* test, but will also provide the techniques for testing planned contrasts, post hoc comparisons, and trend analyses. As noted in the preface and in chapter 1, throughout this book, primarily syntax will be taught, although the PAC methods that can be used with SPSS for Windows will be covered briefly at the end of each chapter. Knowing the syntax will allow the reader to access SPSS from either the mainframe or from Windows.

BASIC ANALYSIS OF VARIANCE COMMANDS

It will be useful to begin by displaying a set of hypothetical data from three groups of participants. The data appear in Fig. 3.1. It should be noted that these identical data were used as the example for the "DATA LIST" command in chapter 2, Fig. 2.1. In what follows, it is assumed that these data were already read into SPSS with a "DATA LIST" command.

a1: Group 1	a2: Group 2	a3: Group 3
5	11	1
6	12	9
3	15	5
8	16	8
10	9	10

FIG. 3.1.   Data from a one-factor between-subjects design with three levels of Factor A.

In the example presented in Fig. 3.1, five different participants are in each of three groups, and there is just one grouping factor in the design. In this example, the data come from an experiment to determine if type of instruction affects false memory production. Each group of five participants first hears a list of words and is then asked to indicate if they have heard the word when it comes up on a computer screen. The number of words they say they have seen but truly have not (i.e., they have a false memory for having seen those words) constitutes the dependent variable. The first group is told to visualize the word (which is termed the Visualize condition), the second group is told to count the number of syllables of each word in the list (Count), and the last group receives no specific instructions (the control group). The study seeks to determine whether the three groups differ in the mean number of words falsely recalled.

Although all of the examples in this chapter have equal cell sizes (i.e., all of the groups have the same sample size, an equal *n* design), SPSS will provide the correct test statistics even if you have an unequal *n* design (interpretation of unequal *n* designs for more than one factor requires care; see chap. 4; also Keppel, 1991, chap. 13). SPSS will do this by default and you do not have to do anything special. When possible, all designs in this book will be analyzed with the SPSS program called MANOVA, which is the most flexible program for a variety of ANOVA designs.

The syntax, presented in Fig. 3.2, is followed by an explanation of the function of the different commands in the program. As in chapter 2, the command specifications that are to be typed into syntax are presented in capital letters and the parts of the command that are specific to the example are in lower case letters. A <RETURN> (or <ENTER>, depending on the keyboard) is assumed to follow each command (program statement). Again, the numbers in the programs that precede each of the program statements are there only for ease of reference within this text and should not be typed in.

```
1.    MANOVA dv BY facta (1,3)

2d.   /OMEANS

3d.   /POWER

4d.   /PRINT=SIGNIF(EFSIZE) HOMO.
```

FIG. 3.2. Syntax commands to conduct a one-factor between-subjects ANOVA.

The command "MANOVA" in line 1 tells SPSS to run the program entitled MANOVA, which conducts (multivariate) analysis of variance. Although the program MANOVA can handle multivariate analyses (i.e., analyses with more than one dependent variable, which are covered in chap. 12), it also handles univariate analyses (i.e., analyses with only one dependent variable, which are covered in chaps. 3–11). You can thus learn one program and be able to analyze both multivariate and univariate designs.

The word directly following the "MANOVA" command is always the dependent variable you wish to analyze; in this example it is called 'dv'. This is followed by the keyword "BY", which in turn is followed by the name of the grouping variable, in this example, 'facta'. In this book, this variable will be referred to as 'facta', 'factb', 'factc', and so on, and you should insert the name(s) of your factor(s) as appropriate. The factor name is immediately followed by a pair of parentheses that contain the information on the levels of the factor. In other words, the levels have to be numbered, and the parentheses contain the range of those numbers. In this example, there are three groups (i.e., levels of 'facta') numbered 1, 2, and 3, so the command line reads '(1,3)'. If there were two groups, it would read '(1,2)', if four '(1,4)', and so on. Putting this all together, the command on line 1 indicates that a one-factor completely randomized analysis of variance is to be conducted on a set of scores from three different groups, identified as levels 1 through 3 of a factor called 'facta' (the grouping or independent variable), where the dependent variable being measured or observed is called 'dv'.

The subcommand "OMEANS" in line 2 is actually optional, but for the sake of interpretation, virtually indispensable (recall that syntax program line numbers with a 'd' after them indicate that the subcommand is optional, meaning the program will run without it, but highly desirable for interpretation). It indicates that you want SPSS to compute and report the group mean on the dependent variable for each of the three groups (the observed means or "OMEANS"). Because it is a subcommand, it is indented and preceded by a "/". Lines 3 and 4 are also optional but desirable; they tell SPSS to compute the observed power and the effect size, respectively, as will be described later. (Because lines 2–4 are all optional, line 1 alone—with a period at the end for most platforms—would produce ANOVA output.) The output resulting from this syntax is shown in Fig. 3.3.

```
The default error term in MANOVA has been changed from WITHIN CELLS to
WITHIN+RESIDUAL.  Note that these are the same for all full factorial
designs.

* * * * * * A n a l y s i s   o f   V a r i a n c e * * * * * *

      15 cases accepted.
       0 cases rejected because of out-of-range factor values.
       0 cases rejected because of missing data.
       3 non-empty cells.

       1 design will be processed.
- - - - - - - - - - - - - - - - - - - - - - - - - - - - - - - - - - - - -
              CELL NUMBER
               1    2    3
Variable
  FACTA        1    2    3

Cell Means and Standard Deviations
Variable .. DV
       FACTOR            CODE              Mean   Std. Dev.          N

  FACTA                   1               6.400    2.702             5
  FACTA                   2              12.600    2.881             5
  FACTA                   3               6.600    3.647             5
  For entire sample                      8.533    4.138            15
- - - - - - - - - - - - - - - - - - - - - - - - - - - - - - - - - - - - -
Univariate Homogeneity of Variance Tests

Variable .. DV

      Cochrans C(4,3) =                      .46021, P =   .724 (approx.)
      Bartlett-Box F(2,324) =               .18602, P =   .830
- - - - - - - - - - - - - - - - - - - - - - - - - - - - - - - - - - - - -

* * * * * * A n a l y s i s   o f   V a r i a n c e -- design  1 * * * *

Tests of Significance for DV using UNIQUE sums of squares
Source of Variation          SS        DF        MS        F  Sig of F
WITHIN CELLS             115.60        12      9.63
FACTA                    124.13         2     62.07     6.44      .013

(Model)                  124.13         2     62.07     6.44      .013
(Total)                  239.73        14     17.12

R-Squared =           .518
Adjusted R-Squared =  .437
- - - - - - - - - - - - - - - - - - - - - - - - - - - - - - - - - - - - -
Effect Size Measures and Observed Power at the .0500 Level
                              Partial Noncen-
Source of Variation      ETA Sqd trality      Power

FACTA                        .518 12.886       .812
```

FIG. 3.3.   Output from a one-factor between-subjects ANOVA.

The first thing seen in the printout is a message from SPSS that the "default error term" (i.e., the term that is used as the denominator of the F ratio) has been changed to "WITHIN+RESIDUAL". This is in contrast to previous versions of MANOVA in which the error term did not include the residual but was just called "WITHIN CELLS", which is often referred to as the *within-groups* or *subjects-within-groups* effect. In the full factorial designs primarily discussed in this book, these two residuals are the same, so the message may be ignored.

The next section of output provides a summary of the analysis and includes number of cases included and excluded and how many cells are in the design. Although this section will not be reprinted in this book on subsequent output, you should always check this section first in order to verify that MANOVA actually used all of your data (e.g., if you accidentally coded a person as being in group 4, this person would not be in the analysis and SPSS would have told you: "1 case rejected because of out-of-range factor values") and that there are as many levels of your independent variable in the analysis as there should be.

The next output is that generated by the "OMEANS" subcommand. (There are a few lines beginning with "CELL NUMBER" before the "OMEANS" output that are generated in response to the keyword "HOMO" on line 4 that can be ignored.) It provides the mean, standard deviation, and N for each group (each group's N is 5). Note that the means are 6.4, 12.6, and 6.6, respectively. Following the output generated by "OMEANS" are the "Univariate Homogeneity of Variance Tests" which were generated by the keyword "HOMO" on line 4 and will be explained later.

Next, the output provides the "Analysis of Variance" results in ANOVA summary table format. For each of the major "Sources of Variation", the computation provides the *SS* (sum of squares), the *DF* (degrees of freedom, usually, except in that portion of output, written in lower case), and the *MS* (mean square). The first row lists these for the error term, "WITHIN CELLS". The next row listed is the one associated with the independent variable, or grouping variable, in this case "FACTA". The "Model" sums of squares and "DF" are frequently known as the between-group sum of squares and degrees of freedom (for the one-factor design, the "Model" sum of squares and degrees of freedom will be equal to that for "FACTA"). The "Total" sum of squares or degrees of freedom, in the case of the one-factor design, will equal the "WITHIN CELLS" plus the "FACTA" sum of squares or degrees of freedom, respectively.

In addition to getting the sum of squares and degrees of freedom associated with each source, you will also get the mean square ("MS"; they always equal the respective sum of squares divided by its degrees of freedom) and the *F* value (which was obtained by dividing the "FACTA MS" by the "WITHIN CELLS MS"). The *F* test and significance ("Sig") of that test are listed on the right side of the output. In this example, the obtained *F* was 6.44, with a significance level of .013. Because this "Sig of *F*" is less than the traditional cutoff, .05, the *F* test shows the difference between the three means to be statistically significant. In APA publication format, it is conventional practice to describe this result as follows: **The difference between the groups was significant, $F(2, 12) = 6.44$, $p = .013$.**[1] The first number within the parentheses is the degrees of freedom for "FACTA", and the second is the degrees of freedom for "WITHIN CELLS".

Note there is an *F* test for the effect of "FACTA", as well as the *F* test for "Model". As noted earlier, in a one-factor design, these two are the same thing. The MANOVA program also gives you "*R*-squared" and "Adjusted *R*-squared". *R* squared (in this case, .518) is simply the proportion of variance in the dependent variable explained by the independent variable and is equal to sum of squares Model divided by sum of squares Total (124.13/239.73). The adjusted $R^2 = [1 - (1 - R^2)(n - 1)/(n - k)] = .437$, where n = the total number of participants (15 in this case) and k = the number of groups (3 here).

Lines 3 and 4 of the program syntax generate the final output on the printout. Although, as noted previously, both of these lines of syntax are optional, it is highly recommended that they be included. Specifically, in addition to getting the overall *F* test, you should also obtain estimates of both power and effect size. Power is the ability to detect a false null hypothesis when it is in fact false, in other words, the probability of correctly obtaining significance. Ideally, to detect an effect if one exists, your power should be .80 or above (Cohen, 1988). In this case, power did achieve that level (power = .812), under the assumption that the effect size in your sample is the true effect size.

In addition to reporting whether or not the overall *F* is significant, it is now standard practice to include a measure of effect size (APA, 2001). An effect size is a measure of the impact of a treatment on the dependent variable. Although various indices of effect size are commonly in use, the effect size index reported by MANOVA is partial eta squared, which provides the effect size in terms of the proportion of variance in the dependent variable explained by the grouping factor. Thus the partial eta squared will be a number between 0 and 1 inclusive, with higher scores representing more desirable, larger effect sizes. Partial eta squared is a bit of an overestimate of the actual population effect

---

[1]The fifth edition of the *Publication Manual of the American Psychological Association* (APA, 2001), in contrast with previous editions, suggested that when conducting statistical tests with software packages "in general it is the exact probability (*p* value) that should be reported" (p. 25). In this method, the *p* value is reported exactly as it appears in the printout, as was done in the example with "*p* = .013." Normally, however, although there are exceptional circumstances, the report should only be to "two decimal places (i.e., the lowest reported significance probability being *p* < .01)" (p. 129). Thus, to be in conformity with the publication manual, the "*p* = .013" should be replaced with "*p* = .01." However, the manual also allows the older alpha-level alternative for reporting statistical significance: After the comma, the *p* level is reported as either "*p* < .05" or "*p* < .01," the lowest of these two that applies. In this style, in the example, again, the "*p* = .013" would be replaced by "*p* < .05." If "Sig of *F*" had been larger than .05 (or perhaps .01 if you explicitly declare it; cf. APA, 2001, p. 25), in the alpha-level method of reporting, in addition to providing the exact *p* value, you would describe the difference as nonsignificant, assuming that it was earlier indicated that the .05 level was the alpha value you were abiding by. In the remainder of this book, where APA-style sentences are used, we use the exact probability method; however, to aid in clarity, we will deviate from the manual and display *p* values to three decimal places throughout.

size. The formula for partial eta squared is $F/[F + (\text{"DF WITHIN CELLS"}/\text{"DF FACTA"})]$. Another formula that provides the same answer is "SS FACTA"/"SS Total". In the one-factor ANOVA, R squared and partial eta squared have the same value. **Here the partial eta squared is .518, thus 51.80% of the variance in the dependent variable is explained by the independent variable.**

If your F is nonsignificant, you can look at the power value to determine if that nonsignificance is due to inadequate power to detect the difference. Inadequate power is most easily corrected by increasing sample size (assuming the same effect size). In determining if an effect is nonsignificant due to a lack of power, both power and eta squared should be examined together. If eta squared is large, but power is small, then increasing sample size will help to make the effect statistically significant. However, if eta squared is small, it would be very difficult to make the effect become significant without very large sample sizes (see Cohen, 1988; Keppel, 1991, for more details about power and effect sizes). You can also conduct a power analysis prior to conducting the experiment (see Keppel, 1991; Stevens, 1999) to determine what sample size is necessary to detect the effect.

TESTING THE HOMOGENEITY OF VARIANCE ASSUMPTION

One important assumption of ANOVA is the homogeneity of variance assumption, which posits that the various groups all have identical values for their population variances. To test this assumption, you can use a "PRINT" subcommand with the keyword "HOMO" as was done on line 4 (this can either be added onto the existing "PRINT" statement or be a new statement, e.g., on line 5, "PRINT=HOMO"). This syntax leads to printout with two variants of such a test, the "Cochran's" and the "Bartlett-Box" tests. The assumption is violated if the "P" value is small (generally less than .05), thus for this test you want nonsignificance and if the "P" value is larger than .05, retention of the assumption is warranted. In addition to the actual tests, you will also obtain the output associated with "CELL NUMBER" (located directly above the "OMEANS" output). This is simply telling you how many levels of the grouping variable the assumption is being tested for. In Fig. 3.3, you can see that the "P" = .724 for Cochran's and .830 for Bartlett-Box, thus the assumption is not violated in this example. If the assumption is violated, the F test will be positively biased, thus a more stringent alpha level should be employed. Although the question of how much to adjust alpha is complicated and depends on several factors (e.g., equal vs. unequal N's, sample size, degree of heterogeneity present), Keppel (1991) suggested adjusting from $p = .05$ to .025 when the ratio of the largest to smallest group variance is greater than 3 to 1.

COMPARISONS

The omnibus or overall F test discussed previously will tell you only if all the group means are roughly equal or if there are some significant differences among them. In the latter case, it will not tell you which groups are different from which other groups. Analyses to accomplish tests detailing where differences lie are commonly called *analytic comparisons* or, simply, *comparisons*. There are two main classes of comparisons that may be made with any set of data: planned comparisons (which hereafter primarily are called *planned contrasts* or, more simply, *contrasts*) and post hoc comparisons. Of course, if there are only two levels of the independent variable Factor A, the only difference that could possibly account for the significant F test is the difference between Group 1 and Group 2. In such a case, none of the remainder of this chapter is relevant, nor are discussions or tests of comparisons and associated tests relevant in any subsequent chapter when the factor in question has only two levels.

Planned contrasts are those analyses conducted to test relevant hypotheses that a researcher had a priori (i.e., before the experiment was run). In the previous example, for instance, the researcher may have decided a priori on two hypotheses: (a) that the average of the Visualize and the Count groups is greater than the control group and (b) that the Visualize group will do better than the Count group. In post hoc comparisons, on the other hand, the researcher has no prior hypotheses about the group differences and is simply exploring the data to ascertain which group differences are driving the significance of the overall F test. Whenever possible, it is desirable to conduct a priori hypotheses tests instead of post hoc tests, largely in order to avoid making a large number of tests and thereby helping to control the familywise error rate. An excellent discussion of these concepts can be found in Keppel (1991, chaps. 6 and 8). He also covered the issue of orthogonality of the contrasts, as well as the number of contrasts that can be conducted.

Planned Contrasts

Figure 3.4 shows the general commands necessary to conduct a planned contrast.

1.   MANOVA dv BY facta (1,3)

2d.   /OMEANS

3.   /CONTRAST(facta)=*type (name the type of contrast you want, with*

       associated specifications)

4.   /DESIGN=facta(1), facta(2), *etc. (one less than the number of levels of*

       the factor).

FIG. 3.4.   Syntax to conduct planned contrasts in a one-factor between-subjects ANOVA.

Lines 1 and 2 are the same as those in the overall or main effects analysis. Of course, you would substitute the actual name of your dependent variable and factor name for 'dv' and 'facta', respectively, on these and the remaining lines. Note that the optional commands requesting power and effect size output were omitted here for simplicity, but could have been included. Line 3 is the line that constructs the contrasts. After the subcommand "CONTRAST", specify which factor the contrast is to be conducted on. In a one-factor analysis of variance, of course, there is only one factor and thus the factor here is 'facta'. After the equal sign, specify the type of contrast you wish to do, which will be discussed in more detail later. Line 4 indicates the command to SPSS to conduct the tests of the contrasts constructed. After the keyword "DESIGN" and the equal sign, repeatedly insert the factor name followed by successive numbers in parentheses, beginning with 1. The number of times the factor name should be given is one less than the number of levels of the factor, in other words, the number of degrees of freedom (df) of the factor. In the present example, because Factor A has three levels, the subcommand would be 'DESIGN=facta(1), facta(2)'.[2] Imagine, however, that the factor name was 'groups' and it had five levels (i.e., the "MANOVA" command was 'MANOVA dv BY groups (1,5)'). Then the "DESIGN" subcommand would be 'DESIGN=groups(1) groups(2) groups(3) groups(4)'. Although SPSS will run and provide numeric output without giving you an error message even if you do not repeat the factor name the same number of times as the degrees of freedom on the "DESIGN" subcommand, the significance tests may be numerically wrong.

Probably the most common and useful type of contrast is "SPECIAL", a user-defined contrast. After the keyword "SPECIAL", you must enter a set of numerical weights enclosed in parentheses. The number of weights must be the square of the number of levels of the factor. For the example just discussed, where Factor A has three levels, this means 9 coefficients. Although you can enter all the weights on the same line (as shown in the gray box on page 26), it is most clear if you enter these weights (or coefficients) in a square matrix (as shown in the gray box on page 28), with the number of rows and columns each equal to the number of levels of the factor. The first row should contain all 1s and represents the mean effect of the factor, which is generally ignored. The succeeding rows contain each of the contrasts of interest, in each case, one weight for each group.

The set of contrast weights for any given contrast can be determined by the application of a set of simple rules. Any contrast compares the mean of a certain group to the mean of a certain other

---

[2]Although commas are frequently used to separate elements of the specifications in commands (e.g., 'DESIGN=facta(1), facta(2)'), in SPSS syntax they are actually optional.

group, or it compares the average mean of a certain subset of groups to the mean of another group or to the average mean of a certain other subset of groups. For instance, two comparisons of interest were described earlier: The first contrast compared the average of the means of Groups 1 and 2 to the mean of Group 3 (control), whereas the second contrast compared the mean of Group 1 (Visualize) with the mean of Group 2 (Count). The general form is "x versus y," where x and y each represent either a certain group or the average of a certain subset of groups. Thus, the second example is "1 versus 2", whereas the first example is "average of 1 and 2 versus 3." The simple rules are these:

1. Groups named on the left side of the word *versus* each get the same positive contrast weight.
2. Groups on the right side of the word *versus* each get the same negative weight.
3. Groups not mentioned on either side get a weight of 0.
4. For rules (1) or (2) the weight is equal to the number of groups named on the other side of the word *versus*.

For example, to apply these four rules to the case of five groups and the contrast "average of Groups 1 and 5 versus average of Groups 2, 3, and 4," Groups 1 and 5 would each get the weight +3 (positive because they are on the left side, the same weight as one another because they are on the same side of the word *versus*, and both have the value 3 because there are 3 groups named on the right side of the word *versus*), whereas Groups 2, 3, and 4 each get the weight −2 (negative because they are on the right side of *versus*, 2 because there are two groups named on the left side). The weights for the groups, in order, would therefore be: 3, −2, −2, −2, 3.

In the first contrast described previously with three groups, "average of 1 and 2 versus 3," the two groups on the left of the *versus* both get coefficients of +1 (positive because they are on the left side, they get the same weight as one another because they are on the same side of the *versus*, and both have the value 1 because there is 1 group named on the right side of the word *versus*), whereas Group 3 gets the weight −2 (negative because it is on the right side of the *versus*, 2 because there are two groups named on the left side). In the second contrast, 1 versus 2, Group 1 gets a weight of 1, Group 2 gets a weight of −1, and Group 3 gets a weight of 0, because it is not mentioned on either side. Thus, lines 3 and 4 of the syntax in Fig. 3.4 for these examples would be as follows:

```
/CONTRAST(facta)=SPECIAL (1 1 1, 1 1 −2, 1 −1 0)
/DESIGN=facta(1), facta(2).
```

The output for the above "SPECIAL" contrasts is shown in Fig. 3.5.

```
Tests of Significance for DV using UNIQUE sums of squares

Source of Variation        SS       DF        MS        F   Sig of F
WITHIN+RESIDUAL         115.60      12       9.63
FACTA(1)                 28.03       1      28.03     2.91    .114
FACTA(2)                 96.10       1      96.10     9.98    .008

(Model)                 124.13       2      62.07     6.44    .013
(Total)                 239.73      14      17.12

R-Squared =               .518
Adjusted R-Squared =      .437
- - - - - - - - - - - - - - - - - - - - - - - - - - - - - - - - - -
Estimates for DV
--- Individual univariate .9500 confidence intervals

FACTA(1)

Parameter     Coeff.   Std. Err.    t-Value    Sig. t Lower -95% CL- Upper

       2   5.80000000   3.40000    1.70588     .11375   -1.60796   13.20796

FACTA(2)

 Parameter     Coeff.   Std. Err.    t-Value    Sig. t Lower -95% CL- Upper

       3  -6.2000000    1.96299   -3.15845     .00824  -10.47699   -1.92301
```

FIG. 3.5.   Output for a SPECIAL user-defined contrast.

After the "WITHIN+RESIDUAL" line, instead of the overall or omnibus test of "FACTA", as in Fig. 3.3, each contrast has a line and a significance test. The "DESIGN" subcommand that follows the "CONTRAST" subcommand is what causes these individual sum of squares, degrees of freedom, mean square, and F tests to be printed out. If the "DESIGN" subcommand is left off, only the overall sum of squares, degrees of freedom, mean square, and so on will be printed out. In this example, the sum of squares for the first contrast, "FACTA(1)" (i.e., 28.03), and that for the second contrast, "FACTA(2)" (i.e., 96.10), add up to the sum of squares for the overall "Model" (i.e., 124.13; also see the sum of squares for "FACTA" in Fig. 3.3). This will be true when the contrasts are orthogonal[3] and the groups have equal sample sizes, but generally false otherwise. In the orthogonal case, the contrasts are said to partition the overall sum of squares.

Here, contrast 1 (1 1 −2; i.e., the average of Groups 1 and 2 vs. Group 3) is nonsignificant (p = .114), but contrast 2 (1 −1 0; i.e., Group 1 vs. Group 2) is significant (p = .008). The output below the F tests gives you information about the contrasts that is largely redundant. The coefficient ("Coeff.") is often denoted $\hat{\Psi}$ and pronounced "Psi hat," and is the sum of each group mean multiplied by its appropriate contrast weight. Because the weights in contrast 1 were 1 1 −2 and the group means were 6.4, 12.6, and 6.6, respectively, the coefficient is 1(6.4) + 1(12.6) + −2(6.6) = 5.8. The t test associated with the contrast (1.70588) is simply the square root of the corresponding F value (2.91), with its sign matching the sign of the coefficient. Note that the "Sig t" is the same as the "Sig of F", only carried to more significant digits (e.g., .11375 vs. .114). Finally, the output includes the 95% confidence interval around Psi hat. The "Lower -95%" is the Psi hat value minus the standard error ("Std. Err.") of the test multiplied by the tabled t value for your degrees of freedom, and the "CL- upper" adds rather than subtracts the latter.

"SPECIAL" contrasts need not be orthogonal, although you can specify an orthogonal set. It is also important to note that you need to specify exactly $k - 1$ contrasts, where k is the number of groups. If you are interested in less than $k - 1$ contrasts, simply make up additional ones whose output you subsequently ignore. On the other hand, if you have more than $k - 1$ (but see the discussion in Keppel, 1991, pp. 166–167), repeat the "CONTRAST" and "DESIGN" subcommands a second time with appropriate substitutions. Finally, it must be noted that SPSS has the annoying tendency here that not all contrasts go together. Sometimes the set of contrasts produces the error message that "The special contrast matrix for FACTA is SINGULAR. The analysis is terminated." Trial and error is sometimes necessary to arrive at a "legal" set of contrasts.[4]

Sometimes the contrasts you are interested in can be obtained slightly more easily from the built-in (or "canned") contrasts MANOVA contains, instead of needing to use "SPECIAL". First, there is "SIMPLE (refcategory)", in which each level of a factor is compared in turn to group number 'refcategory'. For example, if Factor A had five groups, 'SIMPLE (3)' would yield, as the first contrast, Group 1's mean compared to Group 3's, as the second contrast, Group 2's mean compared to Group 3's, as the third contrast, Group 4's mean compared to Group 3's, and, as the final contrast, Group 5's mean contrasted with Group 3's. The last contrast would be identified on the printout as "FACTA (4)". Thus the following "CONTRAST" syntaxes yield identical results:

---

[3]Orthogonal contrasts provide completely nonredundant, or statistically independent, information. Whether any given pair of contrasts is orthogonal (assuming equal group sizes) is determined by multiplying the two contrasts' weights for each group, then summing these products over groups. If and only if the sum is 0, the contrasts are orthogonal. Consider the two contrasts 3 −2 −2 −2 3 and 0 2 −1 −1 0. To determine whether these are orthogonal you would multiply the 3 by the 0, the first −2 by the 2, and so on, then sum. The result is (3)(0) + (−2)(2) + (−2)(−1) + (−2)(−1) + (3)(0) = 0. Hence they are orthogonal.

[4]An alternative SPSS program to analyze one-way ANOVAs, ONEWAY, has a method of specifying contrasts that is considerably simpler and only requires weights for 1, rather than $k - 1$, contrasts and therefore avoids this "SINGULAR" problem. For example, the syntax for the contrast "average of 1 and 2 versus 3," with three groups, would be:

```
1. ONEWAY dv BY facta
2. /CONTRAST= 1 1 −2.
```

Additional contrasts would simply require additional lines like line 2. Note that a "DESIGN" subcommand is also not necessary in this method.

Because ONEWAY cannot be used in factorial designs, only in one-way ANOVAs, the more general methods using MANOVA are provided in the main text.

```
/CONTRAST(facta)=SIMPLE (3)
```

and

```
/CONTRAST(facta)=SPECIAL
 (1 1 1 1 1,
  1 0 –1 0 0,
  0 1 –1 0 0,
  0 0 –1 1 0
  0 0 –1 0 1)
```

The 'refcategory' defaults to the last group if you do not specify a group. Thus, with 5 groups, 'CONTRAST(facta)=SIMPLE (5)' and 'CONTRAST(facta)=SIMPLE' are functionally identical. Note that "SIMPLE" contrasts are not orthogonal.

A second contrast is "REPEATED", where each level of the factor except the first is compared to that of the previous level. These contrasts are not orthogonal. In other words, if Factor A had included five groups, the first contrast, identified on the printout as 'FACTA(1)', would have compared Group 2 with Group 1, 'FACTA(2)' refers to Group 3 compared to Group 2, 'FACTA(3)' to Group 4 compared to Group 3, and 'FACTA(4)' to Group 5 compared to Group 4. 'CONTRAST (facta)= REPEATED' is therefore equivalent to the "SPECIAL" contrast:

```
/CONTRAST(facta)=SPECIAL
 (1 1 1 1 1,
 –1 1 0 0 0,
  0 –1 1 0 0,
  0 0 –1 1 0,
  0 0 0 –1 1)
```

In the contrast "HELMERT", each level of the factor except the last is compared in turn to the mean of all of the subsequent levels. Thus, 'CONTRAST(facta)=HELMERT' is equivalent to the "SPECIAL" contrast:

```
/CONTRAST(facta)=SPECIAL
 (1 1 1 1 1,
 –                   4 1 1 1,
  0 –3 1 1,
  0 0 –2 1 1,
  0 0 0 –1 1)
```

In the contrast "DIFFERENCE", each level of the factor except the first is compared to the mean of all of the previous levels. These contrasts are the opposite of the "HELMERT" contrasts just discussed.

Finally, for "POLYNOMIAL", the first contrast produced by this keyword is the linear effect, the second is the quadratic, and so on. More detail is given about this type of contrast in the Trend Analysis section.

Post Hoc Tests

In contrast to the tests described previously, post hoc tests are not specified by the researcher a priori. Rather, they are tests that are conducted when you have a significant overall F, but have no a priori hypotheses about which group differences might be causing that effect. Generally, you compare each group's mean with the others to discern where the pairwise group differences lie. The reason to use post hoc tests, rather than a series of *t* tests, is that almost all of the post hoc tests control for alpha inflation (i.e., familywise error rate exceeds the stated alpha level; for a more detailed treatment of this subject see Keppel, 1991). The only test that does not make an adjustment for alpha inflation is Fisher's Least Significant Difference (LSD) test, one of several discussed later.

The MANOVA program, unlike some others in SPSS,[5] does not have syntax that directly computes post hocs. Although MANOVA does not run the post hocs for you, you can use "SIMPLE" contrasts to obtain the necessary information to conduct the post hoc, with the finishing steps conducted manually. To do this, you would simply run the tests of interest as if they were a priori contrasts. Then you compare either the *F* or its significance value from the printout to a criterion value you specially (and manually) calculate to see whether the pair should be declared different. Depending on the test, if the *F* value obtained is equal to or larger than the specially computed criterion *F* value, or if the "Sig of *F*" is smaller than the specially computed criterion significance value, then you declare the pair of means different.

Tukey's Test

The general technique will be illustrated with Tukey's Honestly Significant Difference (HSD) test, one of the most common and desirable post hoc tests (see Fig. 3.6). This test uses the Studentized range statistic instead of the *F* value to test all possible mean differences (i.e., all pairwise comparisons).

```
1.    MANOVA dv BY facta(1,3)

2d.      /OMEANS

3.       /CONTRAST(facta)=SIMPLE(1)

4.       /DESIGN=facta(1) facta(2)

5.       /CONTRAST(facta)=SIMPLE(2)

6.       /DESIGN=facta(1) facta(2).
```

FIG. 3.6.   Syntax to obtain information necessary to conduct a Tukey's HSD test.

Note that there are two sets of "CONTRAST" and "DESIGN" subcommands that look identical, except that the first specifies 'SIMPLE(1)' and the second specifies 'SIMPLE (2)'. This elicits two segments of output labeled "design 1" and "design 2" as shown in Fig. 3.7 (the portions of output not relevant to the following discussion have been omitted).

The "design 1" output was elicited by the first "CONTRAST" subcommand, where the 'refcategory' was Group 1, and "design 2" was elicited by the second "CONTRAST" subcommand, where the 'refcategory' was Group 2. Thus, in "design 1", "FACTA(1)" refers to the first contrast, which tests Group 2 versus Group 1 and has an *F* = 9.98, and "FACTA(2)" refers to the second contrast, which tests Group 3 versus Group 1, and has an *F* = .01. In "design 2", however, each group is compared in turn to Group 2 (the 'refcategory'), so that "FACTA(1)" refers to the test of Group 1 versus Group 2 and has an *F* = 9.98 (note that this is redundant with the test of "FACTA(1)" in "design 1"), and "FACTA(2)" refers to the test of Group 3 versus Group 2, with an *F* = 9.34.

---

[5]The program "ONEWAY" does. There are 20 post hoc tests available in ONEWAY. For example, Tukey and Bonferroni tests in the one-way design may be obtained with the following syntax:

```
ONEWAY dv BY facta
  /POSTHOC=TUKEY BONFERRONI
```

The subcommand to run the tests is "POSTHOC" followed by the specific test you wish to conduct. You can have multiple post hocs per "ONEWAY" command, but each test must be specified on the same "POSTHOC" subcommand line. See Fig. 3.20 later in this chapter for a discussion of the printout for post hocs.

```
* * * * * * A n a l y s i s    o f    V a r i a n c e -- design  1 * * * *

Tests of Significance for DV using UNIQUE sums of squares
Source of Variation         SS        DF        MS          F    Sig of F
WITHIN+RESIDUAL          115.60        12       9.63
FACTA(1)                  96.10         1      96.10       9.98     .008
FACTA(2)                    .10         1        .10        .01     .921

(Model)                  124.13         2      62.07       6.44     .013
(Total)                  239.73        14      17.12

R-Squared =              .518
Adjusted R-Squared =     .437
- - - - - - - - - - - - - - - - - - - - - - - - - - - - - - - - - - - - -
Estimates for DV
--- Individual univariate .9500 confidence intervals

FACTA(1)

 Parameter     Coeff.    Std. Err.    t-Value     Sig. t Lower -95% CL- Upper

       2     6.20000000   1.96299     3.15845      .00824   1.92301   10.47699

FACTA(2)

 Parameter     Coeff.    Std. Err.    t-Value     Sig. t Lower -95% CL- Upper

       3     .200000000   1.96299      .10189      .92053  -4.07699    4.47699
* * * * * * A n a l y s i s    o f    V a r i a n c e -- design  2 * * * * * *

Tests of Significance for DV using UNIQUE sums of squares
Source of Variation         SS        DF        MS          F    Sig of F
WITHIN+RESIDUAL          115.60        12       9.63
FACTA(1)                  96.10         1      96.10       9.98     .008
FACTA(2)                  90.00         1      90.00       9.34     .010

(Model)                  124.13         2      62.07       6.44     .013
(Total)                  239.73        14      17.12

R-Squared =              .518
Adjusted R-Squared =     .437
- - - - - - - - - - - - - - - - - - - - - - - - - - - - - - - - - - - - -
Estimates for DV
--- Individual univariate .9500 confidence intervals

FACTA(1)

 Parameter     Coeff.    Std. Err.    t-Value     Sig. t Lower -95% CL- Upper

       2    -6.2000000    1.96299    -3.15845      .00824 -10.47699   -1.92301

FACTA(2)

 Parameter     Coeff.    Std. Err.    t-Value     Sig. t Lower -95% CL- Upper

       3    -6.0000000    1.96299    -3.05656      .00996 -10.27699   -1.72301
```

FIG. 3.7.   Output necessary to conduct a Tukey's HSD test.

Following is a more comprehensive example with five groups. With five groups, you would need four sets of "CONTRAST" subcommands, differing only in that they use as 'refcategory' the successive integers from 1 to 4 (one less than the number of groups). Each "CONTRAST" would be paired with an identical "DESIGN" subcommand, each specifying 'facta(1) facta(2) facta(3) facta(4)'. Each set would elicit a separate portion of printout labeled "design 1" through "design 4", each one having a test of "FACTA(1)", "FACTA(2)", "FACTA(3)", and "FACTA(4)". These tests, however, refer to different comparisons, as depicted in Table 3.1.

As seen in Table 3.1, many of the tests are redundant. For example, Group 4 versus Group 2 ("FACTA(3)" in "design 2") is referred to in the fourth column as (F), but it gives results identical to Group 2 versus Group 4 ("FACTA(2)" in "design 4") as noted in the third row from the bottom, column 5. There are 10 nonredundant tests, referred to in column 4 as tests (A) through (J). Ten is precisely how many distinct pairs there are with 5 groups.

To conduct Tukey tests requires another step. To establish significance using Tukey's criterion, you do not use the F test itself, but instead calculate a special criterion, F_T, to compare with. As Keppel (1991, p. 175) explained, this quantity is obtained by the formula

$$F_T = \frac{(q_T)^2}{2},$$

where q_T is found in the Studentized range tables. Such tables are found in many textbooks, and must be looked up with three parameters, alpha (which is virtually always set to .05), the number of groups, and the df_{error}. In the main example, there are three groups and df_{error} = "DF WITHIN+RE-

TABLE 3.1
"CONTRAST" Specifications and Interpretations for a Five-Group Pairwise Comparison Example

Contrast Subcommand	Design	Output	Refers to	Redundant With
CONTRAST(facta)=SIMPLE(1)	1	FACTA(1)	Group 2 vs. Group 1 (A)	
		FACTA(2)	Group 3 vs. Group 1 (B)	
		FACTA(3)	Group 4 vs. Group 1 (C)	
		FACTA(4)	Group 5 vs. Group 1 (D)	
CONTRAST(facta)=SIMPLE(2)	2	FACTA(1)	Group 1 vs. Group 2	(A)
		FACTA(2)	Group 3 vs. Group 2 (E)	
		FACTA(3)	Group 4 vs. Group 2 (F)	
		FACTA(4)	Group 5 vs. Group 2 (G)	
CONTRAST(facta)=SIMPLE(3)	3	FACTA(1)	Group 1 vs. Group 3	(B)
		FACTA(2)	Group 2 vs. Group 3	(E)
		FACTA(3)	Group 4 vs. Group 3 (H)	
		FACTA(4)	Group 5 vs. Group 3 (I)	
CONTRAST(facta)=SIMPLE(4)	4	FACTA(1)	Group 1 vs. Group 4	(C)
		FACTA(2)	Group 2 vs. Group 4	(F)
		FACTA(3)	Group 3 vs. Group 4	(H)
		FACTA(4)	Group 5 vs. Group 4 (J)	

SIDUAL" = 12. According to the table in Keppel (1991, p. 523), q_T for this case is 3.77. Thus, F_T is 7.106. (This compares with 4.75 as an overall F criterion.) Of the F values in the output, only the first, 9.98, pertaining to "FACTA(1)" in "design 1" (see also the same test in "design 2"), in other words, Group 2 versus Group 1, the mean of 12.6 versus the mean of 6.4, and the second F from "design 2" of 9.34 pertaining to "FACTA(2)" (i.e., Group 3 versus Group 2, the mean of 6.6 versus the mean of 12.6) are greater than F_T and so would be declared significantly different by Tukey's test. For convenience, a table of F_T values (in other words, Studentized range statistics, q_T, squared and divided by 2) is provided as appendix A. Examining at the intersection of number of groups being compared for Tukey's test = 3, df_{error} = 12, and α_{FW} = .05, you find the value 7.11, which is used for declaring significant by Tukey's test any of the printed-out F tests from the "SIMPLE" contrasts.

Other Pairwise Tests: LSD, Student-Newman-Keuls, and Duncan's Tests

Two of the other three common pairwise tests can be used in analogous fashion, comparing the output F values with specially calculated criteria. The Student-Newman-Keuls (SNK) test uses the Studentized range test statistic and therefore calculates q_T and F_T as previously described, but computes a different value for each pair of means depending on how many means are intermediate between the two being compared, using that number plus 2 as the "number of groups" in the table lookup. For example, if there are six groups overall, when you are comparing the second highest mean to the second lowest, there are two groups intermediate between these two. Thus, you would use 4 as the number of groups when looking up q_T in the Studentized range tables or when looking up F_T in appendix A. (See Kirk, 1982, pp. 123–125, or Winer, 1971, pp. 191–196, for additional information.) In the main example, when comparing Group 1 to Group 2's mean (the 6.4 to the 12.6), because they are the largest and smallest, there is one group intermediate, thus you would use 3 as the number of groups, but when comparing Group 1 to Group 3 (the smallest to the second smallest) or when comparing Group 2 to Group 3 (the largest to the second largest) there are no groups intermediate, so you would use the value 2 as the number of groups, with a smaller critical value, 4.74. Duncan's test (also called the New Multiple Range test) is conducted analogously to SNK, but the analyst uses his specialized tables instead of the Studentized range tables. An adaptation of his table, which transforms the Duncan values into F_D values, suitable for comparing the F from MANOVA, is in appendix B. This table is used similarly to appendix A. It shows that the critical value for assessing the comparison of Groups 1 and 3 or 2 and 3 is 4.74, as with the SNK test, but the critical value for evaluating the difference between Groups 1 and 2 is smaller than with SNK, 5.22. Fisher's Least Significant Difference (LSD) test, on the other hand, simply uses the F value MANOVA computes as the test criterion. To determine whether a pair of means is significantly different, simply examine whether the "Sig of F" is less than .05. It should be noted that, although the LSD, SNK, and Duncan tests are in common use, few statistical authorities regard them as acceptable post hoc tests.

Scheffé Test

A procedure that can be used to test both pairwise and other contrasts is the Scheffé test. The critical value for any such comparison, F_S, is found by $F_S = (k - 1)F_{\text{tabled}}(df_{\text{Model}}, df_{\text{error}})$, where F_{tabled} is found in virtually any statistics text, and looked up with two degrees of freedom values (Keppel, 1991, p. 172). In the main example, where $k = 3$, $df_{\text{Model}} = 2$, and $df_{\text{error}} = 12$, assuming alpha at .05, $F_{\text{tabled}} = 3.89$, F_S would be 7.78. Therefore, any difference found with a contrast, whether pairwise or of a more complex nature, would be compared with this value.

Dunnett's Test

This test is designed for the case in which exactly one of the groups is compared to each of the others. The most common example of this application is when one of the groups is a control group and the remaining (experimental) groups are each compared to it. The simplest way to conduct these tests in MANOVA is to specify them as "SIMPLE" contrasts, then compare the resulting "t-Values" that arise in the "Estimates" section of the printout to Dunnett's special tables. For example, in Fig. 3.7, two sets of simple contrasts were conducted; consider just the first one, which compared each of the groups against Group 1, 'SIMPLE(1)'. Had Group 1 been the control group, and had Dunnett's tests thus been desired, the two contrast "t-Values" (3.15845 and .10189, respectively) would have been compared against the critical value from Dunnett's table (for example, Table A-6 from Keppel, 1991), with $df_{\text{error}} = 12$, and number of groups = 3. For $\alpha = .05$, two-tailed tests (see Keppel, p. 176, for a discussion of one- vs. two-tailed tests in the context of Dunnett's tests), the critical value found from the table is 2.50. Because only the obtained t value for the first contrast exceeds this value, only that test is significant.

Bonferroni Test

In this test, alpha is adjusted to take into account the number of comparisons being conducted. That is, the test simply reduces the per comparison Type I error probability as the number of comparisons are increased in order to maintain a constant familywise Type I error that equals the stated alpha level. This test is used to test for pairwise as well as more complex comparisons. Specifically, to find the alpha to use for each test, you divide the familywise alpha desired (almost always between .05 and .10) by C, the number of tests conducted. Consider conducting all pairwise tests for five groups, for example. As seen previously, there are 10 such distinct tests, so $C = 10$. If you were conducting these as Bonferroni tests, you would declare a pair significantly different by the Bonferroni criterion only if the "Sig of F" were less than .10/10, in other words, .01.

Modified Bonferroni Test

The final post hoc test that will be presented is a modified version of the Bonferroni test. In the modified version of the test, the researcher takes into account that doing a certain number of planned contrasts is reasonable and thus no adjustments are necessary. Keppel (1991) suggested that a reasonable number of planned contrasts is $k - 1$ (i.e., the degrees of freedom associated with between groups). To calculate your new alpha level, you first calculate a new familywise error rate as $\alpha_{\text{FWplanned}} = (k - 1)(\alpha)$, where α is the per contrast α you want. You then divide this new $\alpha_{\text{FWplanned}}$ by the number of contrasts you plan on conducting. If you were conducting the analysis of all pairwise comparisons for a factor that had 5 groups described in the Bonferroni section, assuming a per contrast α of .05, $\alpha_{\text{planned}} = ([5 - 1][.05])/10 = .02$.

TREND ANALYSIS

A trend analysis is appropriate when the independent variable can be meaningfully described quantitatively. For example, Keppel (1991, p. 56) described an experiment varying the number of hours the participants in each group were required to go without sleep, from 4 to 12 to 20 to 28 hours.

Here, as in all trend analyses, the independent variable is a meaningful number (e.g., 4, 12, 20, 28). The idea is to fit what is called a *polynomial function* to the means from these four conditions. The lowest of these functions is called the *linear* function: It is a straight line. The next lowest is a *quadratic* function, which has one bend in the middle—that is, it is either U-shaped or inverted U-shaped. The next lowest is *cubic*, which has two bends (e.g., up-down-up, and so on). Each trend function can be understood as a test of a specific contrast.

In MANOVA, the request for a trend analysis is initiated in a "CONTRAST" subcommand under "MANOVA", as seen in Fig. 3.8. The data is from Keppel (1991, p. 161). In this experiment, a researcher was studying the effects of anxiety on performance of a complex task. The levels of anxiety factor is called 'facta', and has six levels: low anxiety (a1) to high anxiety (a6). The dependent variable is called 'score'.

```
1.    MANOVA score BY facta(1,6)

2d.   /OMEANS

3.    /CONTRAST(facta)=POLYNOMIAL

4.    /DESIGN=facta(1) facta(2) facta(3) facta(4) facta(5)

5o.   /DESIGN.
```

FIG. 3.8. Syntax to conduct a trend analysis in a one-factor ANOVA.

The "CONTRAST" subcommand requires the use of the keyword "POLYNOMIAL" when a trend analysis is desired. Similar to the syntax in Fig. 3.4, in line 4, in order to obtain the significance tests for each trend, each trend must be designated by the numbers 1, 2, and so on, in parentheses, each following the factor name. Again, the number of such specifications must equal the number of levels of the factor minus one (i.e., this is the number of trend orders being tested). For example, with four levels, the linear, quadratic, and cubic trends would each be tested, requiring 'facta(1)', 'facta(2)', and 'facta(3)' following the equal sign in the "DESIGN" subcommand. The values for the levels of the trend factor in a trend analysis are important. For example, the factor could be number of milligrams of a drug, with the dosages being .5, 1.0, 1.5, and 2.0 mg. These four dosages are each separated by .5 mg. If the intervals are all identical, the values for the individual intervals do not have to be specified. The example in Fig. 3.8 is written under the assumption of equal intervals. When no specific metric is specified, equal intervals are assumed. However, if the intervals are not equal, their values must be specified in parentheses. For example:

```
MANOVA score BY facta(1,4)
   /CONTRAST(facta)=POLYNOMIAL (1, 2, 2.5, 3)
```

would be appropriate if the dosages were 1, 2, 2.5, and 3 mg, that is, unequally spaced.

If you wish to also obtain the omnibus F test, add a "DESIGN" subcommand without an equal sign and without further specifications (as in line 5). This additional "DESIGN" subcommand is needed only if the omnibus F test is also desired and can immediately precede, or immediately follow, the "DESIGN" subcommand with the specifications. Figure 3.9 shows the output from the syntax in Fig. 3.8.

The omnibus F test is presented after the trend analysis because the "DESIGN" statement without any specifications follows the "DESIGN" statement with the trend specifications. Overall, "FACTA" has a significant effect: $F(5, 24) = 7.53$, $p = .001$. Similar to the output in Fig. 3.5 for the "SPECIAL" contrasts, the coefficients and t tests follow the omnibus test, with the same significance values as their matching tests that came earlier (as "design 1"). The tests for the trends are presented in order, namely linear, quadratic, cubic, fourth order, and fifth order. The t test associated with the contrast is simply the square root of the previous F value, with its sign matching the sign of the coefficient. The output shows that the linear and quadratic trends are significant ($p = .000$ and $p = .001$, respectively). It should be noted that the means (as produced by "OMEANS") first increase, then

```
Cell Means and Standard Deviations
Variable .. SCORE
        FACTOR              CODE                  Mean  Std. Dev.              N

   FACTA                    1                     .800      .447               5
   FACTA                    2                    1.600      .548               5
   FACTA                    3                    3.400     1.140               5
   FACTA                    4                    3.600     1.342               5
   FACTA                    5                    3.200      .837               5
   FACTA                    6                    2.800      .837               5
For entire sample                               2.567     1.331              30

    * * * * * * A n a l y s i s   o f   V a r i a n c e -- design  1 * * *

Tests of Significance for SCORE using UNIQUE sums of squares
Source of Variation            SS        DF        MS          F  Sig of F
WITHIN+RESIDUAL             20.00        24       .83
FACTA(1)                    16.07         1     16.07      19.29      .000
FACTA(2)                    13.04         1     13.04      15.65      .001
FACTA(3)                      .11         1       .11        .13      .718
FACTA(4)                     1.83         1      1.83       2.19      .152
FACTA(5)                      .32         1       .32        .38      .543

(Model)                     31.37         5      6.27       7.53      .000
(Total)                     51.37        29      1.77

R-Squared =         .611
Adjusted R-Squared = .530

* * * * * * A n a l y s i s   o f   V a r i a n c e -- design  2 * * * * *

Tests of Significance for SCORE using UNIQUE sums of squares
Source of Variation            SS        DF        MS          F  Sig of F
WITHIN CELLS               20.00        24       .83
FACTA                      31.37         5      6.27       7.53      .000

(Model)                     31.37         5      6.27       7.53      .000
(Total)                     51.37        29      1.77

R-Squared =         .611
Adjusted R-Squared = .530
- - - - - - - - - - - - - - - - - - - - - - - - - - - - - - - - - - -
Estimates for SCORE
--- Individual univariate .9500 confidence intervals

FACTA
Parameter     Coeff.   Std. Err.    t-Value    Sig. t Lower -95%  CL- Upper

       2   1.79284291    .40825    4.39155    .00020    .95026   2.63543
       3  -1.6148124     .40825   -3.95547    .00059  -2.45740    -.77223
       4   -.14907120    .40825    -.36515    .71820    -.99165    .69351
       5    .604743157   .40825    1.48131    .15153    -.23784   1.44733
       6   -.25197632    .40825    -.61721    .54291  -1.09456    .59061
```

FIG. 3.9. Output for a trend analysis, including omnibus *F* test.

decrease after Group 4. Thus the means appear as an inverted U, which is why the quadratic trend is significant. However, they do not fall (Group 6) as low as they were for Group 1. Thus, the means also appear to be generally rising as anxiety increases; hence the linear trend is significant as well.

There is another subcommand that might be useful when performing a trend analysis and that is the "PARTITION" subcommand. This subcommand would be used if you wanted to test the previous linear trend, but then really were not interested in the other trends individually, so wished to lump together the remaining tests into one additional significance test. The syntax and output are given in Figs. 3.10 and 3.11, respectively.

```
1.    MANOVA score BY facta(1,6)

2d.   /OMEANS

3.    /CONTRAST(facta)=POLYNOMIAL

4.    /PARTITION(facta)=(1, 4)

5.    /DESIGN=facta(1) facta(2).
```

FIG. 3.10. Syntax to conduct a trend analysis using the PARTITION subcommand.

The "PARTITION" subcommand is on line 4. It can be seen that the word "PARTITION" is followed by the name of the factor that you are doing the partitioning on in parentheses, here, '(facta)'. The factor name is followed by an equal sign and in parentheses you specify how you want to divide up (i.e., partition) the degrees of freedom. Here you partition them into 1 (the linear trend) and 4 (the remaining trends). In general, these two should sum to one less than the number of levels of the factor. In line 5, you specify which partitions you want significance tests for, typically one for each partition.

```
Tests of Significance for SCORE using UNIQUE sums of squares
Source of Variation          SS       DF        MS         F  Sig of F

WITHIN+RESIDUAL           20.00       24       .83
FACTA(1)                  16.07        1     16.07     19.29      .000
FACTA(2)                  15.30        4      3.82      4.59      .007

(Model)                   31.37        5      6.27      7.53      .000
(Total)                   51.37       29      1.77

R-Squared =           .611
Adjusted R-Squared =  .530
```

FIG. 3.11.   Output from a trend analysis using the PARTITION subcommand.

In Fig. 3.11 you see that you obtain a significance test for the linear trend that is identical to the test when you requested a trend analysis without using the "PARTITION" subcommand, that is, $F(1, 24) = 19.29$, $p = .001$ in both cases. However, "FACTA(2)", which simultaneously tests all trend orders above the linear, is also significant, $F(4, 24) = 4.59$, $p = .007$.

Some writers (e.g., Keppel, 1991, pp. 156–158) recommend a procedure of determining which trend orders are necessary to describe the means by repeatedly estimating or pulling out lower order trends, then testing the remaining higher order trends simultaneously for significance until they are no longer significant. Although this could be done in a series of analyses in which you look at the output, then decide whether to repeat another cycle, it can also be done all at once, as seen in Fig. 3.12.

```
1.    MANOVA score BY facta(1,6)

2d.    /OMEANS

3.     /CONTRAST(facta)=POLY

4.     /PARTITION(facta)=(1,4)

5.     /DESIGN=facta(1) facta(2)

6.     /PARTITION(facta)=(1,1,3)

7.     /DESIGN=facta(1) facta(2) facta(3)

8.     /PARTITION(facta)=(1,1,1,2)

9.     /DESIGN=facta(1) facta(2) facta(3) facta(4)

10.    /PARTITION(facta)

11.    /DESIGN=facta(1) facta(2) facta(3) facta(4) facta(5).
```

FIG. 3.12.   Syntax to simultaneously test the significance of higher order trends using the PARTITION subcommand.

Note that the last "PARTITION" can simply be written as in Fig. 3.12, because the default specification for "PARTITION" is a series of $k - 1$ single df tests. The output is in Fig. 3.13, edited to retain only what is salient for the discussion.

```
* * * * * A n a l y s i s   o f   V a r i a n c e -- design  1 * * * *

Tests of Significance for SCORE using UNIQUE sums of squares
Source of Variation          SS       DF        MS          F  Sig of F

WITHIN+RESIDUAL            20.00       24       .83
FACTA(1)                  16.07        1     16.07      19.29     .000
FACTA(2)                  15.30        4      3.82       4.59     .007

* * * * * A n a l y s i s   o f   V a r i a n c e -- design  2 * * * *

Tests of Significance for SCORE using UNIQUE sums of squares
Source of Variation          SS       DF        MS          F  Sig of F

WITHIN+RESIDUAL            20.00       24       .83
FACTA(1)                  16.07        1     16.07      19.29     .000
FACTA(2)                  13.04        1     13.04      15.65     .001
FACTA(3)                   2.26        3       .75        .90     .454

* * * * * A n a l y s i s   o f   V a r i a n c e -- design  3 * * * *

Tests of Significance for SCORE using UNIQUE sums of squares
Source of Variation          SS       DF        MS          F  Sig of F

WITHIN+RESIDUAL            20.00       24       .83
FACTA(1)                  16.07        1     16.07      19.29     .000
FACTA(2)                  13.04        1     13.04      15.65     .001
FACTA(3)                    .11        1       .11        .13     .718
FACTA(4)                   2.15        2      1.07       1.29     .294

* * * * * A n a l y s i s   o f   V a r i a n c e -- design  4 * * * *

Tests of Significance for SCORE using UNIQUE sums of squares
Source of Variation          SS       DF        MS          F  Sig of F

WITHIN+RESIDUAL            20.00       24       .83
FACTA(1)                  16.07        1     16.07      19.29     .000
FACTA(2)                  13.04        1     13.04      15.65     .001
FACTA(3)                    .11        1       .11        .13     .718
FACTA(4)                   1.83        1      1.83       2.19     .152
FACTA(5)                    .32        1       .32        .38     .543
```

FIG. 3.13. Output for simultaneously testing the significance of higher order trends using the PARTITION subcommand.

At each step (i.e., each "design"), examine the last entry. If it is significant, this tells you that you need to go to the next step; if not, stop and interpret the present step. In "design 1", "FACTA(2)" is significant, telling you that you need to proceed to "design 2". In "design 2", "FACTA(3)" is not significant; therefore you can stop here and ignore later output. Within "design 2", both "FACTA(1)" (the linear trend) and "FACTA(2)" (the quadratic trend) are significant. This is what would be reported.

MONOTONIC HYPOTHESES

Often you might have a specific hypothesis about the order of the group means, for example, that Group 1's should be the lowest, Group 2's next lowest, which should in turn be lower than Group 3's, and Group 4's is highest. Such a hypothesis is termed a *monotonic* or *ordinal* hypothesis (Braver & Sheets, 1993). In order to test this hypothesis, you actually proceed in three steps. In Step 1, you test the linear trend as described earlier. If the linear trend is nonsignificant, declare the monotonic hypothesis not supported and stop there. If it is significant, proceed to Step 2. In Step 2, you examine the sample means to determine if they are in the hypothesized order. If the linear trend is significant and your sample means are in hypothesized order, you can stop there and declare your monotonic hypothesis supported. However, if the linear trend is significant but the sample means are not in the correct order, it is important to proceed to Step 3, to test whether or not this incorrect ordering reflects a true rejection of the monotonic hypothesis, or if the means are out of order due to sampling error. As it is unlikely that the sample means will order exactly like the population means, you need to test if any of the reversals in the data are substantial enough to reject the monotonic hypothesis. In Step 3, you test for significant reversals by testing each adjacent pair of means. Specifically, 1 versus 2, 2 versus 3, and 3 versus 4 (you can use "REPEATED" contrasts to do this if you have numbered your groups in the predicted order). The null hypothesis is that there are no reversals, thus you wish to retain the null. You would use an alpha adjustment similar to the Bonferonni adjustment. The formula for the adjusted alpha level is: $\alpha_{adj} = 1 - (1 - \alpha)^{1/k - 1}$, where $\alpha = .5$ and $k =$ the number of groups ($k = 4$ in the example; Braver & Sheets, 1993). If all of the contrasts are nonsignificant, then you do not have any significant reversals and the monotonic hypothesis is supported.

PAC

All of the PAC sequences are from Version 11.0. To run a one-factor ANOVA, click Analyze and then obtain the GLM analysis by clicking General Linear Model–Univariate. Unlike MANOVA, GLM uses different programs to run univariate and multivariate designs (see chap. 13), so for this univariate example, you must use the pulldown menu for the Univariate option in PAC (see Fig. 3.14).

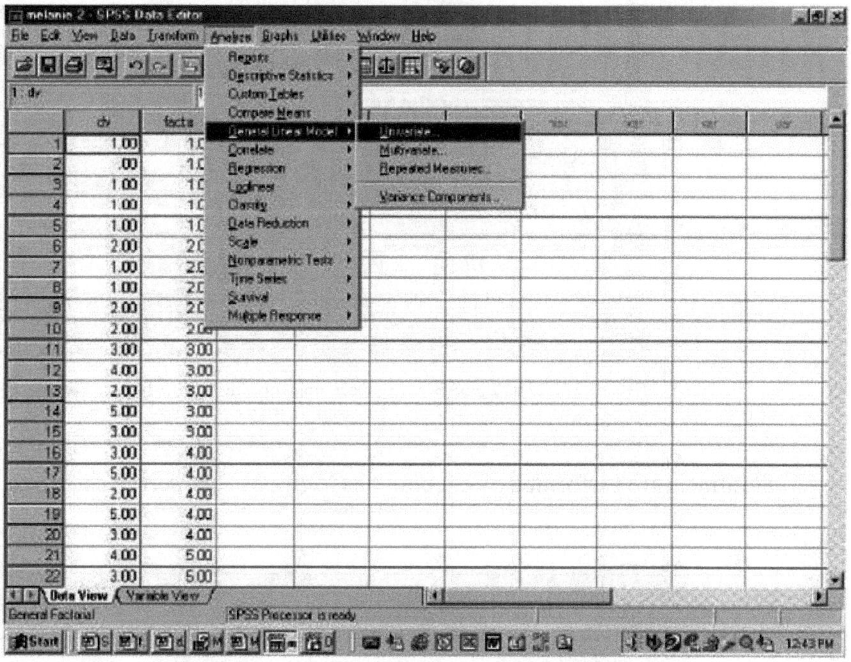

FIG. 3.14.   PAC menus to perform an ANOVA.

A screen like the one seen in Fig. 3.15 will pop up that will allow you to enter your dependent variable and independent variable.

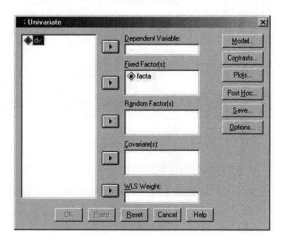

FIG. 3.15.   The dialogue box to select independent and dependent variables.

You simply highlight the variable on the left and hit the little arrow key in front of the box on the right where you want it to go. Here, your independent variable is Fixed Factor(s). You can also do post hoc tests and planned comparisons. For each type of contrast, a menu will pop up and you can select the type of contrast or post hoc you wish to conduct. Post hocs are performed by clicking on the Post Hoc button. At the post hoc screen seen in Fig. 3.16, highlight the factor ('facta') and click the arrow to move it into the Post Hoc Tests For box, and simply check the post hoc tests you desire. In the example, a Tukey test will be performed.

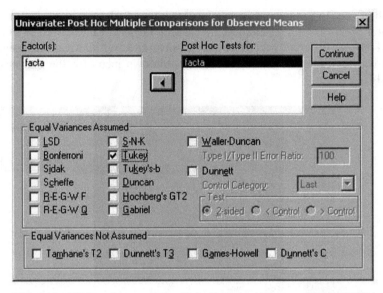

FIG. 3.16.   Dialogue box to select post hoc tests in a between-subjects ANOVA.

Contrasts are performed by clicking on Contrasts. The screen shown in Fig. 3.17 will pop up.

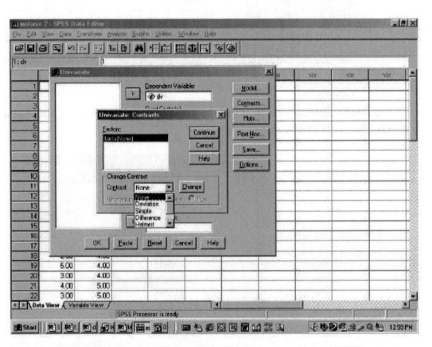

FIG. 3.17.   Contrasts dialogue box for a between-subjects ANOVA.

After choosing the contrast you want from the pull-down menu, you have to click on the Change button before clicking Continue. For contrasts that have reference groups, only the first or last group can be used in PAC menus. It should be noted, however, that the Contrasts menu does not permit "SPECIAL" contrasts, the type that is of most general use (you can obtain these user-defined contrasts through the use of syntax; see chap. 13). This is one of the reasons MANOVA is explicated as the program of choice throughout this book.

If you would like to obtain power, effect size, homogeneity of variance tests, or observed means, click on the Options button (see Fig. 3.18). Note that the homogeneity of variance test is the Levene test, not the Cochran's or Bartlett-Box, but it is interpreted in the same way: High values for "Sig" are compatible with retention, which indicates that the homogeneity of variance assumption appears to have been met. To obtain means (and standard deviations) highlight 'facta' and click it over to the Display Means for box. In the example, the little boxes for power and effect size were also checked. After clicking Continue, click OK on the main screen to conduct the analysis.

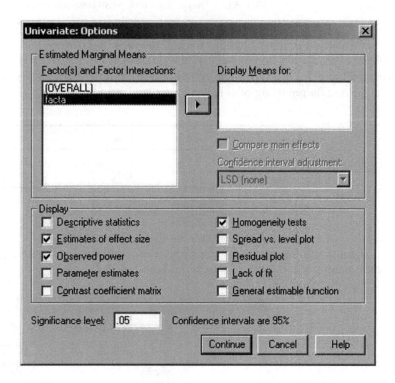

FIG. 3.18.   Dialogue box to obtain observed means, homogeneity tests, power, and effect size in a between-subjects ANOVA.

Having discussed the output from MANOVA, most of the output from PAC will be similar, albeit in somewhat changed form. Requiring special mention is some output concerning post hocs. It will appear as in Fig. 3.19.

Homogeneous Subsets

DV

Tukey HSD[a,b]

FACTA	N	Subset 1	Subset 2
1.00	5	6.4000	
3.00	5	6.6000	
2.00	5		12.6000
Sig.		.994	1.000

Means for groups in homogeneous subsets are displayed.
Based on Type III Sum of Squares
The error term is Mean Square(Error) = 9.633.
   a. Uses Harmonic Mean Sample Size = 5.000.
   b. Alpha = .05.

FIG. 3.19.   Output from PAC SPSS concerning post hoc tests.

This output is conveying that the 6.4 and the 6.6 (Group 1 and Group 3) are not significantly different (i.e., are in a homogeneous subset). Because Group 2 is in its own subset, it is different from Groups 1 and 3. This is the same conclusion reached from the analogous analysis with MANOVA. The APA-style reporting of this analysis would be as follows:

Group		
1	2	3
6.4$_a$	12.6$_b$	6.6$_a$

Note.   Means having the same subscript are not significantly different at $p <$ .05 in the Tukey honestly significant difference comparison.

If you would like to display the syntax PAC produces for any analysis, simply click on the Paste button seen in the bottom row of buttons in Fig. 3.20.

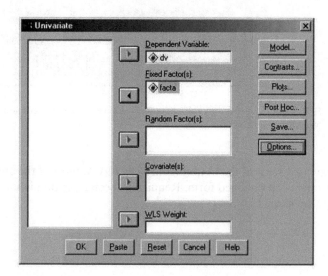

FIG. 3.20.   Screen showing the location of the Paste button.

SPSS for Windows will automatically open a syntax window and display the syntax it produced to conduct the analysis you selected. This is a good idea if you are unsure of which defaults the computer is using or if you would like to add more complicated analyses into the program. To run the syntax program, simply click Run–All (see Fig. 3.21).

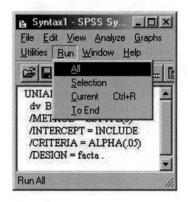

FIG. 3.21.   Running syntax from PAC.

Be aware that the PAC method uses GLM or UNIANOVA rather than MANOVA syntax to run its analyses, so the syntax is different (see chap. 13). However, the "MANOVA" command will work in SPSS for Windows if typed into syntax. Thus, all of the examples in this book can be typed into a syntax window and run.

4 Two-Factor Between-Subjects Analysis of Variance

In chapter 3 you learned how to analyze data from a one-factor completely randomized ANOVA. Studies with more than one factor (or independent variable) are called *factorial* designs. In this chapter, you will learn how to analyze the simplest factorial design, a two-factor completely randomized design. In such designs, participants serve in a *cell*, which is simultaneously a certain level of one factor combined with a certain level of a second factor. Commands for the basic *F* tests and various kinds of follow-up tests are described.

BASIC ANALYSIS OF VARIANCE COMMANDS

Figure 4.1 shows hypothetical data from an investigation of the effects of type of training and type of team on basketball performance. The dependent variable is number of free throw shots made in a training session. There are two independent variables. Factor A is the type of training: no special training (Control), imagine making baskets (Imagine), or practice making baskets (Practice). Factor B is type of team (varsity or nonvarsity). Because Factor A has three levels and Factor B has two levels, this is often called a 3 × 2 factorial design (three levels of Factor A crossed, or combined, with two levels of Factor B). Five different players are in each of the six groups in this 3 × 2 ANOVA. Each cell in Fig. 4.1 is labeled with a designation (e.g., a2b3) indicating which level of Factor A was involved with which level of Factor B.

Control varsity a1b1	Imagine varsity a2b1	Practice varsity a3b1	Control non-varsity a1b2	Imagine non-varsity a2b2	Practice non-varsity a3b2
4	3	8	3	6	7
5	4	6	4	4	6
3	2	8	2	5	5
5	4	7	3	5	5
6	4	4	4	3	5

FIG. 4.1.   Data from a two-factor between-subjects design with three levels of Factor A and two levels of Factor B.

The program, presented in Fig. 4.2, is followed by an explanation of the function of the different commands in the program.

```
1.    MANOVA shots BY facta(1,3) factb(1,2)

2d.   /OMEANS=TABLES (facta, factb, facta BY factb)

3d.   /POWER

4d.   /PRINT=SIGNIF(EFSIZE).
```

FIG. 4.2.   Syntax commands to conduct a two-factor between-subjects ANOVA.

The setup for the two-factor ANOVA is very similar to that of the one-factor ANOVA. The "MANOVA" command is first, followed by the name of the dependent variable, in this case, 'shots'. After the keyword "BY", you identify the between-subjects factors called 'facta' and 'factb'. The names designating the factors are immediately followed by parentheses that contain the levels of the factor. For example, Factor A has three levels, so for Factor A the command line reads 'facta(1,3)' and Factor B has two levels, thus 'factb(1,2)'.

Putting this all together, the syntax statement in line 1 indicates that a two-factor completely randomized analysis of variance is to be conducted on a set of scores from six different groups, identified as levels 1 through 3 of a factor called 'facta', crossed with 'factb', which has two levels (i.e., crossed indicates that each level of Factor A is combined with each level of Factor B, thus the 6 possible groups [$3 \times 2 = 6$]), where the dependent variable is called 'shots'.

The "OMEANS" command in line 2 is slightly altered, because, in a two-way design, it is usually desirable to obtain not only each of the six cell means, but also the three marginal means for Factor A (i.e., the means for each type of training averaged over the two types of teams) and the two marginal means for Factor B (i.e., the means for team type averaged over the three training conditions). To accomplish this, add the keyword "TABLES" to the "OMEANS" subcommand after an equal sign, then in parentheses put the names of the two factors, then the two factors connected by the keyword "BY" (the commas in the subcommand are optional and added for readability). The output from the "OMEANS" subcommand is in Fig. 4.3.

```
Combined Observed Means for FACTA
Variable .. SHOTS
        FACTA
          1         WGT.      3.90000
                    UNWGT.    3.90000
          2         WGT.      4.00000
                    UNWGT.    4.00000
          3         WGT.      6.10000
                    UNWGT.    6.10000
- - - - - - - - - - - - - - - - - - - - - - - - - - - - - - - -
Combined Observed Means for FACTB
Variable .. SHOTS
        FACTB
          1         WGT.      4.86667
                    UNWGT.    4.86667
          2         WGT.      4.46667
                    UNWGT.    4.46667
- - - - - - - - - - - - - - - - - - - - - - - - - - - - - - - -
Combined Observed Means for FACTA BY FACTB
Variable .. SHOTS
              FACTA       1         2         3
        FACTB
          1         WGT.      4.60000   3.40000   6.60000
                    UNWGT.    4.60000   3.40000   6.60000
          2         WGT.      3.20000   4.60000   5.60000
                    UNWGT.    3.20000   4.60000   5.60000
```

FIG. 4.3.   Output for OMEANS in a two-factor between-subjects ANOVA.

When the cell Ns are equal, as in most of the factorial designs in this book, the weighted (abbreviated "WGT.") and the unweighted means (abbreviated "UNWGT.") will be identical, so either one may be examined. The values presented previously are rearranged in an easier to follow form in Table 4.1.

TABLE 4.1
Marginal and Cell Means in a Two-Factor Between-Subjects ANOVA

FACTB: Team Type	FACTA: Training			Average
	Control	Imagine	Practice	
Varsity	4.6	3.4	6.6	4.87
Nonvarsity	3.2	4.6	5.6	4.47
Average	3.90	4.00	6.10	

The values in the middle portion of Table 4.1 come from the "Combined Observed Means for FACTA BY FACTB" portion of printout and are the cell means. The column marginals are provided in the "Combined Observed Means for FACTA" section. For example, the 3.90 in the first column is the average of the 4.6 and 3.2 in its column. Similarly, row marginals come from the "Combined Observed Means for FACTB" section, and the 4.87 in the first row is the average of the 4.6, the 3.4, and the 6.6 cell means in its row.

Just as in the one-factor design, it is highly desirable, but not mandatory, to request observed power and the effect sizes as in lines 3 through 4, respectively. The remaining output is in Fig. 4.4.

```
Tests of Significance for SHOTS using UNIQUE sums of squares
Source of Variation        SS        DF        MS         F   Sig of F

WITHIN CELLS             30.80       24      1.28
FACTA                    30.87        2     15.43      12.03      .000
FACTB                     1.20        1      1.20        .94      .343
FACTA BY FACTB            9.80        2      4.90       3.82      .036

(Model)                  41.87        5      8.37       6.52      .001
(Total)                  72.67       29      2.51

R-Squared =             .576
Adjusted R-Squared =    .488

- - - - - - - - - - - - - - - - - - - - - - - - - - - - - - - - - - - - -

Effect Size Measures and Observed Power at the .0500 Level
                        Partial Noncen-
Source of Variation     ETA Sqd trality     Power

FACTA                      .501  24.052      .989
FACTB                      .037    .935      .163
FACTA BY FACTB             .241   7.636      .637
```

FIG. 4.4.   Output from a two-factor between-subjects ANOVA.

In the output, there is a separate sum of squares, degrees of freedom, mean square, F, and "Sig of F" for each of the two factors, called the "main effects," as well as output for "FACTA BY FACTB", the "interaction." The "FACTA" main effect tests whether the column marginal means (3.90, 4.0, and 6.10, respectively, for the Control, Imagine, and Practice conditions) are significantly different. The output shows that the "Sig of F" is .000, exceeding the conventional .05 significance level. The "FACTB" main effect tests whether the row marginal means (4.87 and 4.67, respectively, for varsity and nonvarsity) are significantly different. The output shows that this is clearly a nonsignificant difference ($p = .343$). The "FACTA BY FACTB" interaction also reaches significance and will be explained in more detail later. In APA format, these results might be summarized with the following language: **The Factor A main effect, $F(2, 24) = 12.03$, $p = .001$, was significant, the Factor B main effect was nonsignificant, $F(1, 24) = .94$, $p = .343$, and the Factor A by Factor B interaction was also significant, $F(2, 24) = 3.82$, $p = .036$.** For a two- (or more) factor design, the "Model" sum of squares equals what some texts call the between-groups sum of squares and is the sum of the sum of squares for "FACTA", "FACTB", and "FACTA BY FACTB"; $30.87 + 1.20 + 9.80 = 41.87$. The same is true for the "Model" degrees of freedom ($5 = 2 + 1 + 2$). The "Total" sum of squares equals that for "Model" plus "WITHIN CELLS" ($72.67 = 41.87 + 30.80$). An analogous computation applies to "Total" degrees of freedom. R-squared and Adjusted R-squared are automatically output, and computed by the same formula as in chapter 3. Power and effect sizes are provided in response to the respective optional subcommands in lines 3 and 4. The formula for partial eta squared in factorial designs is $SS_{\text{Factor name}}/(SS_{\text{Factor name}} + SS_{\text{Within Cells}})$. APA guidelines call for routine reporting of the effect sizes for significant effects. Accordingly, the APA format sentence at the end of the previous paragraph ought also to add language something like: **Specifically, 24.10% of the variance in the number of shots made is explained by the interaction according to the partial eta squared.**

THE INTERACTION

One of the most important reasons to conduct a two-factor ANOVA (rather than two separate studies, one using type of training as the independent variable, the other using type of team as the independent variable each analyzed by one-way ANOVAs) is that you can test for the interaction between the two factors. Specifically, the interaction examines whether the effect of one factor on the dependent variable is different depending on which level of the other factor is being considered. For example, in the previous design, the interaction investigates whether the effect of type of training on the number of shots made is approximately the same (which would imply no significant interaction) or quite different (which would imply that the interaction is significant) for the varsity and nonvarsity players. The analysis shows that the interaction is statistically significant: The pattern of differences shown in Table 4.1 among training conditions for the varsity players (4.6, 3.4, and 6.6 mean shots) is not the same as the pattern of differences among the nonvarsity players (3.2, 4.6, and 5.6 mean shots). Thus, the effect of training is different depending on whether you are a varsity or nonvarsity player. Alternatively, the effect of type of team could be examined and it would be noted that the difference for the control group (from 4.6 to 3.2) is slightly larger than the difference in the Practice condition (from 6.6 to 5.6), and the difference in the Imagine condition (from 3.4 to 4.6) is actually in the opposite direction. Thus, you could also say that the effect of type of team is different depending on which training method is being considered.

When the interaction is significant, it is usually inappropriate to simply examine and report the main effects (i.e., the marginal means), because a significant interaction suggests that the effects of each factor are different depending on which level of the other factor is being considered. Recall that the marginal means average over the cell means. For instance, in the previous example, where the interaction is significant, it appears misleading to simply conclude that training type made a significant difference, as implied by the significant main effect for training, because, in actuality, the training effect differed for varsity and nonvarsity players. As in the present example, when the interaction is significant, the next step for the researcher would be to explore this significant interaction.

On the other hand, when the interaction is not significant, it is appropriate to explore differences among the row or column marginals with planned contrasts or post hoc comparisons when the factor has more than two levels (and often considered inappropriate when the interaction is clearly nonsignificant to explore cell mean differences within a row or within a column, as will be explained in the Exploring a Significant Interaction section). To illustrate, consider the example in Keppel (1991, p. 230). As shown in Keppel's answers (p. 536), for the Factor A main effect, $F(2,18) = 41.39$, $p < .001$; for the Factor B main effect, $F(2, 18) = .27$, *ns*,[1] and, most importantly for present purposes, the interaction is not significant, $F(4,18) = 1.81$, *ns*. Thus, analyses of the Factor A marginal means are appropriate.

UNEQUAL *N* FACTORIAL DESIGNS

Most of what has been covered in this chapter so far assumes that each cell has exactly the same sample size (N) as every other cell. In this section, the analysis when the groups or cells have unequal group sizes (i.e., the unequal N or unbalanced design) is discussed. Before proceeding to analyze an unequal N experiment, the researcher should first ascertain whether or not "missingness" is related to the experimental conditions (see Keppel, 1991; also Tabachnick & Fidell, 2001). For example, if you have an experiment with four conditions and find that one and only one of them has a lot of

---

[1]Exact *p* values cannot be reported as Keppel (1991) did not provide them.

missing data, being missing is quite plausibly related to being in that condition. In this event, it is questionable whether the data can be appropriately analyzed at all (Keppel, 1991). However, if you are convinced that missingness is haphazard and accidental and therefore not meaningfully related to condition, then you can proceed with the analysis, but you have several statistical issues to grapple with.

First, violations of certain ANOVA assumptions are more serious, leading to alpha inflation. There are no useful rules of thumb regarding when these violations become fatal, and thus Keppel (1991) urged caution in interpreting any effects from an unequal N design.

The second issue is that you have two choices regarding how to compute the marginal means. Specifically, you can calculate them by adding the mean values in each cell and dividing by the number of cells involved in the respective marginal means, or you can add up all the scores of the participants in that particular row or column and divide by the number of those participants. The first approach is called the *unweighted* approach, because you are giving equal weight to each cell (or, more to the point, not giving more weight to the cells that have a larger number of participants) and the second approach is termed the *weighted* approach, as the cells with more participants end up influencing the marginal mean more. In a one-factor design, or an equal N factorial design, these two approaches give identical answers. In unequal N factorial designs, however, they give different answers.

As an example, reconsider the data set of Fig. 4.1, this time with three of the scores deleted. The resulting data set is in Fig. 4.5.

Control varsity a1b1	Imagine varsity a2b1	Practice varsity a3b1	Control non-varsity a1b2	Imagine non-varsity a2b2	Practice non-varsity a3b2
4	3	8	3	6	--
5	4	6	--	4	6
3	2	8	2	5	5
5	4	7	3	5	5
--	4	4	4	3	5

FIG. 4.5. The data set of Fig. 4.1 with missing data, an unequal N design.

The subcommand "OMEANS" (by itself) would yield the cell means, standard deviations, and, especially, N found in the printout of Fig. 4.6, whereas 'OMEANS=TABLES (facta, factb)' would yield the marginal means found in Fig. 4.7.

```
Cell Means and Standard Deviations
 Variable .. SHOTS
        FACTOR              CODE              Mean   Std. Dev.          N

    FACTA              1
      FACTB                1               4.250      .957             4
      FACTB                2               3.000      .816             4
    FACTA              2
      FACTB                1               3.400      .894             5
      FACTB                2               4.600     1.140             5
    FACTA              3
      FACTB                1               6.600     1.673             5
      FACTB                2               5.250      .500             4
 For entire sample                         4.556     1.577            27
```

FIG. 4.6. Cell means and Ns obtained with OMEANS in an unequal N design.

```
Combined Observed Means for FACTA
 Variable .. SHOTS
         FACTA
              1         WGT.      3.62500
                        UNWGT.    3.62500
              2         WGT.      4.00000
                        UNWGT.    4.00000
              3         WGT.      6.00000
                        UNWGT.    5.92500
 - - - - - - - - - - - - - - - - - - - - - - - - - - - - - - - - - - - -
Combined Observed Means for FACTB
 Variable .. SHOTS
         FACTB
              1         WGT.      4.78571
                        UNWGT.    4.75000
              2         WGT.      4.30769
                        UNWGT.    4.28333
```

FIG. 4.7.   Weighted and unweighted marginal means in an unequal *N* design.

For example, the weighted ("WGT.") marginal mean for the third level of Factor A is shown to be 6.00000, found by weighting the respective cell means (of 6.6 and 5.25, respectively) by their *N*s (5 and 4, respectively[2]), whereas the unweighted ("UNWGT.") mean of 5.92500 simply adds the 6.6 and 5.25 and divides by 2. Most but not all applied statisticians prefer the report of the weighted means.

The final issue is that the three effects (the two main effects and the interaction) are no longer orthogonal in an unequal *N* design. Thus, the sums of squares for these three sources as normally computed will not add up to the sum of squares "Model", because the three effects have shared or overlapping variance. Thus, in the present example, the subcommand 'DESIGN=facta' would yield *SS* for Factor A = 28.79; the subcommand 'DESIGN=factb' would yield *SS* for Factor B = 1.54; "DESIGN" (with no specification, thereby yielding the default "full factorial") would yield *SS* for interaction = 9.85 and *SS* for "Model" = 39.57. Note that Model's SS of 39.57 is less than 28.79 + 1.54 + 9.85 = 40.18 (these same subcommands in the equal *N* case would add up). This overlapping variance situation gives rise to ambiguity in interpretation.

There are two general approaches to analysis in this case. The first is what Keppel (1991) termed the "unweighted means" approach. In this approach, the cell means are multiplied by the harmonic *N* (p. 289) and then standard analyses are conducted on the resulting matrix of adjusted cell sums. This approach cannot be implemented in SPSS (or most other software); it must be completed by hand and is no longer recommended by statisticians.

The second general approach is termed the *General Linear Model* or *least squares* approach and is quite easily implemented with computer software (and not easily calculated without a computer). A complication, however, is that there are several variants of this approach that yield different results, and the variant that is preferred depends on the type of experiment, which is often related to why data are missing (see Tabachnik & Fidell, 2001). The preferred variant for experimental designs (in which you assume your missingness is completely random and does not reflect true population differences in group sizes) is what Keppel termed "the analysis of unique scores" approach (Tabachnick & Fidell termed this approach the "unweighted-means" approach, not to be confused with Keppel's unweighted means approach, see previous discussion) and is often also called the *SS Type III* approach. This approach does not assign the overlapping variance to any effect; the overlapping variance between effects is simply discarded and not used by any effect. Put another way, the test for each effect, 'facta', 'factb', and their interaction, partials (or corrects or adjusts for) the variance of each of the other two effects. In MANOVA, the subcommand "METHOD=UNIQUE" directs

---

[2]The weighted mean formula for unequal *N* is:

$$\frac{\sum N\overline{Y}}{\sum N}.$$

For the second marginal,

$$\frac{\sum N\overline{Y}}{\sum N} = \frac{6.6 \cdot 5 + 5.25 \cdot 4}{5 + 4} = \frac{54}{9} = 6.00.$$

SPSS to perform this analysis. However, because "UNIQUE" is the default "METHOD" in MANOVA, you do not actually have to specify the previous syntax to obtain this analysis unless you have previously overridden the default with some other "METHOD" subcommand. Fig. 4.8 contains the results for this method.

```
Tests of Significance for SHOTS using UNIQUE sums of squares
  Source of Variation            SS        DF        MS           F    Sig of F

  WITHIN CELLS                25.10        21      1.20
  FACTA                       26.66         2     13.33       11.15        .001
  FACTB                        1.45         1      1.45        1.21        .283
  FACTA BY FACTB               9.85         2      4.92        4.12        .031

  (Model)                     39.57         5      7.91        6.62        .001
  (Total)                     64.67        26      2.49

  R-Squared =           .612
  Adjusted R-Squared =  .519
```

FIG. 4.8.   Output for METHOD=UNIQUE (the default) for an unequal N design.

Note that the sums of squares for "FACTA" and "FACTB" are different from those in Fig. 4.4 and the three effects' sums of squares do not add up to the sum of squares "Model". Keppel (1991) cautioned that F may be slightly positively biased with this method and thus a slightly more stringent alpha level should be adopted.

The second variant, sometimes termed the *SS Type II* approach, the preferred variant for nonexperimental studies in which unequal cell sizes are meaningful and reflect real-world differences, partials both main effects from the interaction (as does the unique approach), but from each main effect only partials the other main effect (not also the interaction). Thus, the test of significance for Factor A is adjusted for Factor B and the test of Factor B is adjusted for Factor A. In MANOVA, this is accomplished by specifying "ERROR=WITHIN" and two consecutive "DESIGN" statements as follows:

```
/ERROR=WITHIN
/DESIGN
/DESIGN=facta, factb.
```

The first "DESIGN" statement gives you the same printout as Fig. 4.8. From it, you examine only the interaction, in this case, with $F(2, 21) = 4.12$. The second "DESIGN" statement yields the results seen in Fig. 4.9.

```
Tests of Significance for SHOTS using UNIQUE sums of squares
  Source of Variation            SS        DF        MS           F    Sig of F

  WITHIN CELLS                25.10        21      1.20
  FACTA                       28.18         2     14.09       11.79        .000
  FACTB                         .93         1       .93         .78        .388
```

FIG. 4.9.   Output for SS Type 2 method for main effects in an unequal N design.

The results in response to the second "DESIGN" statement (i.e., Fig. 4.9) would be where you obtain the main effect results, which are somewhat changed from Fig. 4.8. Many writers believe that this approach ought not to be used to evaluate main effects when the interaction is large or significant. Of course, most writers recommend not analyzing main effects at all when the interaction is large and significant, instead preferring to explore the interaction.

In the third variant, which might be called the *hierarchical* or *SS Type I* method, the overlapping variance is given to whichever main effect the researcher has greater interest in (Tabachnick & Fidell, 2001, called this approach the "weighted n" approach, but it is not the weighted n approach discussed by Keppel, 1991). Assigning the overlapping variance to a particular effect requires adding a new subcommand, namely the "METHOD=SEQUENTIAL" subcommand. Each sum of squares would then be adjusted for the effects that precede it. The order of testing may be controlled by a

"DESIGN" subcommand. For example, the syntax 'DESIGN=factb, facta, facta BY factb' would produce a test for Factor B not adjusted for anything else, a test for Factor A adjusted for the effects of Factor B, and a test of the interaction adjusted for Factor A and Factor B. The results are shown in Fig. 4.10.

```
Tests of Significance for SHOTS using SEQUENTIAL Sums of Squares
Source of Variation        SS      DF        MS        F   Sig of F

WITHIN+RESIDUAL          25.10      21      1.20
FACTB                     1.54       1      1.54     1.29     .269
FACTA                    28.18       2     14.09    11.79     .000
FACTA BY FACTB            9.85       2      4.92     4.12     .031

(Model)                  39.57       5      7.91     6.62     .001
(Total)                  64.67      26      2.49
```

FIG. 4.10.   Output for hierarchical method, with Factor B requested to precede Factor A in an unequal *N* design.

Note that the *F* value for Factor B in this method is the highest of any of the other variants (though still very small). This is because, generally, by testing an effect first in a sequential test, you maximize the power of the test. In the absence of an explicit "DESIGN" subcommand (or of an explicit specification on the "DESIGN" subcommand), the specification would default to testing first whichever main effect was specified first on the "MANOVA" command after the "BY". In this approach, the sums of squares for the three effects will add up to the sum of squares "Model" (i.e., 1.54 + 28.18 + 9.85 = 39.57).

The fact that there are several approaches to significance testing, as well as issues surrounding why the cell *N*s are unequal, whether cells within a row or column have cell *N*s that are in the same proportion as in every other row or column, whether cell *N*s are proportional to their representation in the population, and whether some cells have zero *N*s, make unequal *N* factorial designs a rather thorny problem. Extrapolation to larger factorials multiply these problems. Additionally, when other analyses explored in this chapter, such as simple effects and simple comparisons, are desired in the context of unequal *N* factorials, the problems get so complicated that most writers advise unfactorializing: Treat each cell as if it was derived from a one-way design.

PLANNED CONTRASTS AND POST HOC ANALYSES OF MAIN EFFECTS

Basically, when exploring main effects on marginal means, you may include "CONTRAST" subcommands for each factor. Then the "DESIGN" subcommand requests tests of significance for each contrast, as shown in the syntax presented in Fig. 4.11 to analyze a hypothetical 3 × 3 example.

```
1.    MANOVA score BY facta(1,3) factb(1,3)

2d.   /OMEANS=TABLES (facta, factb, facta BY factb)

3.    /CONTRAST(facta)=SPECIAL

4.      (1 1 1

5.       1 0 -1

6.      -1 2 -1)

7.    /CONTRAST(factb)=DIFFERENCE

8.    /DESIGN=facta(1), facta(2), factb(1), factb(2), facta BY factb.
```

FIG. 4.11.   Syntax commands to conduct planned contrasts on main effects in a two-factor between-subjects ANOVA.

As Fig. 4.11 shows, contrasts are requested on both Factor A and Factor B, a "SPECIAL" contrast on Factor A and the "DIFFERENCE" contrast set on Factor B. The "DESIGN" subcommand requests tests of significance for both Factor A contrasts—the 'facta(1) facta(2)' part of the "DESIGN" subcommand—as well as the Factor B contrasts—the 'factb(1) factb(2)' part of the "DESIGN" subcommand. Additionally, the test of the interaction is requested—the 'facta BY factb' part of the "DESIGN" subcommand. Although the latter is not one of the contrasts, omitting it will cause problems for the error term and the accuracy of the analyses. An alternative to its inclusion, therefore, is to insert the subcommand:

/ERROR=WITHIN

Unless the "DESIGN" statement accounts for all orthogonal degrees of freedom between groups, which it would not do if you left out the 'facta BY factb', you have to specify that you want the "WITHIN" error term and not the default, which is "WITHIN+RESIDUAL". If you do not specify this, your tests will be incorrect. The salient parts of the output are in Fig. 4.12.

```
Tests of Significance for SCORE using UNIQUE sums of squares
  Source of Variation          SS        DF        MS          F   Sig of F

WITHIN+RESIDUAL             194.00        18     10.78
FACTA(1)                     68.06         1     68.06       6.31      .022
FACTA(2)                     20.17         1     20.17       1.87      .188
FACTB(1)                      8.00         1      8.00        .74      .400
FACTB(2)                      6.00         1      6.00        .56      .465
FACTA BY FACTB               76.44         4     19.11       1.77      .178
```

FIG. 4.12.   Output for planned contrasts on main effects in a two-factor between-subjects ANOVA.

As Fig. 4.12 shows, the only significant contrast is "FACTA(1)", $F(1, 18) = 6.31$, $p = .022$, which compares the marginal mean of the first Factor A group to the third Factor A group's mean.

Virtually the same method is used if trend analyses rather than typical planned contrasts are required. In this case, simply specify "POLYNOMIAL" contrasts.

If you were performing post hoc tests rather than planned contrasts on marginal means, the general method is the same. For example, because only the Factor A main effect was significant, you would probably conduct "SIMPLE" contrasts on Factor A, then use the manual calculation discussed in chapter 3 to obtain special criterion values (which specific criterion values depend on whether Tukey, Bonferroni, Scheffé, or other tests are desired), then compare the SPSS output to these special criteria to establish significance. Figure 4.13 shows the syntax for the original 3 × 2 design presented in Fig. 4.1 (not the previous 3 × 3 example).

```
1.    MANOVA score BY facta(1,3) factb(1,2)

2d.   /OMEANS=TABLES(facta, factb, facta by factb)

3.    /CONTRAST(facta)=SIMPLE (1)

4.    /ERROR=WITHIN

5.    /DESIGN=facta(1) facta(2)

6.    /CONTRAST(facta)=SIMPLE(2)

7.    /DESIGN=facta(1) facta(2).
```

FIG. 4.13.   Syntax commands to conduct post hoc tests on main effects in a two-factor between-subjects ANOVA.

EXPLORING A SIGNIFICANT INTERACTION

As mentioned earlier, post hoc or planned tests on marginals are generally considered appropriate only when the interaction is not significant. When it is significant, it is more common and appropriate to explore this interaction. There are two general approaches to probing a significant interaction. You can conduct either a simple effects analysis or an interaction comparison analysis (Keppel, 1991, pp. 236–237).

Simple Effects

Simple effects (some authors use the term *simple main effects*, however, in this manual, the term *simple effects*, following Keppel, 1991, will be used) test the effect of one factor at each level of the other factor. For example, in this type of analysis, as applied to the example in Fig. 4.1, you could look at the simple effects of type of training at the two different levels of type of team or you could look at the simple effects of type of team at each of the three levels of type of training. Typically, you either look at the simple effects of Factor A at Factor B or the simple effects of Factor B at Factor A and usually not both, because they would provide redundant information and therefore result in alpha-inflation problems. Although you would not typically request both simple effects, the syntax for both will be presented here for illustrative purposes. Which simple effect you choose should be determined by the purpose of the study. The syntax to run simple effects analyses on Factor A is in Fig. 4.14.

```
1.    MANOVA shots BY facta(1,3) factb(1,2)

2.        /ERROR=WITHIN

3.        /DESIGN=facta WITHIN factb(1), facta WITHIN factb(2).
```

FIG. 4.14.   Syntax commands to test the simple effects of Factor A at the two levels of Factor B.

Simple effects are specified on the "DESIGN" subcommand. If you want the overall ANOVA results, as well as the results from a contrast, simple effect, and so on, you need to add a blank "DESIGN" statement before or after line 3. A "DESIGN" statement with nothing after it tells SPSS to run the full factorial model, which will give the overall ANOVA table. Notice in line 2 that the "ERROR=WITHIN" subcommand was used because all orthogonal degrees of freedom between groups were not specified on the "DESIGN" subcommand. Unless you are sure your request includes all orthogonal degrees of freedom between groups, inclusion of the "ERROR=WITHIN" subcommand is generally a wise precaution.

To test a simple effect in SPSS, you simply specify on the "DESIGN" statement that you want to test the simple effects of that factor at each level of the other. Thus, the statement to get the simple effects of Factor A at each level of Factor B is seen in Fig. 4.14, line 3, where the numbers in parentheses after 'factb' specify the level of Factor B for the simple effect. The first part of the "DESIGN" statement in the previous example, 'facta WITHIN factb(1)', directs SPSS to test the means of the control group, Imagine group, or Practice group for the varsity players, in other words, if the 4.6, 3.4, and 6.6 are significantly different from one another. The second part of the "DESIGN" statement, 'facta WITHIN factb(2)', directs SPSS to test whether the analogous means for the nonvarsity players, in other words, the 3.2, 4.6, and 5.6, are significantly different from one another. The results are in Fig. 4.15.

```
Tests of Significance for SHOTS using UNIQUE sums of squares
  Source of Variation          SS       DF        MS          F  Sig of F

WITHIN CELLS                 30.80       24      1.28
FACTA WITHIN FACTB(1)        26.13        2     13.07      10.18     .001
FACTA WITHIN FACTB(2)        14.53        2      7.27       5.66     .010
```

FIG. 4.15.   Output for the simple effects of Factor A at both levels of Factor B.

The simple effect of Factor A was significant for the varsity, $F(2, 24) = 10.18$, $p = .001$, as well as the nonvarsity players, $F(2, 24) = 5.66$, $p = .010$. This indicates that the means of 4.6, 3.4, and 6.6 were statistically different from one another and the means of 3.2, 4.6, and 5.6 were also significantly different. Thus, type of training made a difference for both the varsity and nonvarsity players.

You could have tested instead the simple effects of Factor B at each level of Factor A, as seen in Fig. 4.16.

```
1.    MANOVA shots BY facta(1,3) factb(1,2)

2.        /ERROR=WITHIN

3.        /DESIGN=factb WITHIN facta(1), factb WITHIN facta(2), factb

4.        WITHIN facta(3).
```

FIG. 4.16.   Syntax commands to test the simple effects of Factor B at the three levels of Factor A.

The "DESIGN" statement to obtain the simple effects of Factor B at each level of Factor A starts on line 3, where again the numbers in parentheses after 'facta' specify the level of Factor A for the test of simple main effects. This example tests whether or not type of team makes a difference for players in the control group, 'factb WITHIN facta(1)'; whether or not type of team makes a difference for players in the Imagine group, 'factb WITHIN facta(2)'; and whether or not type of team makes a difference for players in the Practice group, 'factb WITHIN facta(3)'.

```
Tests of Significance for SHOTS using UNIQUE sums of squares
Source of Variation          SS        DF        MS          F   Sig of F

WITHIN CELLS               30.80       24      1.28
FACTB WITHIN FACTA(1)       4.90        1      4.90       3.82      .062
FACTB WITHIN FACTA(2)       3.60        1      3.60       2.81      .107
FACTB WITHIN FACTA(3)       2.50        1      2.50       1.95      .176
```

FIG. 4.17.   Output for the simple effects of Factor B at the three levels of Factor A.

As shown in Fig. 4.17, the simple effect of type of team is nonsignificant for the players in all conditions (though it is near significant, $p = .062$, for the control group), thus type of team did not have an effect for players in the control group, the Practice group, or the Imagine group.

For the sake of simplicity, assume you are interested in the first set of simple effects, the effect of type of training at each of the different team types (simples of Factor A at levels of Factor B). From the analysis, you learned that type of training makes a difference for both types of players, but you do not know yet which group differences account for those simple effects. To answer that question, you may next turn to simple comparisons.

Simple Comparisons and Simple Post Hocs

These are programmed quite similarly to the contrasts from the previous chapter. To proceed, assume that you were only interested in the effect of type of training on the varsity players. In this case, you might be interested in finding out if the control group is significantly different from the Imagine group and if the Imagine group is different from the Practice group. Notice that you need only do these tests in the varsity group, as that is the only group you are interested in. Thus, you are comparing the 4.6 to the 3.4 and the 3.4 to the 6.6. The first step in conducting a simple comparison is to write a "CON-TRAST" statement that gives you the contrasts of interest. The syntax to do this is in Fig. 4.18.

```
1.   MANOVA shots BY facta(1,3) factb(1,2)

2.       /ERROR=WITHIN

3.       /CONTRAST(facta)=SPECIAL  (1 1 1, 1 -1 0, 0 -1 1)

4.       /DESIGN=facta(1) WITHIN factb(1), facta(2) WITHIN factb(1).
```

FIG. 4.18.   Syntax commands to conduct simple comparisons on Factor A at the first level of Factor B.

The "CONTRAST" statement looks the same as it did in chapter 3. There is a row of 1s, the same number of them as the number of groups of the factor on which you are doing the simple comparison (in this case Factor A) and then $k - 1$ contrasts.[3] As usual, a "DESIGN" statement is included with the "CONTRAST" statement. In line 4, the number in parentheses after the 'facta' refers to which contrast from the "SPECIAL" contrast you are specifying, whereas the number in parentheses after the 'factb' is the level of Factor B in which the contrast is tested. Thus, in this example, you are testing the control versus Imagine for the varsity players with the statement 'facta(1) WITHIN factb(1)' and the Imagine versus Practice for the varsity players with the statement 'facta(2) WITHIN factb(1)'. The "ERROR=WITHIN" subcommand is necessary because the contrasts requested do not exhaust the degrees of freedom. The output is in Fig. 4.19.

```
Tests of Significance for SHOTS using UNIQUE sums of squares
   Source of Variation         SS       DF       MS        F   Sig of F

   WITHIN CELLS               30.80     24     1.28
   FACTA(1) WITHIN FACTB(1)    3.60      1     3.60     2.81     .107
   FACTA(2) WITHIN FACTB(1)   25.60      1    25.60    19.95     .000
```

FIG. 4.19. Output for the simple comparisons on Factor A at the first level of Factor B.

You can see that, within the varsity players group, there is a difference between the Imagine and Practice groups (i.e., between the 3.4 and the 6.6), $F(1, 24) = 19.95$, $p = .001$, but not between the control group and the Imagine group.

It is sometimes desirable to conduct simple post hoc tests, post hocs of the differences of all pairs of cell means within a given row or column. The methods described previously are generally used with sets of "SIMPLE" contrasts.

Interaction Contrasts

Instead of analyzing simple effects and then simple comparisons, you could test an interaction contrast. In this type of analysis, you are asking if a contrast on Factor A acts differently at one level of Factor B versus another level of Factor B. Typically, interaction contrasts would be specified a priori. For example, you might be interested in a pairwise contrast testing whether the difference between the Imagine group and Practice group for the varsity players is the same as the difference between the Imagine group and Practice group for the nonvarsity players. In another interaction contrast, you could test whether the differences between the control and the average of the two other types of training groups act differently across levels of Factor B. The syntax to test this when the factor you are looking at (Factor B here) has two levels is given in Fig. 4.20. An example of how to do this when this factor has more than two levels can be seen in Fig. 4.22. To test the interaction contrast, you first write a "CONTRAST" statement with $k - 1$ contrasts. In this example, there are two contrasts, the Imagine versus Practice contrast and the control versus the average of the two types of training.

```
1.   MANOVA errors BY facta(1,3) factb(1,2)

2.       /CONTRAST(facta)=SPECIAL (1 1 1, 1 –1 0, 2 –1 –1)

3.       /DESIGN=facta (1), facta (2), factb, facta(1) BY factb,

4.       facta(2) BY factb.
```

FIG. 4.20. Syntax commands to test interaction contrasts when one factor has only two levels.

First, the contrasts are defined in line 2, then a "DESIGN" statement is written to test them. In line 3, the first Factor A contrast, the second Factor A contrast, the Factor B effect (there is no con-

---

[3]'CONTRAST(facta)=REPEATED' would work the way line 3 does, so could have been substituted.

trast possible on Factor B because Factor B has only two levels), and then the two interaction contrasts are specified. The number in parentheses after 'facta' refers to the contrast being tested and the 'BY factb' tells SPSS to test whether that contrast is acting differently at the different levels of Factor B. You can think of this "DESIGN" statement as being similar to the one to run the overall ANOVA, where you specify main effect Factor A, main effect Factor B, and then the interaction. You are essentially doing the same thing here by specifying the main contrast effects and then the interaction contrast effects. If you do not specify all of the effects (here all of the effects were specified), the tests of the interaction contrasts will be incorrect, unless you add "ERROR=WITHIN". The output is in Fig. 4.21.

```
Tests of Significance for SHOTS using UNIQUE sums of squares
Source of Variation          SS        DF        MS          F     Sig of F

WITHIN+RESIDUAL             30.80       24       1.28
FACTA(1)                      .05        1        .05        .04      .845
FACTA(2)                     8.82        1       8.82       6.87      .015
FACTB                        1.20        1       1.20        .94      .343
FACTA(1) BY FACTB            8.45        1       8.45       6.58      .017
FACTA(2) BY FACTB            3.75        1       3.75       2.92      .100
```

FIG. 4.21.   Output for an interaction contrast where Factor A has three levels and Factor B has two levels.

The difference between the control group and Imagine group on the marginal means, that is, the difference between the 3.90 and the 4.00, the "FACTA(1)" effect, is nonsignificant, $F(1, 24) = .04$, $p = .845$. However, there is a significant difference between the control group and the average of the other two training groups, that is, the "FACTA(2)" effect, which tests whether the 3.90 differs from the average of the 4.00 and the 6.10, $F(1, 24) = 6.87$, $p = .015$. The "FACTB" main effect is nonsignificant, with exactly the same values as in the overall output, Fig. 4.4. Turning now to the two interaction contrasts, the first, "FACTA(1) BY FACTB", is significant, $F(1, 24) = 6.58$, $p = .017$. Because "FACTA(1)" tests the difference between the control and Imagine groups, the interpretation of this is that the difference between the control and Imagine groups is different for the varsity and nonvarsity players. Specifically, for the varsity players, this difference is 1.20, or 4.6 (the mean of the control condition) minus 3.4 (the mean of the Imagine condition). For the nonvarsity players, this difference is −1.4, or 3.2 (the mean of the control condition) minus 4.6 (the mean of the Imagine condition). The significant interaction contrast tells you that the 1.20 is significantly different from the −1.40.

The second interaction contrast, "FACTA(2) BY FACTB", does not reach significance, $F(1, 24) = 2.92$, $p = .100$. Because "FACTA(2)" examines the difference between the control group and the average of the two other training groups, the interpretation of this is that the extent of this difference does not depend on whether you are considering the varsity or the nonvarsity players. For the varsity players, this difference is −.40, or 4.6 (the mean of the control condition) minus 5.0 (the average of the 3.4 and the 6.6, the two other training conditions). For the nonvarsity players, this difference is −1.9, or 3.2 (the mean of the control condition) minus 5.1 (the average of the 4.6 and the 5.6, the other two training conditions). The nonsignificant interaction contrast tells you that the −.40 is not significantly different from the −1.9.

Interaction Contrasts When Both Factors Have More Than Two Levels

Although more complicated than the previous design, you can also conduct interaction contrasts when both factors have more than two levels. Keppel (1991, p. 254) distinguished two types of such interaction contrasts: $A_{Comp} \times B$ and $A_{Comp} \times B_{Comp}$. Although the former type represents no special issues—the syntax discussed earlier, e.g., 'facta(1) BY factb', works appropriately—the latter type, in which you wish to explore how a contrast on each of the factors interacts, has not been previously covered. To test it, you have to decide which contrasts you will examine in Factor A, as well as which contrasts you will examine in Factor B. An example of how to set up such a design is in Fig. 4.22, assuming that Factors A and B have three levels.

```
1.    MANOVA score BY facta(1,3) factb(1,3)

2.       /CONTRAST(facta)=SPECIAL (1 1 1, 1 –1 0, 2 –1 –1)

3.       /CONTRAST(factb)=SPECIAL (1 1 1, 1 0 –1, 0 1 -1)

4.       /DESIGN=facta (1), facta (2), factb(1), factb(2), facta(1) BY factb(1),

5.          facta(2) BY factb(1), facta(1) BY factb(2), facta(2) BY factb(2).
```

FIG. 4.22.   Syntax commands to conduct $A_{Comp} \times B_{Comp}$ interaction contrasts when both factors have three levels.

In this example, for Factor A, you are looking at Group 1 versus Group 2 and Group 1 versus the average of Groups 2 and 3, and for Factor B, you are looking at Group 1 versus Group 3 and Group 2 versus Group 3. You set up contrasts on Factor B the same way you set them up on Factor A (see line 3). On the "DESIGN" statement, the main effects contrasts must be specified before the interaction contrasts.

Suppose the means are as in Table 4.2. The first interaction contrast in the "DESIGN" statement, 'facta(1) BY factb(1)', tests whether the difference between a1 versus a2, as the first Factor A contrast has the weights 1 –1 0, is different at b1 versus b3, as 'factb(1)' has the weights 1 0 –1 (the numbers in parentheses refer to the contrast numbers for both factors). In other words, this interaction contrast tests whether the 5 minus the 8 difference is similar to the 7 minus 11 difference. Now consider 'facta(2) BY factb(2)'. Because 'facta(2)' is 2 –1 –1, this explores the first Factor A group as compared to the average of the second and third Factor A groups. Because 'factb(2)' has the weights 0 1 –1, this explores whether the second Factor B group differs from the third Factor B group. Thus, putting these two together, 'facta(2) BY factb(2)' tests whether the 9 minus the average of 2 and 10, that is $9 - [(2 + 10)/2] = 9 - 6 = 3$, differs from the 7 minus the average of 11 and 3, that is, $7 - [(11 + 3)/2] = 7 - 7 = 0$. As always, if every degree of freedom is not accounted for (i.e., all possible interaction contrasts as well as all main effect contrasts), the results will be incorrect unless "ERROR=WITHIN" is specified. In this case, all possible interaction contrasts are the first contrast on Factor A interacting with the first contrast of Factor B, the second contrast on Factor A interacting with the first contrast of Factor B, the first contrast on Factor A interacting with the second contrast of Factor B, and the second contrast on Factor A interacting with the second contrast of Factor B.

TABLE 4.2
Hypothetical Marginal and Cell Means for a 3 × 3 ANOVA

FACTB	FACTA			
	a1	a2	a3	Average
b1	5	8	14	9
b2	9	2	10	7
b3	7	11	3	7
Average	7	7	9	

Trend Interaction Contrasts and Simple Trend Analysis

Just as you can conduct a trend analysis in a one-factor ANOVA, you can also examine trends in a two-factor design. To do this, you specify a "POLYNOMIAL" contrast for the quantitative factor. Earlier in this chapter you considered trends on marginal means. Now the interaction of a particular trend with the other factor, for example, the interaction of the linear trend of Factor A with Factor B, is examined. If the interaction of the linear trend of Factor A with Factor B was statistically significant, it would indicate that there are different linear trends of Factor A at the different levels of Factor B, or linear trends of Factor A at some levels of Factor B, but not at others. To test this interaction, still assuming Factor A is the quantitative factor, the "DESIGN" subcommand would specify 'facta(1) BY factb'.

There are other possible interactions of interest, for example, the interaction of two trends if both factors are quantitative. Specifically, if the interaction of the linear trend of Factor A with the linear trend of Factor B was statistically significant, it would indicate that the linear trend of Factor A increases (or decreases) linearly over levels of Factor B. This would be tested with the specification 'facta(1) BY factb(1)'. All such further specifications would be added to the "DESIGN" subcommand. The only requirement is that the total of all degrees of freedom for interaction questions being tested should not add up to more than the number of degrees of freedom in the interaction term. An example of the "DESIGN" subcommand that includes requests for trend interactions in a 4 × 3 design is as follows:

/DESIGN=facta(1), facta(2), facta(3), factb(1), factb(2),
    facta(1) BY factb(1), facta(2) BY factb(1), facta(3) BY factb(1),
    facta(1) BY factb(2), facta(2) BY factb(2), facta(3) BY factb(2).

All of these designs can easily be extended to designs with three or more factors, as you will see in chapter 5.

You can also examine simple trends, that is, trends on one factor within levels of the other factor by "DESIGN" specifications of the form 'facta(2) WITHIN factb(3)', which would test the quadratic trend on Factor A within the third level of Factor B.

PAC

A two-factor ANOVA can be easily run using the PAC pull-down menus in SPSS for Windows. You would access the exact same menus as in the one factor, but this time, you would send two variables over to the Fixed Factor(s) box as seen in Fig. 4.23.

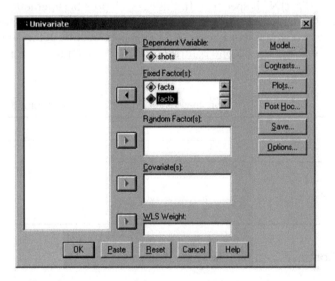

FIG. 4.23.   Dialogue box for a two-factor between-subjects ANOVA.

You can conduct post hocs and trend analyses using the same menus as in the one factor. Specifically, to conduct post hocs, you would select the factor you wanted the post hoc test on along with the test itself (see Fig. 4.24). You could request post hocs on both factors, but if you wanted different types of post hoc tests on the two factors (Duncan tests are selected in the example of Fig. 4.24), you would have to run the analyses separately.

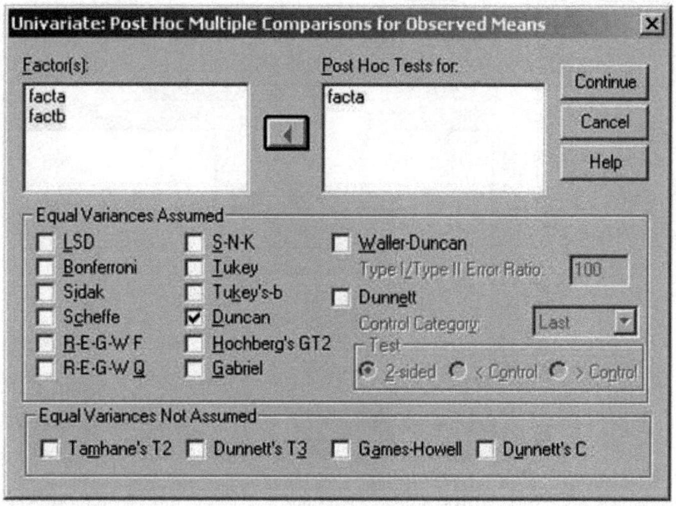

FIG. 4.24.   Dialogue box to conduct post hoc tests in a two-factor between-subjects ANOVA.

To conduct any of the canned contrasts, you would use the Contrast button and select the contrast you desired, as outlined in chapter 3. Simple effects, simple comparisons, and interaction contrasts would have to be conducted with syntax. The syntax to accomplish these analyses is somewhat more difficult than MANOVA's (which was another reason to work primarily with MANOVA in this text) and is detailed in chapter 13 for the interested reader. Power, effect size estimates, and means can be obtained in the Options submenu as seen in Fig. 4.25.

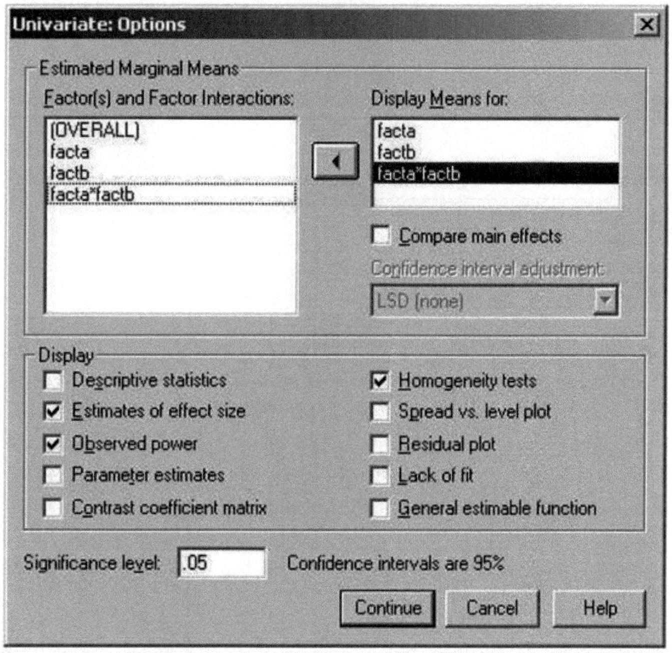

FIG. 4.25.   Options dialogue box.

You would send 'facta', 'factb', and 'facta*factb' over to the Display Means for box in order to obtain both cell and marginal means. The boxes for power, effect size, and homogeneity are also checked, thus providing you with that information, as outlined in chapter 3.

If you would like to run an unequal *N* analysis using something other than *Type III SS*, click on the Model button at the top right of Fig. 4.23. You will get a dialogue box as seen in Fig. 4.26.

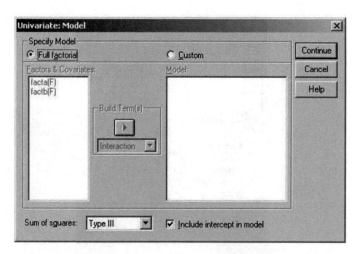

FIG. 4.26.   Dialogue box to change the type of Sum of squares.

On the bottom left-hand side of the Model screen is another pull-down menu for Sum of squares. By default, this is set to Type III. Other options include Type II (detailed earlier), Type I, which is the approach labeled as "sequential" by MANOVA, and Type IV (a similar approach to Type III that is sometimes used if any of the cells have $N = 0$).

5 Three (and Greater) Factor Between-Subjects Analysis of Variance

In chapter 4 you learned how to analyze a two-factor completely randomized ANOVA. In this chapter, those commands are extended to a three-factor design (and beyond).

BASIC ANALYSIS OF VARIANCE COMMANDS

The data for this example are from Stevens (1999, p. 174). In order to make the output more understandable, the variables have been renamed from Stevens' original terms. In this study, the researcher investigated the effects of grade and gender of the participant and type of feedback on memory. The dependent variable is 'score', the participant's score on a memory test. There are three independent variables: Factor A is grade (either first grade, coded 1, or third, coded 2), Factor B is the gender of the participant (either boy, coded 1, or girl, coded 2), and Factor C is the type of feedback a person received (either positive, coded 1, negative, coded 2, or none, coded 3). This design is a 2 × 2 × 3 analysis of variance. Each participant of a certain level of age ('facta') and a certain gender ('factb') received a certain level of feedback ('factc'). For example, one group of participants was male first graders receiving positive feedback. There are 12 (= 2 × 2 × 3) such groups of participants in all.

The syntax, presented in Fig. 5.1, is followed by an explanation of the function of the different commands in the program.

```
1.    MANOVA score BY facta(1,2) factb(1,2) factc(1,3)

2d.      /OMEANS=TABLES(facta, factb, factc, facta by factb, facta by factc,

3.          factb by factc, facta by factb by factc)

4d.      /POWER

5d.      /PRINT=SIGNIF(EFSIZE)
```

FIG. 5.1. Syntax commands to conduct a three-factor between-subjects ANOVA.

The syntax for the three-factor ANOVA is very similar to that of the two-factor ANOVA. The "MANOVA" command is followed by the dependent variable, in this case, 'score'. Next is the keyword "BY", which in turn is followed by the names of the factors, here, 'facta', 'factb', and 'factc'. The variable names designating the factors are each immediately followed by parentheses that contain the information on the levels of the factor. If you had wished to include a fourth, a fifth, or even more such factors or independent variables, they would simply each follow 'factc' and be defined in the same manner. In order to obtain the means for each factor, for each combination of two factors, and for the combination of 3 factors, you have to ask for them after the keyword "TABLES" on the "OMEANS" subcommand in line 2. Effect sizes and power analyses were requested on lines 4 through 5. If you leave off the "DESIGN" subcommand, as was done here, SPSS will automatically generate the full factorial model, which gives the results in Fig. 5.2. The output generated by "OMEANS" has been omitted for now.

```
Tests of Significance for SCORE using UNIQUE sums of squares
Source of Variation           SS        DF        MS         F    Sig of F
WITHIN CELLS               217.33        24      9.06
FACTA                         .11         1       .11       .01    .913
FACTB                       36.00         1     36.00      3.98    .058
FACTC                       24.89         2     12.44      1.37    .272
FACTA BY FACTB                .11         1       .11       .01    .913
FACTA BY FACTC              80.89         2     40.44      4.47    .022
FACTB BY FACTC               4.67         2      2.33       .26    .775
FACTA BY FACTB BY FACTA     74.89         2     37.44      4.13    .029

(Model)                    221.56        11     20.14      2.22    .049
(Total)                    438.89        35     12.54

R-Squared =           .505
Adjusted R-Squared =  .278
- - - - - - - - - - - - - - - - - - - - - - - - - - - - - - - - - - - - -
Effect Size Measures and Observed Power at the .0500 Level
                       Partial Noncen-
Source of Variation    ETA Sqd trality     Power

FACTA                     .001    .012      .042
FACTB                     .142   3.975      .481
FACTC                     .103   2.748      .266
FACTA BY FACTB            .001    .012      .042
FACTA BY FACTC            .271   8.933      .710
FACTB BY FACTC            .021    .515      .088
FACTA BY FACTB BY FACTA   .256   8.270      .674
```

FIG. 5.2.   Output from a three-factor between-subjects ANOVA.

This output is an extension of that for the two-factor ANOVA. First, there is an F test for each of the main effects, then F tests for each of the three possible two-way interactions, and finally an F test for the three-way interaction. In this design, whether grade has an effect averaging over gender and type of feedback is being tested as the "FACTA" main effect, whether gender has an effect averaging over grade and all types of feedback is tested as the "FACTB" main effect, and whether type of feedback has an effect averaging over all levels of grade and gender is the "FACTC" main effect. You can observe that none of these effects is significant at the .05 level. You also receive the effect size and power estimates for each effect, in response to lines 4 through 5. Recalling that the formula for partial eta squared in factorial designs is $SS_{Factor\ name}/(SS_{Factor\ name} + SS_{Within\ Cells})$, Factor A, disregarding Factors B and C, accounts for 0.10% of the variance in the dependent variable; Factor B, disregarding Factors A and C, accounts for 14.2% of the variance in the dependent variable; and, finally, Factor C, disregarding Factors A and B, accounts for 10.3% of the variance in the dependent variable.

Here is the first part of the "OMEANS" output:

```
Combined Observed Means for FACTA
 Variable .. SCORE
         FACTA
           1        WGT.      8.61111
                  UNWGT.      8.61111
           2        WGT.      8.50000
                  UNWGT.      8.50000
```

As seen, the "WGT." (weighted) and "UNWGT." (unweighted) means are identical, as they will always be for equal N designs. To save space, however, the "OMEANS" portion of output deleting the "UNWGT." line will be reprinted in Fig. 5.3.

```
Combined Observed Means for FACTA
 Variable .. SCORE
        FACTA
          1         WGT.      8.61111
          2         WGT.      8.50000
- - - - - - - - - - - - - - - - - - - - - - - - - - - - - -
Combined Observed Means for FACTB
 Variable .. SCORE
        FACTB
          1         WGT.      7.55556
          2         WGT.      9.55556
- - - - - - - - - - - - - - - - - - - - - - - - - - - - - -
Combined Observed Means for FACTC
 Variable .. SCORE
        FACTC
          1         WGT.      7.66667
          2         WGT.      8.33333
          3         WGT.      9.66667
- - - - - - - - - - - - - - - - - - - - - - - - - - - - - -
Combined Observed Means for FACTA BY FACTB
 Variable .. SCORE
                   FACTA         1            2
        FACTB
          1         WGT.      7.55556      7.55556
          2         WGT.      9.66667      9.44444
- - - - - - - - - - - - - - - - - - - - - - - - - - - - - -
Combined Observed Means for FACTA BY FACTC
 Variable .. SCORE
                   FACTA         1            2
        FACTC
          1         WGT.      7.83333      7.50000
          2         WGT.      6.50000     10.16667
          3         WGT.     11.50000      7.83333
- - - - - - - - - - - - - - - - - - - - - - - - - - - - - -
Combined Observed Means for FACTB BY FACTC
 Variable .. SCORE
                   FACTB         1            2
        FACTC
          1         WGT.      6.50000      8.83333
          2         WGT.      7.83333      8.83333
          3         WGT.      8.33333     11.00000
- - - - - - - - - - - - - - - - - - - - - - - - - - - - - -
Combined Observed Means for FACTA BY FACTB BY FACTC
 Variable .. SCORE
                             FACTA         1            2
        FACTC     FACTB
          1         1         WGT.      6.33333      6.66667
          1         2         WGT.      9.33333      8.33333
          2         1         WGT.      4.33333     11.33333
          2         2         WGT.      8.66667      9.00000
          3         1         WGT.     12.00000      4.66667
          3         2         WGT.     11.00000     11.00000
```

FIG. 5.3.   Output generated by OMEANS in a three-factor between-subjects ANOVA.

In Table 5.1 you will find the final set of means (for "FACTA BY FACTB BY FACTC").

TABLE 5.1
Means for FACTA BY FACTB BY FACTC

	factc1		factc2		factc3	
	facta1	facta2	facta1	facta2	facta1	facta2
factb1	6.33	6.67	4.33	11.33	12.00	4.67
factb2	9.33	8.33	8.67	9.00	11.00	11.00

The nonsignificant main effects in the ANOVA printout suggest that the marginal means, printed out first, are all not significantly different. For example, the means for the two Factor B conditions, according to the printout, are 7.55556 and 9.55556, respectively. The nonsignificant ($p = $.058) F value of 3.98 for "FACTB" suggests that these two means are not significantly different.

The two-way interactions each explore whether two of the factors interact, averaged over all levels of the third factor. Consider, for example, the "FACTA BY FACTC" interaction, which the ANOVA revealed to be significant at the .022 level, with an F value of 4.47 and 27.10% of the variance in the dependent variable accounted for by this interaction (note that the other 2 two-way interactions are nonsignificant). The means being compared are displayed in the output section entitled "Combined Observed Means for FACTA BY FACTC". For the Positive Feedback condition (= 1), the means are 7.83333 and 7.50000, for the first and third grades of Factor A, respectively. The respective means for the Negative feedback condition (= 2) are 6.50000 and 10.16667 and for the No Feedback condition (= 3) they are 11.50000 and 7.83333. The entries in this table can also be obtained by averaging the values in Table 5.1 over Factor B. For example, the value in the cell at the intersection of 'facta2' and 'factc2' is 10.17. This comes from averaging the two values in the fourth column in Table 5.1, the 11.33 and the 9.00 (20.33/2), all of which are 'facta2' and 'factc2'. This two-factor interaction therefore examines whether type of feedback has a different effect for the two grade levels, averaging over gender. The significant "FACTA BY FACTC" two-way interaction is thus telling you that the pattern across type of feedback for the first graders is different from the pattern for the third graders. Each of the other means in each two-way table (actually, they are called *subtables*) can likewise be found by averaging over the relevant means in the three-way table. In turn, the marginal means are the average of the relevant means from the relevant two-way tables. For example, the first-grade marginal mean ("FACTA=1") of 8.61111, found in the "Combined Observed Means for FACTA" printout portion, can also be found by averaging the 7.83, 6.50, and 11.50 from the "FACTA BY FACTC" table or by averaging the 7.56 and the 9.67 from the "FACTA BY FACTB" table.

New in this design is the three-way (or triple) interaction. The three-way interaction is a reflection of whether one of the two-way interactions is different or has a different pattern at each of the levels of the third factor. For example, the "FACTA BY FACTB BY FACTC" interaction can be interpreted as asking if the "FACTA BY FACTC" interaction is the same for the boys and girls ("FACTB"). Alternatively, it can be interpreted as inquiring whether the "FACTB BY FACTC" interaction has the same or different patterns for each level of "FACTA", or whether the "FACTA BY FACTB" interaction has the same or different patterns for each level of "FACTC". All of these questions have the same answer: Either they all have the same pattern or they all have different patterns. In the current example, you would report the three-way interaction as significant, $F(2, 24) = 4.13$, $p = .029$, implying that these two-way interaction patterns are different over levels of the third factor.

In the presence of a significant interaction, it is usually inappropriate to interpret the lower order effects (i.e., main effects and interactions with fewer ways). In the case of the three-factor design, if you do not have any a priori hypotheses, this means that you would first look at the three-way interaction. If that is significant, you would proceed to explore within this significant interaction. If it is not significant, instead turn to looking at the significance of the two-way interactions. Again, if those are significant, explore those (exactly like you explored the significant interaction in a two-factor ANOVA). If no interactions are significant, then you would interpret the main effects.

You can also interpret a significant main effect if any interactions with that term are not significant. To interpret this main effect, you would either conduct a post hoc analysis on that factor or, if you had a priori hypotheses, you could run the appropriate planned contrasts as in chapter 3.

EXPLORING A SIGNIFICANT THREE-WAY INTERACTION

Simple Two-Way Interactions

If the three-way interaction is significant, you would then look at one of the following:

The simple Factor A × Factor B two-way interaction at the different levels of Factor C.
The simple Factor A × Factor C two-way interaction at the different levels of Factor B.
The simple Factor B × Factor C two-way interaction at the different levels of Factor A.

Similar to looking at simple effects, you would typically choose one of these interactions to analyze, and not all three. Your choice would depend on your interests. If you were interested in the simple Factor A × Factor C two-way interaction at each of the different levels of Factor B, you would test this interaction at the two levels of Factor B to examine its nature. The syntax to do that is in Fig. 5.4.

```
1.    MANOVA score BY facta(1,2) factb(1,2) factc(1,3)

2.      /ERROR=WITHIN

3.      /DESIGN=facta*factc WITHIN factb(1), facta*factc WITHIN factb(2).
```

FIG. 5.4. Syntax commands to analyze a simple two-way interaction in a three-factor between-subjects ANOVA.

The "DESIGN" statement is similar to the "DESIGN" statement to conduct a simple effects analysis in a two-factor ANOVA (this time the optional "*" keyword instead of the equivalent "BY" keyword is used). You simply tell SPSS which effect you want to test (in this case the Factor A × Factor C interaction) at which level(s) of another factor (in this case, each of the two levels of Factor B). If you had an interest in this test at only one level of Factor B, then you would simply run the test at that level only. Notice the "ERROR=WITHIN" subcommand in line 2. As before, unless the "DESIGN" statement accounts for all orthogonal degrees of freedom between groups, you have to specify that you want the "WITHIN" error term and not the default, which is "WITHIN+RESIDUAL". If you do not specify this, your tests will be incorrect.

The output in Fig. 5.5 looks very similar to the output seen previously for the between-subjects designs. Here you can see that the Factor A × Factor C interaction is significant at the first level of Factor B, $F(2, 24) = 8.52$, $p = .002$, but not at the second level, $F(2, 24) = .08$, $p = .924$.

```
Tests of Significance for SCORE using UNIQUE sums of squares
Source of Variation                    SS       DF       MS       F  Sig of F
WITHIN CELLS                        217.33      24     9.06
FACTA * FACTC WITHIN FACTB(1)       154.33       2    77.17    8.52     .002
FACTA * FACTC WITHIN FACTB(2)         1.44       2      .72     .08     .924
```

FIG. 5.5. Output for testing a simple two-way interaction in a three-factor between-subjects ANOVA.

Simple Simple Effects

If one of the tests of a simple two-way interaction is significant, as is "FACTA BY FACTC WITHIN FACTB(1)", you would follow it up with a simple effects test. Now, however, because the test would be within a level of both Factor B and another factor, such effects are often termed *simple simple effects*. For example, because the interaction of Factor A by Factor C was significant at the first level of Factor B (i.e., there is an interaction between grade and feedback for boys), you could then examine either the simple simple effects of Factor A within levels of Factor C or the simple simple effects of Factor C within levels of Factor A, in both cases restricting yourself to the first level of Factor B. The "DESIGN" statement to test the simple simple effects of Factor C at both levels of Factor A at the first level of Factor B is:

```
/ERROR=WITHIN
/DESIGN=factc WITHIN facta(1) WITHIN factb(1), factc WITHIN
    facta(2) WITHIN factb(1).
```

Simply use double "WITHIN"s to tell SPSS that you want the effects of Factor C within the first level of Factor A at the first level of Factor B and the effects of Factor C within the second level of Factor A at the first level of Factor B. If you wanted to look at the simple simple effects of Factor A, you would look at the effects of Factor A within the three levels of Factor C, all at the first level of Factor B.

A NONSIGNIFICANT THREE-WAY: SIMPLE EFFECTS

If the three-way interaction was nonsignificant, it would then be appropriate to examine the tests for the simple two-way interactions. You should also look at the results of the power analysis to see if you had enough power to detect the effect. If the power to detect the three-way interaction is low, it is possible that there is a three-way interaction, but there is not enough power to detect it. This power analysis illustrates why it is important to do a power analysis before you start the project, so you will have enough participants to detect the effects you are interested in.

If one of the two-way interactions was significant, you would simply proceed as you did in a two-factor ANOVA when the interaction was significant. You would examine either the simple effects or specific interaction contrasts. In this example, the Factor A × Factor C interaction was significant, so you could analyze the simple effects of Factor A at Factor C or the simple effects of Factor C at Factor A. The syntax to test these effects is the same as it was in a two-factor ANOVA. Namely, if you are testing the effects of Factor A at Factor C:

```
/ERROR=WITHIN
/DESIGN=facta WITHIN factc(1), facta WITHIN factc(2), facta
    WITHIN factc(3).
```

The output would look identical to that presented in chapter 4 for simple effects. If one of these simple effects was significant, you would likely wish to follow it up with simple comparisons of interest.

Interaction Contrasts, Simple Comparisons, Simple Simple Comparisons, and Simple Interaction Contrasts

An alternative analysis track to the one just presented is to do a series of planned interaction contrasts, specifically looking at those that are of theoretical interest to you (Keppel, 1991). You would follow the logic of setting up contrasts that was presented in chapter 4. For example, you might be interested in whether a certain contrast on Factor C interacts with Factor A and Factor B. Suppose the contrast you were interested in on Factor C was comparing the positive and negative Factor C groups, but omitting the No Feedback group. The syntax to test this three-way interaction contrast is in Fig. 5.6.

```
1.    MANOVA score BY facta(1,2) factb(1,2) factc(1,3)

2.    /CONTRAST(factc)=SPECIAL(1 1 1, 1 –1 0, 2 –1 –1)

3.    /ERROR=WITHIN

4.    /DESIGN=factc(1) BY facta BY factb, factc(2) BY facta BY factb.
```

FIG. 5.6. Syntax commands to conduct an interaction contrast in a three-factor between-subjects ANOVA.

You have to specify $k - 1$ contrasts on the "CONTRAST" subcommand even though you are only interested in one of those contrasts. You must also specify "ERROR=WITHIN" or your significance tests will be incorrect. To be sure the output is correct, you should also specify the remaining interaction contrasts, that is, 'factc(2) BY facta BY factb'.[1] Interaction contrasts are quite flexible and powerful, as you can not only evaluate a Factor C contrast interacting with Factor A and Factor B, but also test Factor C contrasts by Factor A contrasts interacting with Factor B, and even Factor C contrasts by Factor A contrasts by Factor B contrasts. The interested reader is referred to Keppel (1991).

Simple comparisons examine a contrast on one of the factors within levels of one of the other factors. Consider first the "FACTA BY FACTC" subtable of means (Fig. 5.3). The first column of this table (that is, when Factor A has the value 1) contains the means 7.83333, 6.50000, and 11.50000. Suppose you wished to examine whether the average of the first two of these significantly

---

[1]Because of a programming bug in MANOVA, specifying only the first, desired contrast inexplicably yields an incorrect answer.

differed from the third. Because this looks within a column, it is simple. Because it examines a comparison within the column, it is a simple comparison. The syntax[2] is in Fig. 5.7.

```
1.   MANOVA score BY facta(1,2) factb(1,2) factc(1,3)

2.      /CONTRAST(factc)=SPECIAL(1 1 1, -1 -1 2, 0 1 -1)

3.      /ERROR=WITHIN

4.      /DESIGN=factc(1) WITHIN facta (1), factc(2) within facta(1).
```

FIG. 5.7.   Syntax commands to conduct a simple comparison in a three-factor between-subjects ANOVA.

Simple simple comparisons examine a contrast on one of the factors within levels of both of the other factors. For an example, consider the "FACTA BY FACTB BY FACTC" table of means (Table 5.1). The first row, first column of each table (i.e., when 'facta' = 1 and 'factb' = 1) contains the means 6.33, 4.33, and 12.00. Suppose you wished to test whether the difference between the first and last means was significant. Because this is examining a set of cell means at a certain level of both other factors, it is simple simple. Because you are examining a comparison on that set of cell means, it is a simple simple comparison. The syntax[3] to do this is illustrated in Fig. 5.8.

```
1.   MANOVA score BY facta(1,2) factb(1,2) factc(1,3)

2.      /CONTRAST (factc) = SPECIAL (1 1 1, 1 0 –1, 0 1 -1)

3.      /ERROR = WITHIN

4.      /DESIGN = factc(1) WITHIN facta(1) WITHIN factb (1), factc(2)

5.         WITHIN facta(1) WITHIN factb(1).
```

FIG. 5.8.   Syntax commands to conduct a simple simple comparison in a three-factor between-subjects ANOVA.

A simple interaction contrast is an interaction contrast between two of the factors within certain levels of the third factor. Again consider Table 5.1. Suppose you wished to detect whether the difference between the 6.33 and 9.33 ('factc' = 1, 'facta' = 1, 'factb' = 1 and 2) was significantly larger than the difference between the 4.33 and 8.67 ('factc' = 2, 'facta' = 1, 'factb' = 1 and 2). This is simple because it is within 'facta' = 1. It is an interaction contrast because it involves a contrast on Factor C interacting with Factor B. Thus, it is a simple interaction contrast. The syntax is in Fig. 5.9.

```
1.   MANOVA score BY facta(1,2) factb(1,2) factc(1,3)

2.      /CONTRAST(factc)=SPECIAL (1 1 1, 1-1 0, 0 1 -1)

3.      /ERROR=WITHIN

4.      /DESIGN=factc(1) BY factb WITHIN facta(1), factc(2) BY factb

5.         WITHIN facta(1).
```

FIG. 5.9.   Syntax commands to conduct a simple interaction contrast in a three-factor between-subjects ANOVA.

---

[2]Again, simple comparisons require specification of all the contrasts to obtain correct answers because of the programming bug described in fn. 1. That is why 'factc(2) WITHIN facta(1)' is included on the "DESIGN" subcommand even though it was not desired.

[3]Here, the two contrasts are not orthogonal, which does not matter. As long as the second contrast, 'factc(2) WITHIN facta(1) WITHIN factb(1)', is specified on the "DESIGN" command, the answer will be correct.

COLLAPSING (IGNORING) A FACTOR

Assume a three-factor completely randomized design, where one of the factors is gender. Suppose you completed the analysis and found that the main effect of gender was far from statistically significant, no interaction involving gender approached significance, and that the gender-related differences were thus so small that it was clearly not an appropriate variable for this analysis. You might now wish to look at the analysis with gender removed as a variable and ignore gender in any further analyses. Ignoring a factor is quite simple in a completely randomized design. In the program statement containing the "MANOVA" command, simply omit any reference to the factor you wish to ignore. Figure 5.10 gives an example of a three-factor completely randomized design in which Factor C is not mentioned in the "MANOVA" command specification and so is ignored in the analysis. The analysis uses all of the data, but does not separate scores in terms of the levels of Factor C.

1.   MANOVA dv BY facta(1,2) factb(1,2)

2.   /OMEANS

3.   /POWER

4.   /PRINT=SIGNIF(EFSIZE).

FIG. 5.10.   Syntax commands to conduct a three-factor between-subjects ANOVA, collapsing across Factor C.

MORE THAN THREE FACTORS

All of the previous designs and discussions can be extended to include more than three factors. The designs and possible contrasts, interactions, simple effects, and so on simply get more complicated. All of the logic on setting up these designs is the same, however.

PAC

A three-factor ANOVA can be easily run using the PAC pull-down menus. You would access the exact same menus as in the one- and two-factor designs, but this time, you would send three variables over to the Fixed Factor(s) box (see Fig. 5.11). You could run post hocs and trend analyses using the same menus as in the one factor, but all of the simple interactions, simple simple effects, simple effects, simple comparisons, interaction contrasts, simple simple comparisons, and simple interaction contrasts would have to be run using the MANOVA program accessed through syntax or GLM syntax (see chap. 13). Power, effect size estimates, and means can be obtained in the Options submenu, as in the one factor.

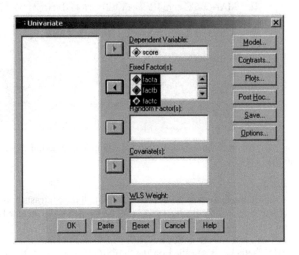

FIG. 5.11.   Dialogue box for a three-factor between-subjects ANOVA.

6 One-Factor Within-Subjects Analysis of Variance

In chapters 3 through 5, the analysis of completely randomized (or between-subjects) ANOVAs was examined, first when there was only one factor (chap. 3), then when there were two (chap. 4) or three or more (chap. 5) factors. Beginning in this chapter, the commands to conduct within-subjects or repeated measures ANOVAs (also called *correlated measures designs*) are covered. The most common example for this kind of data arises when each participant gets each of the treatments or conditions of the independent variable(s) or levels of the factor(s). In contrast, in the between-subjects designs examined earlier, each participant received one and only one of the conditions. As was done for the earlier designs, the simplest version (i.e., only one within-subjects factor) is presented first, in this chapter, followed by more complex variants in subsequent chapters.

BASIC ANALYSIS OF VARIANCE COMMANDS

The data for this example, shown in Fig. 6.1, are from Stevens (1999, p. 207) and have been renamed to make the output more understandable. A researcher investigated the effects of word length on memory. The dependent variable is number of words that participants recall immediately after reading a word list. The independent variable is the length of the words, with three levels, either short, 3 letters or less (a1), medium, 4 to 6 letters (a2), or long, more than 6 letters (a3). As is the hallmark of within-subjects designs, each participant received each of these three levels. Specifically, a participant read a word list with short words and then completed a memory test for that list; the participant

	Length of Words		
	a1: Short	a2: Medium	a3: Long
s_1	30	28	34
s_2	14	18	22
s_3	24	20	30
s_4	38	34	44
s_5	26	28	30

FIG. 6.1. Data from a one-factor within-subjects ANOVA with three levels of Factor A. J. P. Stevens (1999). *Intermediate Statistics: A modern approach* (2nd ed.), p. 207. Copyright by Lawrence Erlbaum Associates. Reprinted with permission.

also read a word list with medium words and took a memory test on that list; finally, the participant read a list with long words and took a memory test on that list. Ideally, the researcher would have randomized the order of the three conditions across participants to remove any order or practice effect. For example, one or more participants would have read and been tested for recall on the list of medium-length words first, then on the short words, and then on the long words; another would have read first short, then medium, and then long; another would have read first long, then short, and then medium, and so on. In this example, there are five different participants, labeled s_1 to s_5. In Fig. 6.1, the data for all participants is rearranged into the order short, medium, long, regardless of the order in which they actually received the word lists.

The data, when entered into SPSS, has three variables for each participant, called a1, a2, and a3, respectively. Because each participant receives every condition, there is no need to add a variable designating which condition the participant receives, the grouping variable that had been the independent variable in examples previously. The syntax, presented in Fig. 6.2, is followed by an explanation of the function of the different commands in the program.

```
1.    MANOVA a1 a2 a3

2.    /WSFACTORS = facta (3)

3d.   /OMEANS

4d.   /POWER

5d.   /PRINT=SIGNIF(EFSIZE)

6o.   /WSDESIGN

7o.   /DESIGN.
```

FIG. 6.2. Syntax commands to conduct a one-factor within-subjects ANOVA.

The setup for the within-subjects ANOVA is somewhat different from that for the between-subjects ANOVAs. You still start with the "MANOVA" command, however, now it is followed by the names of each of the conditions. In this case there are three conditions, so there are three scores named on the "MANOVA" command. There is also no keyword "BY", because there are no between-subjects factors. In order to let SPSS know it is a within-subjects or repeated measures study, a new subcommand is specified, namely the "WSFACTORS" subcommand on line 2 (which stands for "within-subjects factor"). The "WSFACTORS" subcommand must be the first subcommand following the "MANOVA" command. Because the within-subjects factor does not actually exist per se in the raw data, you must assign it a name here to refer to in the printout. This is done by following "WSFACTORS" with an equal sign and, to the right of that equal sign, providing a variable name for the within-subjects factor. The within-subjects factor can be named anything (following SPSS naming conventions) that has not already been used for a variable name. Here the factor is named 'facta'. The number in parentheses after the new name is the number of levels (or conditions) of the within-subjects factor. For a one-factor within-subjects design, this number is the same as the number of variables named earlier on the "MANOVA" command.

Line 3 directs SPSS to print out the observed means, as was done earlier, and in lines 4 and 5 effect size and power analyses have been requested and would be interpreted the same as for the between-subjects ANOVAs. Lines 6 and 7 are each optional and, if left off, SPSS will automatically generate the full factorial model. With a within-subjects design, there are two design statements, a "WSDESIGN" (i.e., the design on the within-subjects factors) and a "DESIGN" (which specifies the design on the between-subjects factors). Although both are optional here, they will be necessary in more complicated designs, so some researchers like to include them to get into the habit of having both statements. The output from this analysis, which is considerably changed from that of between-subjects designs, is in Fig. 6.3.

```
Cell Means and Standard Deviations
Variable .. A1
                                      Mean   Std. Dev.            N

For entire sample                   26.400      8.764             5
- - - - - - - - - - - - - - - - - - - - - - - - - - - - - - - - - - -
Variable .. A2
                                      Mean   Std. Dev.            N

For entire sample                   25.600      6.542             5
- - - - - - - - - - - - - - - - - - - - - - - - - - - - - - - - - - -
Variable .. A3
                                      Mean   Std. Dev.            N

For entire sample                   32.000      8.000             5
- - - - - - - - - - - - - - - - - - - - - - - - - - - - - - - - - - -

Tests of Between-Subjects Effects.

Tests of Significance for T1 using UNIQUE sums of squares
Source of Variation            SS       DF       MS          F  Sig of F

WITHIN CELLS                696.00        4   174.00
CONSTANT                  11760.00        1 11760.00      67.59      .001
- - - - - - - - - - - - - - - - - - - - - - - - - - - - - - - - - - -
Effect Size Measures and Observed Power at the .0500 Level
                                     Partial Noncen-
Source of Variation      ETA Sqd   trality       Power
- - - - - - - - - - - - - - - - - - - - - - - - - - - - - - - - - - -

Tests involving 'FACTA' Within-Subject Effect.

Mauchly sphericity test, W =           .49769
Chi-square approx. =                  2.09336 with 2 D. F.
Significance =                         .351

Greenhouse-Geisser Epsilon =           .66564
Huynh-Feldt Epsilon =                  .87240
Lower-bound Epsilon =                  .50000

AVERAGED Tests of Significance that follow multivariate tests are equivalent to
univariate or split-plot or mixed-model approach to repeated measures.
Epsilons may be used to adjust d.f. for the AVERAGED results.
- - - - - - - - - - - - - - - - - - - - - - - - - - - - - - - - - - -

EFFECT .. FACTA
Multivariate Tests of Significance (S = 1, M = 0, N = 1/2)

Test Name         Value    Exact F Hypoth. DF   Error DF  Sig. of F

Pillais          .93986  23.44186      2.00       3.00       .015
Hotellings     15.62791  23.44186      2.00       3.00       .015
Wilks           .06014  23.44186      2.00       3.00       .015
Roys            .93986
Note.. F statistics are exact.
- - - - - - - - - - - - - - - - - - - - - - - - - - - - - - - - - - -
Multivariate Effect Size and Observed Power at .0500 Level

TEST NAME    Effect Size   Noncent.      Power

 (All)           .940     46.884        .92
- - - - - - - - - - - - - - - - - - - - - - - - - - - - - - - - - - -

Tests involving 'FACTA' Within-Subject Effect.

AVERAGED Tests of Significance for A using UNIQUE sums of squares
Source of Variation            SS       DF       MS          F  Sig of F

WITHIN CELLS                 38.40        8     4.80
FACTA                       121.60        2    60.80      12.67      .003
- - - - - - - - - - - - - - - - - - - - - - - - - - - - - - - - - - -
Effect Size Measures and Observed Power at the .0500 Level
                                     Partial Noncen-
Source of Variation      ETA Sqd   trality       Power

FACTA                        .760    25.333       .964
```

FIG. 6.3. Output from a one-factor within-subjects ANOVA.

Because the subcommand "OMEANS" was used, the means for the different levels of the factor are printed out first, in output that looks slightly different from previous output, because only means "For entire sample" are printed. Next, a table is printed out labeled "Tests Of Between-Subjects Effects", which may be a bit surprising given that there are no between-subjects factors in this design. This table can be ignored for designs like the ones covered in this chapter and in chapter 7 without between-subjects factors. The final portion of output is termed "Tests involving 'FACTA'

Within-Subject Effect". The portion of output beginning "Mauchly sphericity test" will be temporarily skipped and instead the significance tests will be covered.

Analysis of Variance Summary Tables

The significance tests are divided into two types, "Multivariate Tests" and "AVERAGED Tests" (which are also commonly termed *univariate*). The multivariate tests are only present when there are three or more levels of the within-subjects factor and precede the univariate tests. For within-subjects factors with only two levels, only the univariate tests are conducted.

The multivariate tests in the SPSS printout give three significance tests, each with probability values, labeled "Pillais", "Hotellings", and "Wilks".[1] Each test is based on different criteria that are in common use, with no clear consensus as to which is best. However, the multivariate tests tend to give answers that in most instances are all quite similar (or even exactly the same, as here). Generally, they are more conservative and give larger probability values than the "AVERAGED" or univariate tests, although occasionally this will not be the case. The univariate tests, on the other hand, are the ones for which hand calculation methods are typically given in textbooks, such as in Keppel (1991, pp. 346–350) or Stevens (1999, p. 208). The "WITHIN CELLS" line in the univariate summary table is the error term (which, for one-factor within-subjects designs, Keppel referred to as the A × S term and many other texts refer to as the "treatment by subject" term), and the line with the factor name (in this example, "FACTA") offers the sum of squares, mean square, degrees of freedom, and significance level for the test of the within-subjects factor. In the example, the F is significant and, together with the effect size results, would be reported in APA format something like this: **The difference between the three word length conditions is significant, $F(2, 8) = 12.67$, $p = .003$. Specifically, word length accounts for 76.0% of the variance in memory.** If you wish to suppress the multivariate printout, you can do so by using the following subcommand:

/PRINT = SIGNIF (AVONLY)

CORRECTION FOR BIAS IN TESTS OF WITHIN-SUBJECTS FACTORS

The univariate approach to analysis of variance for within-subjects factors is known to result in positively biased F tests, which means statistical significance may be found too often. This is why the multivariate tests are provided, and also why the section of printout beginning "Mauchly sphericity test" is included. The positive bias is primarily due to violations of the univariate test's assumption of homogeneity of the variances of differences among pairs of treatment measures (i.e., between pairs of levels of the within-subjects factor). This assumption is also referred to as the *sphericity assumption*. The multivariate tests do not make this sphericity assumption and so are immune from the positive biasing effect when it is violated. However, as a result, they are somewhat more conservative than the univariate test, as noted earlier, resulting in tests with reduced power (Huynh & Feldt, 1976).

Thus, a reasonable preliminary question would appear to be whether evidence of violation of the sphericity assumption is present. A test for this assumption, the Mauchly sphericity test, is offered in the SPSS printout. In the previous example, this test is not even close to significant ($p = .351$). If the test had been statistically significant, it would suggest that the sphericity assumption had been violated. Unfortunately, problems, primarily involving the test's oversensitivity, reduce its practical value. Kesselman, Rogan, Mendoza, and Breen (1980) demonstrated, with the aid of Monte Carlo data, that no advantage was gained by incorporating the Mauchly sphericity test into the decision process. Violations of the assumption cannot occur if the within-subjects factor has only two levels (because there is only one pairwise variance), which is why neither the multivariate analysis nor the Mauchly test is provided when a within-subjects factor has only two levels.

---

[1]The "Roys" value also has an associated significance value, but it is not printed out by MANOVA. Tables of critical values for Roy's criterion can be found in Rencher (1995).

An alternative to using the multivariate tests is the use of a correction in the degrees of freedom, permitting a choice of a larger critical F value, which, if properly selected, avoids the positive bias problem. Box (1954) developed a correction factor, epsilon, a fractional value that, when multiplying both the numerator and denominator degrees of freedom of the F ratio, yields reduced degrees of freedom. The reduced degrees of freedom pertain to the correct (bias-free) F distribution, which can then be used to obtain the higher, but correct, critical F value for testing the within-subjects factor. The value of epsilon can serve both as a correction factor and as an index of the extent of the violation of the assumption of homogeneity of variances of differences. Epsilon varies between a value of 1 (no violation of the assumptions) and $1/(k - 1)$ (maximum violation of the assumptions, referred to in the printout as "Lower-bound Epsilon"), where k is the number of levels of the within-subjects factor. The true epsilon is never known exactly in actual data collection situations. Fortunately, there are two correction factors that are generally recognized as useful for estimating epsilon: the Greenhouse-Geisser epsilon estimate (Geisser & Greenhouse, 1958) and the Huynh-Feldt epsilon estimate (Huynh & Feldt, 1976). Both epsilon estimates are given in the SPSS printout when within subjects factors with more than two levels are analyzed.

The procedure of Greenhouse and Geisser has been endorsed by others in the field (e.g., Keppel, 1982; Myers, 1979). Following their suggested procedure involves first checking the printout for the univariate F test of the within-subjects factor. If this test, which might be positively biased, is not statistically significant, the issue ends there, with the report that the difference is nonsignificant. If, however, the ordinary univariate F test leads to statistical significance, a more conservative (likely too conservative) test is tried next. The printout, in the same table giving the Greenhouse-Geisser and Huynh-Feldt epsilon estimates, gives the lower bound epsilon. The researcher would multiply this lower bound epsilon by each degrees of freedom, and then use the resulting lower bound degrees of freedom to identify a new criterion F value in an F table (you can also have the computer run this test for you, as discussed later). The printout F would then be compared to this conservative criterion. If the result is significant even with the conservative criterion, then once again the issue is ended (this time with a conclusion that the difference is statistically significant). If the two tests contradict each other, that is, if the uncorrected (positively biased) test yields statistical significance and the conservative (negatively biased) test does not, then the more specific epsilon correction in the degrees of freedom is made, substituting either the Greenhouse-Geisser or Huynh-Feldt epsilon estimate in place of the lower bound epsilon. SPSS will also print out the Greenhouse-Geisser and Huynh-Feldt significance tests (the lower bound F test is also printed out when one of these other tests is requested) with the following subcommand:

/PRINT=SIGNIF (GG HF)

The use of one of these estimates, besides being likely to yield higher degrees of freedom than the lower bound, should yield degrees of freedom for the unbiased F distribution, the distribution that is more likely to represent the true degrees of freedom created by the extent of the violation of the assumption. The new degrees of freedom obtained with one of the estimates should then be used to select a new critical F value, with which a final statistical decision is made. The printout containing these tests is in Fig. 6.4.

It was seen in Fig. 6.3 that the overall F was significant ($p = .003$), thus, you would now turn to whether or not the "Lower bound" test is significant. You can see that this test is significant ($p =$

```
Tests involving 'FACTA' Within-Subject Effect.

AVERAGED Tests of Significance for A using UNIQUE sums of squares
Source of Variation        SS       DF       MS        F   Sig of F

WITHIN CELLS             38.40        8     4.80
     (Greenhouse-Geisser)           5.33
     (Huynh-Feldt)                  6.98
     (Lower bound)                  4.00
FACTA                   121.60        2    60.80    12.67    .003
     (Greenhouse-Geisser)           1.33             12.67    .012
     (Huynh-Feldt)                  1.74             12.67    .005
     (Lower bound)                  1.00             12.67    .024
```

FIG. 6.4.   Output for "corrected" tests in a one-factor within-subjects ANOVA.

.024), thus, you would conclude that word length did have an effect on memory. If the lower bound test had been nonsignificant, you would have turned next to either the test using the Greenhouse-Geisser or Huynh-Feldt epsilon (see later discussion as to which epsilon to use). If that test indicates that the effect is significant, then your final conclusion would be that the effect is indeed significant.

The next issue is the choice of the epsilon estimate. Huynh and Feldt (1976) recommended that their epsilon estimate should be used in most situations, reserving the Greenhouse-Geisser epsilon estimate for use only when the assumptions are strongly violated (when the true epsilon is less than .5). However, the true epsilon value is never known. If the two estimates are close, with both estimates low, you would be justified in using the Greenhouse-Geisser estimate. If both are high, the Huynh-Feldt estimate would be appropriate. If they contradict each other, one high and one low, there would be two different sets of degrees of freedom, which can be used to select a critical F value. In this case it might be useful to try both epsilons, testing the empirical F against the two different tabled critical F values. It would then be appropriate to use a decision procedure analogous to the one used with the lower bound degrees of freedom correction, and the F test with the original degrees of freedom. In this case the two different critical values will be closer together than when using the lower bound epsilon, improving the probability of the two epsilons leading to the same decision. If the two estimates lead to different decisions, this fact might simply be reported in a research report or article.

The procedure for using any of the three epsilons (the lower bound epsilon, the Greenhouse-Geisser epsilon, or the Huynh-Feldt epsilon) is the same and, although the computer will calculate the significance tests for you, it is explained here so that you know what the computer is doing. You multiply the chosen epsilon by both the numerator and denominator degrees of freedom. Because noninteger values of degrees of freedom can occur as the products, it is reasonable to round to the nearest integer. For example, consider a two-factor design with a within-subjects factor, containing three levels and 37 participants. The univariate F test would have (2, 72) degrees of freedom. The lower bound epsilon, displayed in the printout, would be .50. Multiplying this decimal value times 2 and 72 would yield degrees of freedom of (1, 36). If the Huynh-Feldt epsilon was selected from the printout instead and was found to be, say, .68, the resulting nearest integer degrees of freedom would be (1, 49). The F tables would be consulted for the new critical values of the adjusted degrees of freedom. The empirical F ratio would be tested against the new critical value. For (2, 72) df, the critical value for a .05 Type I error probability is 3.13; for (1, 36) df, it is 4.11. A more specific estimate, such as the hypothetical Huynh-Feldt estimate of .68 that results in (1, 49) df, yields a critical value between the other two of 4.04.

PLANNED CONTRASTS

In order to specify contrasts for a within-subjects design, either the "CONTRAST" subcommand (which provides the correct answer only for orthogonal contrasts) or the "TRANSFORM" subcommand may be used. The "TRANSFORM" subcommand is similar to the "CONTRAST" subcommand, but more versatile (because it is also appropriate for nonorthogonal comparisons), so it will be explicated first. Basic syntax is in Fig. 6.5.

1.	MANOVA a1 a2 a3
2d.	/OMEANS
3.	/TRANSFORM(a1 a2 a3)=SPECIAL (1 1 1, 1 -2 1, 0 1 -1)
4d.	/RENAME=skip negvoth negvneut
5o.	/NOPRINT=SIGNIF(MULTIV).

FIG. 6.5. Syntax commands to conduct contrasts in a one-factor within-subjects ANOVA using the TRANSFORM subcommand.

The "TRANSFORM/RENAME" Method for Nonorthogonal Contrasts

To test contrasts with the "TRANSFORM" subcommand, start with the "MANOVA" command, as in line 1, but leave off the "WSFACTORS" subcommand. Then get the means with "OMEANS". Next, the "TRANSFORM" subcommand is used. The specification of the "TRANSFORM" subcommand is very similar to that for the "CONTRAST" subcommand, differing primarily in what is enclosed in the first set of parentheses. Whereas in "CONTRAST" it was the factor name, in "TRANSFORM" it is the names of each of the conditions or variables, as was specified on line 1. You could also use the "TO" convention on the "TRANSFORM" subcommand. Thus, '(a1 a2 a3)' and '(a1 TO a3)' work identically. In this example, "SPECIAL" contrasts are specified: After the obligatory set of 1s, the first contrast compares the medium-length condition to the average of the other two, and the second contrast compares the medium- to long-word conditions. (Note that the contrasts are nonorthogonal.)

The "RENAME" subcommand in line 4 is optional but very useful for labeling output. The specification of "RENAME" requires one new name for each contrast. You can use any meaningful names, but you must follow SPSS variable naming conventions. The set of all 1s must be named as well. Here it is named 'skip' to remind you to ignore it on the printout. The other two contrasts are named 'medvoth' (medium vs. others) and 'medvlong' (medium vs. long), respectively, to be as mnemonic as possible within the confines of eight-character SPSS names. "WSDESIGN" and "DESIGN" subcommands are optional and are not included. The output from the program in Fig. 6.5 is in Fig. 6.6.

```
EFFECT .. CONSTANT (Cont.)
Univariate F-tests with (1,4) D. F.

Variable    Hypoth. SS   Error SS  Hypoth. MS   Error MS         F   Sig. of F

SKIP        35280.0000  2088.00000  35280.0000   522.00000  67.58621      .001
MEDVOTH       259.20000   196.80000   259.20000    49.20000   5.26829      .083
MEDVLONG      204.80000    51.20000   204.80000    12.80000  16.00000      .016
```

FIG. 6.6. Output for contrasts for a one-factor within-subjects ANOVA using the TRANSFORM subcommand.

The multivariate output was suppressed by the use of the "NOPRINT" subcommand in line 5 (the "PRINT" subcommand does not work with the "TRANSFORM" subcommand). The output of interest is the univariate F tests, where the F test for each contrast (as well as the set of 1s now conveniently labeled "SKIP") is given. Notice, however, that this output is arranged somewhat differently; for example, the two df values are at the top. The contrast labeled "MEDVOTH" is nonsignificant, $F(1, 4) = 5.27$, $p = .083$. The difference between the medium and long words, however, is significant, with an F of 16.00 and p value of .016.

Had the "RENAME" subcommand not been used, the three F tests would be labeled "T1", "T2", and "T3", respectively instead of "SKIP", "MEDVOTH", and "MEDVLONG".

Because the test for a contrast does not use the "WSFACTORS" subcommand, you cannot obtain the overall F test here. If you need the overall F test, you would have a separate "MANOVA" like the one in Fig. 6.2 preceding the syntax in Fig. 6.5. In addition to "SPECIAL", the other "canned" sets of weights, such as "SIMPLE", "REPEATED", and "POLYNOMIAL", are applicable to "TRANSFORM". "POLYNOMIAL" is what would be used for trend analysis and useful "RENAME"s for trend analysis would be 'skip, linear, quadratic, cubic', and so on.

If you wanted to specify more than $k - 1$ contrasts, you would need to have multiple "TRANSFORM" subcommands. To get each one to produce printout, include a "DESIGN" subcommand after each one (the final one is not needed, however). The "RENAME" subcommand will, by default, stay in effect until changed with a new "RENAME", so it is a good idea to accompany each "TRANSFORM/DESIGN" set with an interposed appropriate "RENAME". This principle will be illustrated later, for the case of post hocs.

The "CONTRAST/WSDESIGN" Method for Orthogonal Contrasts

For orthogonal contrasts, and only for orthogonal contrasts, you can use the "CONTRAST" subcommand as an alternative to "TRANSFORM". Although it is not particularly easier to use in the present application, there are advantages in terms of ease of use for more complex within-subjects designs. It is set up identically as in between-subjects contrasts. For the previous example contrast (i.e., contrasting the mean of Group a2 with the average of the means of Groups a1 and a3), the analysis is set up as seen in Fig. 6.7.

1.	MANOVA a1 a2 a3
2.	/WSFACTORS=facta(3)
3d.	/OMEANS
4.	/CONTRAST(facta)=SPECIAL (1 1 1, 1 -2 1, 1 0 -1)
5.	/WSDESIGN=facta(1) facta(2).

FIG. 6.7. Syntax commands to conduct orthogonal contrasts using the CONTRAST subcommand in a one-factor within-subjects ANOVA.

Use of the "CONTRAST" subcommand requires that "WSFACTORS" be specified as the first subcommand in the syntax. The "CONTRAST" subcommand itself is set up identically as in the between-subjects design, except that the variable name in parentheses that follows the word "CONTRAST" is the name you specified on the "WSFACTORS" subcommand. As before, you must have a contrast of all 1s, followed by $k - 1$ (in this case, two) orthogonal contrasts. In order to make the contrasts orthogonal, the weights 1 0 −1 were substituted for the nonorthogonal weights 0 1 −1 that appeared in Fig. 6.5. As in between-subjects usage of "CONTRAST", you could also specify any of the canned contrast routines that are orthogonal, including a trend analysis, if appropriate. Line 5 indicates that you want significance tests of both contrasts, hereafter called 'facta(1)' and 'facta(2)'. The form of a specification requesting orthogonal contrasts on within-subjects factors is identical to that for requesting contrasts in between-subjects design (e.g., see line 4 in Fig. 3.4), except that here it is found on the "WSDESIGN" rather than on the "DESIGN" subcommand. Selected output is presented in Fig. 6.8.

```
>Warning # 12252 in column 29.  Text: SPECIAL
>Special contrasts were requested for a WSFACTOR.  MANOVA automatically
>orthonormalizes contrast matrices for WSFACTORS.  If the special contrasts
>that were requested are nonorthogonal, the contrasts actually fitted are
>not the contrasts requested.  See the transformation matrix for the actual
>contrasts fitted.  Use TRANSFORM instead of WSFACTORS to produce
>nonorthogonal contrasts for within subjects factors.  Multivariate and
>averaged tests remain valid.
- - - - - - - - - - - - - - - - - - - - - - - - - - - - - - - - - - - -

Tests involving 'FACTA(1)' Within-Subject Effect.

Tests of Significance for T2 using UNIQUE sums of squares
Source of Variation          SS        DF        MS          F  Sig of F

WITHIN+RESIDUAL           32.80         4      8.20
FACTA(1)                  43.20         1     43.20       5.27      .083
- - - - - - - - - - - - - - - - - - - - - - - - - - - - - - - - - - - -

Tests involving 'FACTA(2)' Within-Subject Effect.

Tests of Significance for T3 using UNIQUE sums of squares
Source of Variation          SS        DF        MS          F  Sig of F

WITHIN+RESIDUAL            5.60         4      1.40
FACTA(2)                  78.40         1     78.40      56.00      .002
```

FIG. 6.8. Output for orthogonal contrasts using the CONTRAST subcommand in a one-factor within-subjects ANOVA.

At the top of the output is a warning that you used a special contrast and the program assumes that contrasts are orthogonal and will test ("fit") different contrasts from those requested if they are not. Next are the significance tests. The first contrast (identical to the one named "MEDVOTH" in Fig. 6.6) is nonsignificant, $F(1, 4) = 5.27$, $p = .083$. The second contrast (note that it is a different contrast having different weights from the second contrast in Fig. 6.6, a contrast chosen to be orthogonal) is significant, $F(1, 4) = 56.00$, $p = .002$.

POST HOC TESTS

Presuming no a priori contrasts had been planned for the previous example, because the overall or omnibus test was significant, it would be appropriate to conduct post hoc tests. Recall that MANOVA does not have special syntax for post hoc tests, but instead requires repeated use of "SIMPLE" contrasts to obtain numerical values, and then manual computation of criterion values for Tukey, Scheffé, and other tests. Because "SIMPLE" weights are nonorthogonal, the "TRANSFORM" method must be used. This is demonstrated in Fig. 6.9.

1.   MANOVA a1 a2 a3

2.   /TRANSFORM(a1 TO a3)=SIMPLE(1)

3.   /RENAME=skip shrtvmed shrtvlon

4.   /DESIGN

5.   /TRANSFORM(a1 TO a3)=SIMPLE (2)

6.   /RENAME=skip medvshrt negvlon.

FIG. 6.9.   Syntax commands to conduct post hocs in a one-factor within-subjects ANOVA.

The F or p values produced by these commands would be compared against special criterion values appropriate to the specific type of post hoc (e.g., Tukey, Bonferroni, etc.) test, as described in chapter 3.

PAC

A one-factor within-subjects ANOVA can be run using the PAC pull-down menus in SPSS for Windows. To do so, select the Analyze option and then choose the General Linear Model (GLM) and, under this menu, choose Repeated Measures (see Fig. 3.14). The first screen you will see is shown in Fig. 6.10.

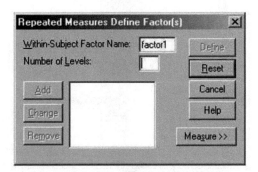

FIG. 6.10.   Dialogue box to define within-subjects factors with the default name of the factor displayed.

This screen asks you to provide a Within-Subjects Factor Name. The name of the factor by default is 'factor1'. You can change this name by typing in any name you want (following SPSS naming conventions), such as 'facta' (see Fig. 6.11). After naming the factor, you have to type in the Number of Levels it has, in this case, '3'. Remember that you need to name the factor here, as there is no within-subjects factor in the raw data.

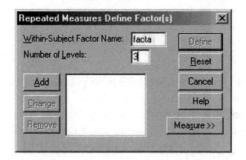

FIG. 6.11.   Dialogue box to define wtihin-subjects factors, with factor name displayed.

Then the Add button will darken so you can click it. Then the Define button will darken so the screen appears as in Fig. 6.12.

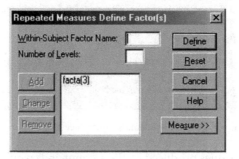

FIG. 6.12.   A completed dialogue box to define a within-subjects factor.

Now click Define. You will get to the screen seen in Fig. 6.13.

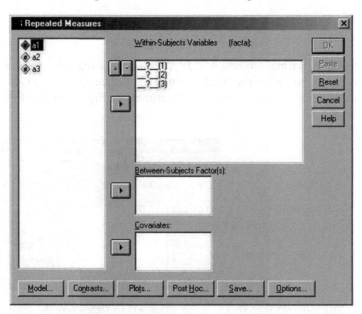

FIG. 6.13.   Dialogue box to analyze a within-subjects ANOVA.

Now you can define which variables from your dataset make up the within-subjects factor 'facta'. You will have the opportunity to pick as many variables as there are levels of the factor. To pick the variables, simply highlight the variables on the left and hit the little arrow key. You may then click OK (see Fig. 6.14).

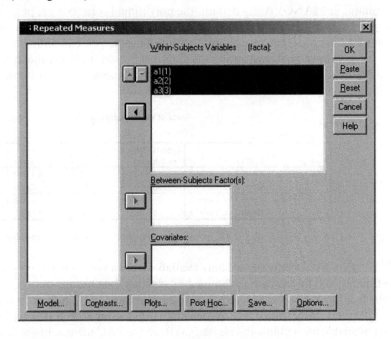

FIG. 6.14.   Dialogue box to analyze a within-subjects ANOVA with variable names inserted.

The printout looks somewhat different from that discussed earlier. For example, the Mauchly test is arrayed as seen in Fig. 6.15.

Mauchly's Test of Sphericity[b]

Measure: MEASURE_1

Within Subjects Effect	Mauchly's W	Approx. Chi-Square	df	Sig.	Epsilon[a]		
					Greenhous e-Geisser	Huynh-Feldt	Lower-bound
FACTA	.498	2.093	2	.351	.666	.872	.500

Tests the null hypothesis that the error covariance matrix of the orthonormalized transformed dependent variables is proportional to an identity matrix.

    a. May be used to adjust the degrees of freedom for the averaged tests of significance. Corrected tests are displayed in the Tests of Within-Subjects Effects table.

   b. Design: Intercept
     Within-Subjects Design: FACTA

FIG. 6.15.   PAC Mauchly sphericity test output.

The significance tests come out quite differently as well, as shown in Fig. 6.16.

Tests of Within-Subjects Effects

Measure: MEASURE_1

Source		Type III Sum of Squares	df	Mean Square	F	Sig.
FACTA	Sphericity Assumed	121.600	2	60.800	12.667	.003
	Greenhouse-Geisser	121.600	1.331	91.341	12.667	.012
	Huynh-Feldt	121.600	1.745	69.693	12.667	.005
	Lower-bound	121.600	1.000	121.600	12.667	.024
Error(FACTA)	Sphericity Assumed	38.400	8	4.800		
	Greenhouse-Geisser	38.400	5.325	7.211		
	Huynh-Feldt	38.400	6.979	5.502		
	Lower-bound	38.400	4.000	9.600		

FIG. 6.16.   PAC output from a within-subjects ANOVA.

The "Sphericity Assumed" test is what was termed a "univariate" or "AVERAGED" test in MANOVA. Here you automatically obtain the Greenhouse-Geisser and Huynh-Feldt epsilon corrected tests, in contrast to needing to specify them with a subcommand in MANOVA. In the multivariate section (not shown) it also gives significance by Roy's (Largest Root) criterion, not available in MANOVA. By default, the polynomial contrasts are printed out and there is no way to suppress this output unless you specify other contrast types (see later discussion). If you are not interested in this output, or the multivariate output, you can simply ignore it.

You may run contrasts using the Contrast button, but only the canned ones, such as Simple and Polynomial. The contrasts do not have to be orthogonal. The printout accompanying Simple is in Fig. 6.17.

Tests of Within-Subjects Contrasts

Measure: MEASURE_1

Source	FACTA	Type III Sum of Squares	df	Mean Square	F	Sig.
FACTA	Level 1 vs. Level 3	156.800	1	156.800	56.000	.002
	Level 2 vs. Level 3	204.800	1	204.800	16.000	.016
Error(FACTA)	Level 1 vs. Level 3	11.200	4	2.800		
	Level 2 vs. Level 3	51.200	4	12.800		

FIG. 6.17.   PAC output for a Simple contrast in a within-subjects ANOVA.

"SPECIAL" contrasts are only available from a syntax window (see chap. 13). Power, effect size estimates, and means can be obtained by clicking the Options button at the lower right of Fig. 6.13, which brings up a window identical in appearance and function to that in Fig. 3.18.

Post hoc tests, one of the real benefits of PAC over MANOVA for between-subjects designs, are not available for within-subjects designs from the PAC menus. Instead, when the Post Hoc button of Fig 6.13 is clicked, you get the window in Fig. 6.18.

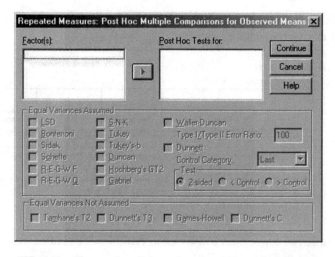

FIG. 6.18.   The post hoc dialogue box for within-subjects designs.

Although you cannot obtain the wide variety of post hoc tests for a within-subjects factor that you can for a between-subjects factor, you can obtain the Bonferroni and Sidak tests through the Options dialogue box. When the Options dialogue box comes up, to obtain post hocs, you need to obtain the means on your factor. Here you would send 'facta' over to the Display Means for box as seen in Fig. 6.19.

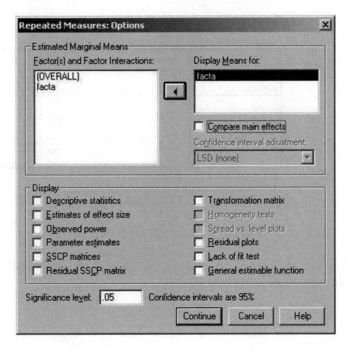

FIG. 6.19.   Options dialogue box in which 'facta' means have been requested.

After requesting the means, you want to click on the Compare main effects box in the upper right. Once you do this, the box labeled Confidence interval adjustment will be usable and you can then select Bonferroni or Sidak tests by pulling down the menu. In Fig. 6.20, Bonferroni tests were selected. In Fig. 6.21, the output is presented.

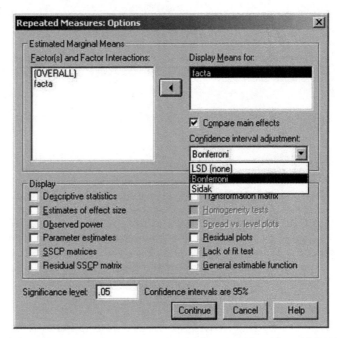

FIG. 6.20.   Running a Bonferroni post hoc test in a one-factor within-subjects ANOVA in PAC.

Pairwise Comparisons

Measure: MEASURE_1

(I) FACTA	(J) FACTA	Mean Difference (I-J)	Std. Error	Sig.[a]	95% Confidence Interval for Difference[a]	
					Lower Bound	Upper Bound
1	2	.800	1.625	1.000	-5.636	7.236
	3	-5.600*	.748	.005	-8.564	-2.636
2	1	-.800	1.625	1.000	-7.236	5.636
	3	-6.400*	1.600	.048	-12.737	-6.274E-02
3	1	5.600*	.748	.005	2.636	8.564
	2	6.400*	1.600	.048	6.274E-02	12.737

Based on estimated marginal means

*. The mean difference is significant at the .05 level.

a. Adjustment for multiple comparisons: Bonferroni.

FIG. 6.21.   PAC output for a Bonferroni post hoc test in a one-factor within-subjects ANOVA.

You can see that Groups 1 and 3 and 2 and 3 are significantly different from one another, but that Groups 1 and 2 are not.

7 Two (or More) Factor Within-Subjects Analysis of Variance

In chapter 6, how to analyze a one-factor within-subjects ANOVA was explained. In this chapter, those commands are extended to a two-factor within-subjects design and beyond, to three or more within-subjects factors.

BASIC ANALYSIS OF VARIANCE COMMANDS

The data for this example are in Fig. 7.1. In this hypothetical study there are two within-subjects factors. Factor A is a list of words, either low or high in concreteness (thus Factor A has two levels) and Factor B is four trials in which the participants study the lists and then recall as many words as they can in 1 minute (thus Factor B has four levels). This is a 2 × 4 ANOVA with repeated measures on both factors.

	a1: Low Concreteness				a2: High Concreteness			
	b: Trials				b: Trials			
	b1	b2	b3	b4	b1	b2	b3	b4
s_1	2	3	4	4	3	4	5	8
s_2	5	7	9	11	5	8	11	13
s_3	6	9	11	12	8	11	13	15
s_4	3	3	5	7	5	7	8	10

FIG. 7.1.   Data from a two-factor within-subjects ANOVA with two levels of Factor A and four levels of Factor B.

The program, presented in Fig. 7.2, is followed by an explanation of the function of the different commands in the program. The "DATA LIST" command is included to demonstrate how the data have been entered into the computer. In the data set, the first score for a participant is their score from the first level of Factor A combined with the first level of Factor B (in other words, Trial 1 of low concrete words), the next number is their score on the first level of Factor A at the second level of Factor B (in other words, Trial 2 of low concrete words), the third number is their score on the first level of Factor A at the third level of Factor B, and so on. The fifth score, therefore, would be the second level of Factor A at the first level of Factor B (in other words, Trial 1 of high concrete words). Thus, Factor A is said to be the factor that is changing the most slowly. In the "DATA LIST" command, the scores are 'a1b1', 'a1b2', 'a1b3', 'a1b4', 'a2b1', and so on.

```
1.    DATA LIST FILE=filename

2.       /a1b1 1-2 a1b2 3-4 a1b3 5-6 a1b4 7-8 a2b1 9-10 a2b2 11-12

3.        a2b3 13-14 a2b4 15-16.

4.    MANOVA a1b1 a1b2 a1b3 a1b4 a2b1 a2b2 a2b3 a2b4

5.    /WSFACTORS=facta(2) factb(4)

6d.   /OMEANS

7d.   /POWER

8d.   /PRINT=SIGNIF(EFSIZE AVONLY)

9o.   /WSDESIGN

10o.  /DESIGN.
```

FIG. 7.2.   Syntax commands to conduct a two-factor within-subjects ANOVA.

The setup for the two-factor within-subjects ANOVA is similar to that for the one-factor within-subjects ANOVA. You start with the "MANOVA" command, followed by each of the scores on the dependent variable. In this case there are eight total scores (two levels of Factor A times four levels of Factor B). There is no keyword "BY" because there are no between-subjects factors.

Just as in the one-factor within-subjects design, in order to let SPSS know this is a within-subjects design, the "WSFACTORS" subcommand is used and has to be the first subcommand following the "MANOVA" command. On the "WSFACTORS" subcommand, you give names to your factors. The order of these factors is important. The factor that changes more slowly is always placed first (Factor A in this example). The phrase "changes more slowly" refers to the levels of the factor as you move from left to right in Fig. 7.1, as summarized in the sequence 'a1b1 a1b2 a1b3 a1b4 a2b1 a2b2 a2b3 a2b4' (see lines 2–4 of Fig. 7.2). Note that the levels of Factor B change in the first four components in the sequence from b1 to b2 to b3 to b4, whereas Factor A remains as a1, not changing until the fifth component (in 'a2b1'). Thus Factor A changes more slowly in this listing of conditions, so that the name you give to Factor A, 'facta', appears first after the equal sign in the "WSFACTORS" subcommand. The numbers in parentheses after the names are, again, the number of levels (or conditions) of the within-subjects factors.

In lines 6 through 8, effect size, power analyses, and means were requested, as in the one-factor within-subjects ANOVA. Additionally, in line 8, the multivariate printout has been suppressed by requesting univariate printout only ("AVONLY"). You could opt to obtain multivariate printout (by omitting the "AVONLY" specification of line 8), and those options and procedures were fully discussed in chapter 6, and will not be repeated here. Lines 9 and 10 are optional and, if left off, SPSS will automatically generate the full factorial model, that is, the printout in Fig. 7.3. The output from the between-subjects test and all sphericity tests have been omitted. If the sphericity tests indicated a violation of the assumption, you would follow the steps outlined in chapter 6 to correct for this.

```
Cell Means and Standard Deviations
Variable .. A1B1
                                      Mean   Std. Dev.         N

For entire sample                    4.000    1.826            4
- - - - - - - - - - - - - - - - - - - - - - - - - - - - - - - -
Variable .. A1B2
                                      Mean   Std. Dev.         N

For entire sample                    5.500    3.000            4
- - - - - - - - - - - - - - - - - - - - - - - - - - - - - - - -
Variable .. A1B3
                                      Mean   Std. Dev.         N

For entire sample                    7.250    3.304            4
- - - - - - - - - - - - - - - - - - - - - - - - - - - - - - - -
Variable .. A1B4
                                      Mean   Std. Dev.         N

For entire sample                    8.500    3.697            4
- - - - - - - - - - - - - - - - - - - - - - - - - - - - - - - -
Variable .. A2B1
                                      Mean   Std. Dev.         N

For entire sample                    5.250    2.062            4
- - - - - - - - - - - - - - - - - - - - - - - - - - - - - - - -
Variable .. A2B2
                                      Mean   Std. Dev.         N

For entire sample                    7.500    2.887            4
- - - - - - - - - - - - - - - - - - - - - - - - - - - - - - - -
Variable .. A2B3
                                      Mean   Std. Dev.         N

For entire sample                    9.250    3.500            4
- - - - - - - - - - - - - - - - - - - - - - - - - - - - - - - -
Variable .. A2B4
                                      Mean   Std. Dev.         N

For entire sample                   11.500    3.109            4
- - - - - - - - - - - - - - - - - - - - - - - - - - - - - - - -


Tests involving 'FACTA' Within-Subject Effect.

AVERAGED Tests of Significance for MEAS.1 using UNIQUE sums of squares
Source of Variation          SS        DF        MS          F  Sig of F

WITHIN CELLS               3.34        3        1.11
FACTA                     34.03        1       34.03      30.53     .012
- - - - - - - - - - - - - - - - - - - - - - - - - - - - - - - -
Effect Size Measures and Observed Power at the .0500 Level
                              Partial Noncen-
Source of Variation       ETA Sqd trality      Power

FACTA                        .911  30.533       .942
- - - - - - - - - - - - - - - - - - - - - - - - - - - - - - - -

Tests involving 'FACTB' Within-Subject Effect.

AVERAGED Tests of Significance for MEAS.1 using UNIQUE sums of squares
Source of Variation          SS        DF        MS          F  Sig of F

WITHIN CELLS              11.28        9        1.25
FACTB                    127.84        3       42.61      34.00     .000
- - - - - - - - - - - - - - - - - - - - - - - - - - - - - - - -
Effect Size Measures and Observed Power at the .0500 Level
                              Partial Noncen-
Source of Variation       ETA Sqd trality      Power

FACTB                        .919 101.992      1.000
- - - - - - - - - - - - - - - - - - - - - - - - - - - - - - - -

Tests involving 'FACTA BY FACTB' Within-Subject Effect.

AVERAGED Tests of Significance for MEAS.1 using UNIQUE sums of squares
Source of Variation          SS        DF        MS          F  Sig of F

WITHIN CELLS               3.03        9         .34
FACTA BY FACTB             3.09        3        1.03       3.06     .084
- - - - - - - - - - - - - - - - - - - - - - - - - - - - - - - -
Effect Size Measures and Observed Power at the .0500 Level
                              Partial Noncen-
Source of Variation       ETA Sqd trality      Power

FACTA BY FACTB               .505   9.186       .518
```

FIG. 7.3.   Output from a two-factor within-subjects ANOVA.

Because the subcommand "OMEANS" was specified, the means for each of the eight combinations of Factor A and Factor B are printed out. Note, however, that with MANOVA in two- (or more) factor within-subjects designs, it is not possible to obtain Factor A and Factor B marginal means, only the previous cell means. Marginals may be obtained by hand calculations (which are presented in Table 7.1) or with other SPSS programs.

TABLE 7.1
Marginal and Cell Means in a Two-Factor Within-Subjects ANOVA

	b1: Trial 1	b2: Trial 2	b3: Trial 3	b4: Trial 4	Average
a1: Low concrete words	4.00	5.50	7.25	8.50	6.31
a2: High concrete words	5.25	7.50	9.25	11.50	8.37
Average	4.63	6.50	8.25	10.00	

Analysis of Variance Summary Tables

Only the univariate tests are obtained because the multivariate output was suppressed on line 8 of Fig. 7.2. Each of the tests is clearly labeled with the name you gave it on the "WSFACTORS" subcommand.[1] There is a significance test, a sphericity test (not printed here), power, and effect size estimates for each of the effects, as well as for their interaction. There is a significant main effect for both Factor A, $F(1, 3) = 30.53, p = .012$, partial eta squared = .911, and Factor B, $F(3, 9) = 34.00, p = .001$, partial eta squared = .919, but a nonsignificant interaction, $F(3, 9) = 3.06, p = .084$, partial eta squared = .505. All of the caveats on the bias in one-factor within-subjects tests apply here and the researcher should keep them in mind.

Because there are two factors, additional analyses could include all the types of analyses discussed in chapter 4: simple effects (if the interaction is significant), contrasts on main effects (including post hocs and trend analysis), simple comparisons, and interaction contrasts. Looking at the power associated with the interaction test, it is fairly low (.52) and, because the test is almost significant, if you had predicted this interaction you might want to explore it in follow-up analyses.

MAIN EFFECT CONTRASTS

If you had a priori hypotheses about differences on a factor and the interaction was nonsignificant, you could examine the main effect contrasts. When the factor has only two levels (such as Factor A), of course, this would be irrelevant, because there is only one possible difference to be significant. However, when the factor has three or more levels, such an analysis would be appropriate. In the previous example, Factor B has four levels, so you could conduct contrasts on it. As was the case for the other designs considered, there are a wide variety of contrasts that can be done. You can do any of the canned contrasts available in SPSS including trend analysis, or you can write "SPECIAL" contrasts of interest.

Orthogonal and nonorthogonal contrasts will be specified differently, as they were in chapter 6. For nonorthogonal contrasts, only the "TRANSFORM" method may be used, whereas for orthogonal contrasts, either the "CONTRAST/WSDESIGN" or the "TRANSFORM" method may be used. In advanced applications, such as the two-factor within-subjects analysis considered in this chapter, the "CONTRAST" subcommand is a bit easier, so it is presented first.

Speaking generally, when contrasts are orthogonal, main effects contrasts, simple comparisons, and interaction contrasts are all handled analogously to the way they were treated in between-subjects designs: First, $k - 1$ contrasts are specified with weights on the "CONTRAST" subcommand, then the ones you want significance tests for are named on the "WSDESIGN" subcommand. The primary difference, then, between within-subjects and between-subjects designs is that the former uses the "WSDESIGN" subcommand, whereas the latter uses the "DESIGN" subcommand. Remember, though, that the statement above applies only when the contrasts are orthogonal.

---

[1]There is also the label "MEAS.1". If "PRINT=SIGNIF(AVONLY)" or "AVERF" is not requested, this will be labeled "T1". This label may be ignored.

Analyzing Orthogonal Main Effect Contrasts (Including Trend Analysis) Using "CONTRAST/WSDESIGN"

Imagine you were interested in the following contrasts on Factor B: (a) the first level versus the average of the last three levels, (b) the fourth level versus the average of the second and third levels; and (c) the second versus the third levels. Thus, the contrast weights are 3 –1 –1 –1, 0 –1 –1 2, 0 1 –1 0, and they are orthogonal. The syntax to test these contrasts is presented in Fig. 7.4.

```
1.    MANOVA a1b1 a1b2 a1b3 a1b4 a2b1 a2b2 a2b3 a2b4

2.      /WSFACTORS = facta(2) factb(4)

3d.    /OMEANS

4o.    /PRINT=SIGNIF(AVONLY)

5.      /CONTRAST(factb)=SPECIAL (1 1 1 1, 3 –1 –1 –1, 0 –1 –1 2, 0 1 –1 0)

6.      /WSDESIGN=factb(1), factb(2), factb(3), facta, factb by facta.
```

FIG. 7.4.   Syntax commands to conduct orthogonal main effect contrasts in a two-factor within-subjects ANOVA using the CONTRAST subcommand.

Note that the "WSDESIGN" specification here is virtually identical to what you might have requested had it been a two-factor between-subjects design, rather than a two-factor within-subjects design (but there it would have been a "DESIGN" specification). For example, 'factb (2)' refers to the second contrast in the list (0 –1 –1 2), comparing the average of the means 6.50 and 8.25 to the mean of 10.00. Even if you do not wish to look at all three of these contrasts, the "SPECIAL" syntax requires specifying exactly $k - 1$ contrasts, where k is the number of levels of the within-subjects factor on which contrasts are to be performed; you must also begin with weights of all 1s and, to use "SPECIAL" "CONTRAST"'s, the contrasts must be orthogonal. Note that "ERROR=WITHIN" is unnecessary in designs with no between-subjects factors. The key parts of the printout are in Fig. 7.5.

```
Tests involving 'FACTB(1)' Within-Subject Effect.

Tests of Significance for T2 using UNIQUE sums of squares
Source of Variation          SS        DF        MS          F  Sig of F

WITHIN+RESIDUAL             8.95         3      2.98
FACTB(1)                   78.84         1     78.84      26.43      .014
- - - - - - - - - - - - - - - - - - - - - - - - - - - - - - - - - - - -

Tests involving 'FACTB(2)' Within-Subject Effect.

Tests of Significance for T3 using UNIQUE sums of squares
Source of Variation          SS        DF        MS          F  Sig of F

WITHIN+RESIDUAL             1.08         3       .36
FACTB(2)                   36.75         1     36.75     101.77      .002
- - - - - - - - - - - - - - - - - - - - - - - - - - - - - - - - - - - -

Tests involving 'FACTB(3)' Within-Subject Effect.

Tests of Significance for T4 using UNIQUE sums of squares
Source of Variation          SS        DF        MS          F  Sig of F

WITHIN+RESIDUAL             1.25         3       .42
FACTB(3)                   12.25         1     12.25      29.40      .012
- - - - - - - - - - - - - - - - - - - - - - - - - - - - - - - - - - - -

Tests involving 'FACTA' Within-Subject Effect.

Tests of Significance for T5 using UNIQUE sums of squares
Source of Variation          SS        DF        MS          F  Sig of F

WITHIN+RESIDUAL             3.34         3      1.11
FACTA                      34.03         1     34.03      30.53      .012
- - - - - - - - - - - - - - - - - - - - - - - - - - - - - - - - - - - -

Tests involving 'FACTB BY FACTA' Within-Subject Effect.

AVERAGED Tests of Significance for MEAS.1 using UNIQUE sums of squares
Source of Variation          SS        DF        MS          F  Sig of F

WITHIN+RESIDUAL             3.03         9       .34
FACTB BY FACTA              3.09         3      1.03       3.06      .084
```

FIG. 7.5.   Output from orthogonal main effect contrasts in a two-factor within-subjects ANOVA using the CONTRAST subcommand.

Thus, the contrast just described, "FACTB(2)", comparing the average of the means 6.50 and 8.25 to the mean of 10.00, is significant, $F(1, 3) = 101.77$, $p = .002$.

Any of the canned orthogonal contrasts, such as "DIFFERENCE" and "HELMERT", might be substituted for "SPECIAL"; the nonorthogonal canned contrasts, such as "SIMPLE" and "RE-PEATED", must, however, be avoided with this technique and analyzed instead with "TRANS-FORM", as described later. Another orthogonal canned contrast is trend analysis, which might be appropriate for Factor B. To accomplish this, simply substitute the keyword "POLYNOMIAL" for "SPECIAL" and its specification (i.e., the contrast weights) on line 5.

Suppose contrasts are also desired on the second factor (Factor A in this example). Of course, in the present example, with Factor A having only two levels, this would be nonsensical. Assume, however, that there are more than two levels for the second factor. An example of this is seen in Fig. 7.6 with a 3 × 3 within-subjects ANOVA.

```
1.    MANOVA a1b1 a1b2 a1b3 a2b1 a2b2 a2b3 a3b1 a3b2 a3b3

2.    /WSFACTORS=facta(3) factb(3)

3.    /CONTRAST(factb)=SPECIAL (3*1, 2 -1 -1, 0 1 -l)

4.    /CONTRAST (facta)=SPECIAL (3* 1, -1 0 1, 1 –2 1)

5d.   /OMEANS

6o.   /PRINT=SIGNIF (AVONLY)

7.    /WSDESIGN=facta(1), facta(2), factb(1), factb(2), facta*factb.
```

FIG. 7.6.   Syntax to conduct orthogonal main effect contrasts when both factors have more than two levels in a two-factor within-subjects ANOVA.

It is irrelevant which "CONTRAST" subcommand is given first (that is, whether contrasts on Factor A or Factor B are requested first). Although in Fig. 7.6 the request for contrasts on Factor B preceded the request for contrasts on Factor A, the order of the two "CONTRAST" subcommands could have been reversed without affecting the program. The order is only crucial on the "WSFACTORS" subcommand, where the most slowly changing factor must be listed first.

Note that, in Fig. 7.6, the two "CONTRAST" subcommands are adjacent and share the same "WSDESIGN" subcommand. This is permissible as long as the contrast requests are for different within-subjects factors. If a second set of contrasts is requested for the same factor, it has to follow the "WSDESIGN" subcommand, have a "DESIGN" subcommand next, and a second set of "WSDESIGN" and "DESIGN" subcommands after the second "CONTRAST". In lines 3 and 4, '3*1' is a shortcut for 1 1 1. Specifically, in this shortcut, the second number (i.e., the one after the "*") is what number you want the computer to use and the first number (i.e., the one before the "*") is how many of them you want. Another shortcut method, introduced in chapter 5, was used in line 7, where "*" was substituted for the keyword "BY".

Nonorthogonal Main Effect Contrasts Using "TRANSFORM/RENAME"

The previous commands for main effect contrasts assumed that the contrasts in the set were orthogonal. When that was true, the "CONTRAST/WSDESIGN" method just described was relatively easy to use. However, if nonorthogonal canned contrasts such as "SIMPLE" and "REPEATED" are used, or if "SPECIAL" contrasts are used (which may or may not be nonorthogonal), a warning appears on the printout telling you, in effect, that the output is wrong. An alternate, somewhat more difficult method is available in this instance, using the "TRANSFORM" subcommand, usually combined with a "RENAME" subcommand. Although, in fact, the "RENAME" subcommand is optional, it helps greatly with the printout interpretation, thus its use is recommended. It is more general to consider this method when both factors have more than two levels, so this is illustrated in Fig. 7.7 with the 3 × 3 example of Fig. 7.6. The main effect contrasts that are illustrated for Factor A are 1 0 −1 and 1 −1 0, in other words, Condition 1 versus 3 and Condition 1 versus 2, respectively (note that they are nonorthogonal), and the main effect contrasts for Factor B are 0 1 −1 and 1 0 −1, in other words, Condition 2 versus 3 and Condition 1 versus 3, respectively (also nonorthogonal).

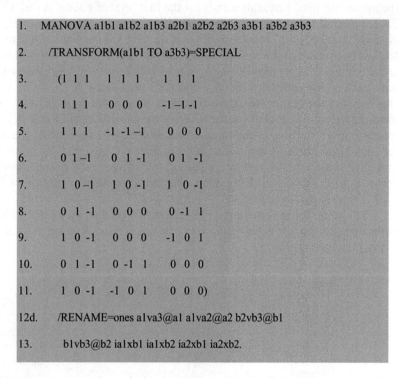

```
1.    MANOVA a1b1 a1b2 a1b3 a2b1 a2b2 a2b3 a3b1 a3b2 a3b3

2.      /TRANSFORM(a1b1 TO a3b3)=SPECIAL

3.      (1 1 1   1 1 1    1 1 1

4.       1 1 1   0 0 0    -1 -1 -1

5.       1 1 1   -1 -1 -1  0 0 0

6.       0 1 -1  0 1 -1   0 1 -1

7.       1 0 -1  1 0 -1   1 0 -1

8.       0 1 -1  0 0 0    0 -1 1

9.       1 0 -1  0 0 0    -1 0 1

10.      0 1 -1  0 -1 1    0 0 0

11.      1 0 -1  -1 0 1    0 0 0)

12d.    /RENAME=ones a1va3@a1 a1va2@a2 b2vb3@b1

13.      b1vb3@b2 ia1xb1 ia1xb2 ia2xb1 ia2xb2.
```

FIG. 7.7. Syntax commands to conduct nonorthogonal main effect contrasts in a two-factor within-subjects ANOVA using the TRANSFORM subcommand.

The "TRANSFORM" subcommand needs to handle all nine original variables and therefore the matrix of weights is 9 × 9. The easiest way to write more complicated contrasts such as these is to write all of the variable names in a horizontal line on a piece of paper and then put the weights in. This is explicated in Table 7.2.

TABLE 7.2
Contrast Weights Table for Nonorthogonal Contrasts in a Two-Factor Within-Subjects ANOVA

Row	RENAME	a1b1	a1b2	a1b3	a2b1	a2b2	a2b3	a3b1	a3b2	a3b3
1	ones	1	1	1	1	1	1	1	1	1
2	a1va3@a1	1	1	1	0	0	0	−1	−1	−1
3	a1va2@a2	1	1	1	−1	−1	−1	0	0	0
4	b2vb3@b1	0	1	−1	0	1	−1	0	1	−1
5	b1vb3@b2	1	0	−1	1	0	−1	1	0	−1
6	ia1xb1	0	1	−1	0	0	0	0	−1	1
7	ia1xb2	1	0	−1	0	0	0	−1	0	1
8	ia2xb1	0	1	−1	0	−1	1	0	0	0
9	ia2xb2	1	0	−1	−1	0	1	0	0	0

To create something like Table 7.2, you first write all the original variable names (i.e., conditions) across the top in the proper order (i.e., the order they are in on the "MANOVA" command). The next line (row 1) is to be called (i.e., "RENAME"d) 'ones' and contains, naturally enough, the line of 1s. Although transformed variables may be "RENAME"d to any legal SPSS variable name (or not "RENAME"d at all), here they are given mnemonic names, names that will be readily identifiable on printout. Next, in row 2, comes the first contrast, which is a contrast on Factor A, comparing the first to the third (last) condition. The weights for all the a1 conditions are +1, for all the a2 conditions the weights are 0, and for all three a3 conditions the weights are −1. Because it is the a1 condition in 'a1b1', 'a1b2', and 'a1b3', the +1 must be given three successive times, as shown in row 2. Similarly, the 0 weights must be given three times and the −1 weights must be given three times, for 'a3b1', 'a3b2', and 'a3b3', respectively. This contrast is called (i.e., "RENAME"d) 'a1va3@a1'. In the mnemonic used here, this stands for the first level of Factor A ('a1') versus ('v') the third level of Factor A ('a3'), hereafter called ('@') contrast 'a1'. Next, in row 3, comes the contrast "RE-NAME"d 'a1va2@a2', which implies that the first level of Factor A is to be compared to the second level of Factor A and this will be called contrast 'a2' in what follows. It has weights of +1 for 'a1b1', 'a1b2', and 'a1b3', weights of −1 for 'a2b1', 'a2b2', and 'a2b3', and weights of 0 for 'a3b1', 'a3b2', and 'a3b3'. This concludes the two contrasts on Factor A.

Next are the two contrasts on Factor B. The first (row 4) is to be "RENAME"d 'b2vb3@b1', meaning the second level of Factor B versus the third level of Factor B, hereafter contrast 'b1'. A +1 weight is given for each of the three b2 conditions, a −1 for each of the three b3 conditions, and a 0 for each of the three b1 conditions. This implies the weights 0 1 −1. Because the conditions b1, b2, and b3 are adjacent, this means the pattern 0 1 −1 must be repeated three times (see row 4). Next, in row 5, is 'b1vb3@b2', which compares the first to the third condition of Factor B. The weights are 1 0 −1, 1 0 −1, and 1 0 −1.

The coding for the remaining rows (rows 6–9) is discussed later with interaction contrasts. The point for now, though, is that nine rows of weights must be given in total. The relevant part of print-out is presented in Fig. 7.8.

```
EFFECT .. CONSTANT
Univariate F-tests with (1,3) D. F.

Variable  Hypoth. SS   Error SS Hypoth. MS   Error MS        F  Sig. of F

ONES      23256.2500 2194.75000 23256.2500  731.58333  31.78893      .011
A1VA3@A1    702.25000  108.75000   702.25000   36.25000  19.37241      .022
A1VA2@A2    272.25000   18.75000   272.25000    6.25000  43.56000      .007
B2VB3@B1     81.00000   65.00000    81.00000   21.66667   3.73846      .149
B1VB3@B2      1.00000   81.00000     1.00000   27.00000    .03704      .860
IA1XB1      225.00000   41.00000   225.00000   13.66667  16.46341      .027
IA1XB2      256.00000   62.00000   256.00000   20.66667  12.38710      .039
IA2XB1       20.25000   34.75000    20.25000   11.58333   1.74820      .278
IA2XB2       20.25000   14.75000    20.25000    4.91667   4.11864      .135
```

FIG. 7.8.   Output for nonorthogonal main effect contrasts in a two-factor within-subjects ANOVA using the TRANSFORM subcommand.

The output you obtain is the univariate F tests for the four contrasts of interest, plus a few others you might choose to ignore (you can ignore the warnings that SPSS will issue). Contrast 'a1' (i.e., a1 vs. a3), for example, would be reported as significant, $F(1, 3) = 19.37$, $p = .022$.

If the interaction from the overall analysis was significant, you could conduct simple effects, simple comparisons, and interaction contrasts instead of main effect contrasts, just as in the two-factor between-subjects design.

SIMPLE EFFECTS

Syntax for simple effects tests (appropriate when the interaction is significant) in a two-factor within-subjects design is very similar to that of simple effects tests in a two-factor between-subjects design. As was the case there, you would normally choose to look at either the simple effects of Factor A at levels of Factor B or the simple effects of Factor B at levels of Factor A. For example, for the data in Fig. 7.1, you might be interested in the simple effects of trials at each of the two different types of words (simple effects of Factor B at Factor A). The near-significant interaction implies that the pattern of means over the four trials might be different depending on whether participants are in the low or high concreteness condition. The syntax to run this analysis is in Fig. 7.9.

```
1.    MANOVA a1b1 a1b2 a1b3 a1b4 a2b1 a2b2 a2b3 a2b4

2.    /WSFACTORS=facta(2) factb(4)

3o.   /PRINT=SIGNIF(AVONLY)

4.    /WSDESIGN=factb WITHIN facta(1), factb WITHIN facta(2).
```

FIG. 7.9   Syntax commands to test the simple effects of Factor B at Factor A in a two-factor within-subjects ANOVA.

Simple effects for a within-subjects design are specified with a "WSDESIGN" subcommand under the "MANOVA" command. To obtain a simple effect, you specify that you want to do the simples of that factor at each level of the other on the "WSDESIGN" subcommand (see line 4). In a simple effects analysis, you can specify the "AVONLY" keyword to suppress the multivariate output. The output from this analysis is in Fig. 7.10.

```
Tests involving 'FACTB WITHIN FACTA(1)' Within-Subject Effect.

AVERAGED Tests of Significance for MEAS.1 using UNIQUE sums of squares
Source of Variation          SS        DF        MS         F      Sig of F

WITHIN+RESIDUAL            8.06         9       .90
FACTB WITHIN FACTA(1)     46.69         3     15.56       17.37      .000
- - - - - - - - - - - - - - - - - - - - - - - - - - - - - - - - - - - - - -
Tests involving 'FACTB WITHIN FACTA(2)' Within-Subject Effect.

AVERAGED Tests of Significance for MEAS.1 using UNIQUE sums of squares
Source of Variation          SS        DF        MS         F      Sig of F

WITHIN+RESIDUAL            6.25         9       .69
FACTB WITHIN FACTA(2)     84.25         3     28.08       40.44      .000
```

FIG. 7.10.   Output for the simple effects of Factor B at Factor A in a two-factor within-subjects ANOVA.

Both of the tests for simple effects were significant. Thus, you know that there is an effect of Factor B at both levels of Factor A; that is, the means 4.0, 5.5, 7.25, and 8.5 differ significantly and the means 5.25, 7.5, 9.25, and 11.5 differ significantly. Your next step would be to look at either simple comparisons on Factor B at the two levels of Factor A or simple post hocs.

Analyzing Orthogonal Simple Comparisons Using "CONTRAST/WSDESIGN"

Simple comparisons that are orthogonal are set up very similarly to between-subjects designs. The purpose is to test a contrast on the means within a row or within a column. Here you could test simple comparisons on Factor B at both levels of Factor A because both simple effects tests were significant. For example, you might want to test whether there was a difference between performance on the first and last trials at each level of Factor A. Assuming the remaining contrasts you would specify are orthogonal, you could set this up using the "CONTRAST" subcommand as seen in Fig. 7.11.

```
1.    MANOVA a1b1 a1b2 a1b3 a1b4 a2b1 a2b2 a2b3 a2b4

2.    /WSFACTORS=facta(2) factb(4)

3o.   /PRINT=SIGNIF(AVONLY)

4.    /CONTRAST(factb)=SPECIAL(1 1 1 1, -1 0 0 1, 0 1 -1 0, 1 -1 -1 1)

5.    /WSDESIGN=factb(1) WITHIN facta(1), factb(1) WITHIN facta(2).
```

FIG. 7.11.   Syntax commands to conduct orthogonal simple comparisons in a two-factor within-subjects ANOVA using the CONTRAST subcommand.

On the "WSDESIGN" subcommand, you specify that you would like only the first contrast on Factor B, 'factb(1)', to be tested at each level of Factor A, 'facta(1)' and 'facta(2)'. The printout is in Fig. 7.12.

```
Tests involving 'FACTB(1) WITHIN FACTA(1)' Within-Subject Effect.

AVERAGED Tests of Significance for MEAS.1 using UNIQUE sums of squares
Source of Variation              SS        DF       MS          F  Sig of F

WITHIN+RESIDUAL                 5.50        3      1.83
FACTB(1) WITHIN FACTA (1)      40.50        1     40.50      22.09      .018
- - - - - - - - - - - - - - - - - - - - - - - - - - - - - - - - - - - - -
Tests involving 'FACTB(1) WITHIN FACTA(2)' Within-Subject Effect.

AVERAGED Tests of Significance for MEAS.1 using UNIQUE sums of squares
Source of Variation              SS        DF       MS          F  Sig of F

WITHIN+RESIDUAL                 3.38        3      1.13
FACTB(1) WITHIN FACTA (2)      78.12        1     78.12      69.44      .004
```

FIG. 7.12.   Output for orthogonal simple comparisons in a two-factor within-subjects ANOVA using the CONTRAST subcommand.

The simple contrast was significant at both levels of Factor A, with p values of .018 and .004. If you wished to examine whether another of the orthogonal simple comparisons listed on the "CONTRAST" subcommand was significant, for example, 'factb(2) within facta(2)' (which compares the 7.5 to the 9.25), you would simply add them to the list on the "WSDESIGN" subcommand.

Analyzing Orthogonal Interaction Contrasts Using "CONTRAST/WSDESIGN"

As explained in chapter 4, interaction contrasts involve evaluating whether a comparison between certain levels of one factor differ depending on which level of the second factor is being considered. For example, suppose you wished to determine whether the difference between the first and last trial of Factor B for words high in concreteness (i.e., the difference between the 5.25 and the 11.5) was statistically larger than the corresponding difference for words low in concreteness (i.e., the difference between the 4.0 and the 8.5). If you had orthogonal contrasts, you could test this interaction contrast with the following:

/WSDESIGN=factb(1) by facta

The '1' in parentheses refers to the contrast number that you are interested in from line 4 of Fig. 7.11. If both factors had more than two levels, an interaction contrast of the type $A_{Comp} \times B_{Comp}$ would be possible. In this case, after defining the orthogonal contrasts of interest on each factor with "CONTRAST" subcommands, the "WSDESIGN" specification would be of the form:

/WSDESIGN=facta(1) by factb(3)

where the numbers in parentheses refer to the contrast numbers for both factors.

Nonorthogonal Simple Comparisons Using "TRANSFORM/RENAME"

Nonorthogonal simple comparisons can also be tested with the "TRANSFORM/RENAME" method. Suppose in the 3 × 3 example you wished to test "SIMPLE" comparisons (which are not only always nonorthogonal, but also especially useful for present purposes, because they are also used in post hoc analyses) using Condition 2 of Factor B as the reference condition, within each of the levels of Factor A. Thus, the comparison on Factor B is 'b1vb2' (weights 1 −1 0) and 'b3vb2' (weights 0 −1 1) tested within 'a1', then within 'a2', and finally within 'a3'. Although you could use the canned routine "SIMPLE" to test this contrast, the weights will be used in Fig. 7.13 to show an example for the more general case when a canned routine is not available.

```
1.    MANOVA a1b1 a1b2 a1b3 a2b1 a2b2 a2b3 a3b1 a3b2 a3b3

2.    /TRANSFORM(a1b1 TO a1b3/a2b1 TO a2b3/a3b1 TO a3b3)=SPECIAL

3.    (1 1 1, 1 –1 0, 0 –1 1)

4d.   /RENAME=onesa1 b1vb2wa1 b3vb2wa1 onesa2 b1vb2wa2 b3vb2wa2

5.    onesa3 b1vb2wa3 b3vb2wa3.
```

FIG. 7.13.   Syntax commands to conduct nonorthogonal simple comparisons in a two-factor within-subjects ANOVA using the TRANSFORM subcommand.

If this was a between-subjects problem, your contrast matrix for Factor B would be '1 1 1, 1 –1 0, 0 –1 1' and you would test that contrast at each level of Factor A. Because here you have within-subjects, and a nonorthogonal set of contrasts, you are actually going to have to repeat the same contrast matrix for each level of Factor A. Thus, when you are testing the contrasts on Factor B within the first level of Factor A, the first level of Factor A gets the contrast matrix and all of the other levels of Factor A get 0s (see rows 1–3 in Table 7.3); when testing the contrasts on Factor B within the second level of Factor A, the second level of Factor A gets the contrast matrix and all of the other levels of Factor A get 0s (see rows 4–6 in Table 7.3); finally, when testing the contrasts on Factor B within the third level of Factor A, the third level of Factor A gets the contrast matrix and all of the other levels of Factor A get 0s (see rows 7–9 in Table 7.3). Instead of writing out the entire 9 × 9 matrix, you can use a shortcut shown in line 2 of Fig. 7.13. Specifically, when the list of variables in parentheses after a "TRANSFORM" command is separated by "/" (e.g., in line 2, 'a1b1 TO a1b3', then "/"), "MANOVA" expects only as many weights as there are variables before the slash (here three variables), and it repeats the contrast for each set of variables. Thus, putting it altogether, the "TRANSFORM" subcommand produces the contrast weights in Table 7.3.

TABLE 7.3
Contrast Weights Produced by Line 2 in Fig. 7.13

Row	RENAME	a1b1	a1b2	a1b3	a2b1	a2b2	a2b3	a3b1	a3b2	a3b3
1	onesa1	1	1	1	0	0	0	0	0	0
2	b1vb2wa1	1	–1	0	0	0	0	0	0	0
3	b3vb2wa1	0	–1	1	0	0	0	0	0	0
4	onesa2	0	0	0	1	1	1	0	0	0
5	b1vb2wa2	0	0	0	1	–1	0	0	0	0
6	b3vb2wa2	0	0	0	0	–1	1	0	0	0
7	onesa3	0	0	0	0	0	0	1	1	1
8	b1vb2wa3	0	0	0	0	0	0	1	–1	0
9	b3vb2wa3	0	0	0	0	0	0	0	–1	1

The "RENAME"s have been chosen to be mnemonic. Thus, row 4 is labeled 'onesa2', since it has all 1s for the a2 variables and 0s elsewhere. Row 5 is "RENAME"d 'b1vb2wa2', to represent Level 1 of b versus Level 2 of b, both within a2. The relevant part of the printout is in Fig. 7.14.

```
EFFECT .. CONSTANT
Univariate F-tests with (1,3) D. F.

Variable    Hypoth. SS   Error SS  Hypoth. MS    Error MS          F  Sig. of F

ONESA1      1332.25000  338.75000  1332.25000   112.91667   11.79852      .041
B1VB2WA1      36.00000   14.00000    36.00000     4.66667    7.71429      .069
B3VB2WA1        .25000   14.75000      .25000     4.91667     .05085      .836
ONESA2      2809.00000  291.00000  2809.00000    97.00000   28.95876      .013
B1VB2WA2       9.00000    1.00000     9.00000      .33333   27.00000      .014
B3VB2WA2      25.00000    9.00000    25.00000     3.00000    8.33333      .063
ONESA3      3600.00000  150.00000  3600.00000    50.00000   72.00000      .003
B1VB2WA3      25.00000    5.00000    25.00000     1.66667   15.00000      .030
B3VB2WA3     306.25000   62.75000   306.25000    20.91667   14.64143      .031
```

FIG. 7.14.   Output for nonorthogonal simple comparisons in a two-factor within-subjects ANOVA using the TRANSFORM subcommand.

For example, the simple comparison of Condition b1 versus Condition b2 within Condition a3 ("RENAME"d "B1VB2WA3") is significant, $F(1,3) = 15.0$, $p = .030$.

Nonorthogonal Interaction Contrasts Using the "TRANSFORM/RENAME" Method

Nonorthogonal interaction contrasts can also be tested using "TRANSFORM/RENAME". In fact, the last four rows in the transformation weight matrix from Table 7.2 are all interaction contrasts. For example, the first, 'ia1xb1', is the interaction (hence the letter 'i') of Contrast 1 on Factor A ('a1') with Contrast 1 on Factor B. Because 'a1' compares the first to the third level of Factor A, whereas 'b1' compares the second to the third level of Factor B, the test shows whether the difference between the two darker cells in Table 7.4 differs from the difference between the two lighter cells.

TABLE 7.4
The Cells Compared for the Interaction Contrast 'ia1b1'

	a1	a2	a3
b1			
b2	▉		▉
b3	▒		▒

To obtain the correct weights in rows 6 through 9 of Table 7.2, simply take the weights from the two rows involved in the interaction and multiply them together for each column. For example, to get row 6, 'ia1xb1', which is the interaction of contrasts 'a1' (row 2) and 'b1' (row 4), you would multiply row 2 by row 4 as follows: Take the 'a1b1' (col. 1) weight from contrast 'a1' (row 2), which is 1, and multiply it by the 'a1b1' (col. 1) weight from contrast 'b1' (row 4), which is 0; the product is 0, which is therefore the first entry in row 6. Next, take the weight from the 'a1b2' column (col. 2) from contrast 'a1' (row 2, the '1') and multiply it by the weight from 'a1b2' (col. 2) from contrast 'b1' (row, the '1') to get the 'a1b2' (col. 2) weight for 'ia1xb1' (row 6); the product is 1. You would continue to do this for all nine columns.

POST HOCS

Post hoc tests are completed in two-factor within-subjects designs in much the same way as they are in between-subjects designs. Generally, all the pairwise comparisons (either between marginal means as main effect contrasts or cell means within a specific row or column as simple comparisons) are generated by sets of "SIMPLE" contrasts. Then, manual calculations are used to identify new criterion or test values and the printed F or p value output is tested against these calculated criterion values. Because "SIMPLE" contrasts are nonorthogonal, the "TRANSFORM" method, rather than the "CONTRAST" method, must be used to generate the SPSS output.

MORE THAN TWO FACTORS

All of the previous designs can be extended to include more than two within-subjects factors. The syntax for a basic analysis of a three-factor within-subjects design is in Fig. 7.15 (Factor A has two levels, Factor B has three, and Factor C has four).

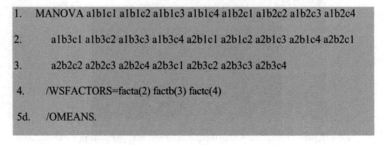

```
1.   MANOVA a1b1c1 a1b1c2 a1b1c3 a1b1c4 a1b2c1 a1b2c2 a1b2c3 a1b2c4

2.       a1b3c1 a1b3c2 a1b3c3 a1b3c4 a2b1c1 a2b1c2 a2b1c3 a2b1c4 a2b2c1

3.       a2b2c2 a2b2c3 a2b2c4 a2b3c1 a2b3c2 a2b3c3 a2b3c4

4.   /WSFACTORS=facta(2) factb(3) factc(4)

5d.  /OMEANS.
```

FIG. 7.15.   Syntax commands to conduct a three-factor within-subjects ANOVA.

The setup for the basic analysis of the three-factor within-subjects ANOVA is very similar to that for the two-factor within-subjects ANOVA. The first score for participants would be their score from the first level of Factor A, the first level of Factor B, and the first level of Factor C; the next number is their score on the first level of Factor A, the first level of Factor B, and the second level of Factor C, and so on. Factor A is said to be the factor that is changing most slowly, Factor B is changing next most slowly, and Factor C is changing fastest. This is reflected on the "WSFACTORS" subcommand, where Factor A is defined first, followed by Factor B, and finally Factor C. If you had more than three factors, you would simply keep adding them in the correct order (by slowest to fastest) on the "MANOVA" command line and "WSFACTORS" subcommand.

The more complicated analyses for three-way designs will be explicated only for orthogonal contrasts, using "CONTRAST" and "WSDESIGN". Basically, all these analyses are directly analogous to the corresponding analysis for three-factor between groups, where these analyses were first covered. For example, simple two-way interactions would have as their "WSDESIGN" specification something of the form:

/WSDESIGN=facta BY factb WITHIN factc(2).

Simple simple effects would have specification of the form:

/WSDESIGN=factb WITHIN facta(2) WITHIN factc(2).

Simple simple comparisons have WSDESIGN subcommands in the form:

/WSDESIGN=factc(1) WITHIN facta(2) WITHIN factb(2).

Simple interaction contrasts are like the following:

/WSDESIGN=facta(2) BY factc WITHIN factb(3).

Finally, interaction contrasts are of the form:

/WSDESIGN=facta(2) BY factc(2) BY factb.

PAC

A two-factor within-subjects ANOVA is run almost exactly like a one-factor. After clicking Analyze and choosing General Linear Model–Repeated Measures, the Define Factors screen (see Fig. 6.10) will pop up. The name of the factor by default is 'factor1'. You can change this name to any name you want (following SPSS naming conventions). After you name the first factor, you have to tell SPSS how many levels it has; in the example from Fig. 7.6, it is three. Then click on the Add button. The cursor then moves back to the Name box and you can add in the second (or subsequent) factor. When you have named all of the factors and specified their number of levels, click the Define button. For a 3 × 3 two-factor within-subjects design, the result is seen in Fig. 7.16.

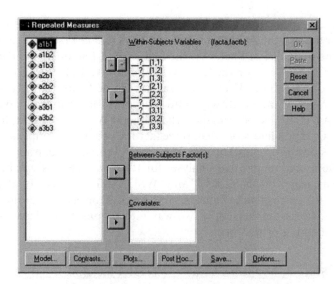

FIG. 7.16. Dialogue box to set up a two-factor within-subjects ANOVA.

You see that you have the opportunity to pick as many variables as there are combinations of the levels of the factors. Similar to the "WSFACTORS" subcommand, the most slowly changing variable is defined first. Thus, the first variable would be 'a1b1', the second 'a1b2', the third 'a1b3', then 'a2b1', 'a2b2', and so on, until all of the variables have been defined (see Fig. 7.17).

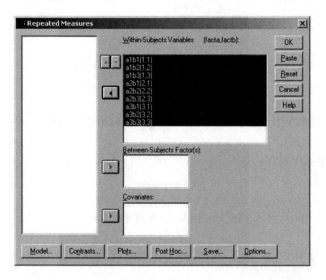

FIG. 7.17. Dialogue box after variables have been defined in a two-factor within-subjects ANOVA.

You could run canned contrasts using the Contrast menu, but all of the more complicated analyses and "SPECIAL" contrasts would have to be run using syntax (see chap. 13). Power, effect size estimates, and means can be obtained in the Options submenu (see Fig. 7.18). The latter is an improvement over MANOVA, because it will calculate marginal as well as cell means.

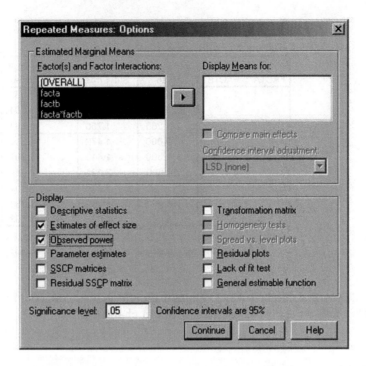

FIG. 7.18. Options dialogue box in a two-factor within-subjects ANOVA.

Select all the Factor(s) and Factor Interactions offered in the box on the left side of the screen (i.e., 'facta', 'factb', and 'facta*factb') and move them to the right box by clicking on the arrow. After clicking Continue, then OK, the means tables print out as seen in Fig. 7.19.

Estimated Marginal Means
1. FACTA

Measure: MEASURE_1

FACTA	Mean	Std. Error	95% Confidence Interval	
			Lower Bound	Upper Bound
1	6.083	1.771	.447	11.720
2	8.833	1.641	3.609	14.057
3	10.000	1.179	6.249	13.751

2. FACTB

Measure: MEASURE_1

FACTB	Mean	Std. Error	95% Confidence Interval	
			Lower Bound	Upper Bound
1	8.083	1.595	3.007	13.159
2	9.417	1.691	4.036	14.798
3	7.417	1.329	3.187	11.646

FIG. 7.19.   *(Continues)*

3. FACTA * FACTB

Measure: MEASURE_1

FACTA	FACTB	Mean	Std. Error	95% Confidence Interval	
				Lower Bound	Upper Bound
1	1	4.000	1.581	-1.032	9.032
	2	7.000	2.273	-.234	14.234
	3	7.250	1.750	1.681	12.819
2	1	9.000	1.472	4.316	13.684
	2	7.500	1.443	2.907	12.093
	3	10.000	2.121	3.249	16.751
3	1	11.250	1.931	5.104	17.396
	2	13.750	1.702	8.334	19.166
	3	5.000	1.080	1.563	8.437

FIG. 7.19.   PAC output of marginal and cell means for a two-factor within-subjects ANOVA.

If you had checked the Compare main effects box, you could then select Bonferroni or Sidak and obtain these post hocs as described in chapter 6.

8 Two-Factor Mixed Designs in Analysis of Variance: One Between-Subjects Factor and One Within-Subjects Factor

In chapters 3 through 7 you learned how to analyze between-subjects and within-subjects (i.e., repeated measures) designs. In this chapter, these two designs are combined to form a *mixed* design (sometimes also called a *split-plot* design). Mixed designs are widely used because of their desirable statistical properties: reduced error variance, owing to the within-subjects factor, and ease of the interpretation of the between-subjects factor's effects. In this chapter, the simplest mixed design, that with two factors, one between- and one within-subjects factor is described. Larger mixed designs are covered in chapter 9.

The hypothetical data for this example are from a smoking cessation study and are shown in Fig. 8.1. There is one between-subjects factor and one within-subjects factor: Factor A, treatment, is the between-subjects factor and Factor B, time, is the within-subjects factor. For the between-subjects factor, participants are assigned to quit smoking using either a nicotine patch (coded 1), group therapy (coded 2), or a no treatment control group (coded 3). For the within-subjects factor, each participant reports the number of cigarettes they smoked in the week before the interventions started, the week after the interventions ended, the week 2 months after the interventions ended, and the week 6 months after the interventions ended (thus, the within-subjects factor of 'time' has four levels).

a1: Nicotine Patch				a2: Group Therapy				a3: Control			
b: Time				b: Time				b: Time			
b1	b2	b3	b4	b1	b2	b3	b4	b1	b2	b3	b4
120	84	47	20	115	50	30	30	125	127	128	120
119	51	40	14	118	30	22	24	120	122	122	124
123	20	18	21	120	0	0	0	114	122	128	128
135	10	9	0	119	4	2	2	108	118	127	128

FIG. 8.1. Data from a one between-, one within-factor ANOVA wih three levels of Factor A and four levels of Factor B.

BASIC ANALYSIS OF VARIANCE COMMANDS

The program, presented in Fig. 8.2, is followed by an explanation of the function of the different commands in the program.

```
1.    MANOVA b1 b2 b3 b4 BY facta(1,3)

2.      /WSFACTORS=factb(4)

3d.    /OMEANS

4d.    /POWER

5d.    /PRINT=SIGNIF(AVONLY EFSIZE)

6o.    /WSDESIGN

7o.    /DESIGN.
```

FIG. 8.2.   Syntax commands to conduct a one between-, one within-factor ANOVA.

The setup for the two-factor mixed design ANOVA is a combination of the one-factor between- and one-factor within-subjects designs. You again start with the "MANOVA" command followed by each of the scores on the within-subjects factor. This sequence is followed by the keyword "BY", which is followed by the name of the between-subjects factor, in this case, 'facta'. Just as in a one-factor between-subjects design, the name designating the between-subjects factor is immediately followed by a pair of parentheses that contains the information on the levels of the factor. In line 2, the within-subjects factor is named on the "WSFACTORS" subcommand just as it was in a one-factor within-subjects design. The observed means are requested in line 3; this optional subcommand is highly recommended. Effect size and power analyses have also been requested in lines 4 and 5, and these subcommands are also optional. Finally, the "WSDESIGN" and "DESIGN" subcommands of lines 6 and 7 are actually also optional. If left off, SPSS will automatically generate the same desired full factorial model output that is shown in Fig. 8.3. Their inclusion is simply good practice, because they are needed for some of the more complex analyses discussed later in the chapter.

```
Cell Means and Standard Deviations
 Variable .. B1
       FACTOR            CODE               Mean   Std. Dev.            N

   FACTA               1              124.250      7.365            4
   FACTA               2              118.000      2.160            4
   FACTA               3              116.750      7.365            4
 For entire sample                   119.667      6.527           12
- - - - - - - - - - - - - - - - - - - - - - - - - - - - - - - - - - - -
 Variable .. B2
       FACTOR            CODE               Mean   Std. Dev.            N

   FACTA               1               41.250     33.420            4
   FACTA               2               21.000     23.466            4
   FACTA               3              122.250      3.686            4
 For entire sample                    61.500     50.459           12
- - - - - - - - - - - - - - - - - - - - - - - - - - - - - - - - - - - -
 Variable .. B3
       FACTOR            CODE               Mean   Std. Dev.            N

   FACTA               1               28.500     17.935            4
   FACTA               2               13.500     14.821            4
   FACTA               3              126.250      2.872            4
 For entire sample                    56.083     53.631           12
- - - - - - - - - - - - - - - - - - - - - - - - - - - - - - - - - - - -
 Variable .. B4
       FACTOR            CODE               Mean   Std. Dev.            N

   FACTA               1               13.750      9.674            4
   FACTA               2               14.000     15.232            4
   FACTA               3              125.000      3.830            4
 For entire sample                    50.917     55.556           12
- - - - - - - - - - - - - - - - - - - - - - - - - - - - - - - - - - - -

Tests of Between-Subjects Effects.

Tests of Significance for T1 using UNIQUE sums of squares
 Source of Variation          SS       DF        MS          F  Sig of F

 WITHIN CELLS              3976.63       9     441.85
 FACTA                    62107.29       2   31053.65      70.28      .000
```

FIG. 8.3.   *(Continues)*

```
Effect Size Measures and Observed Power at the .0500 Level
                              Partial Noncen-
      Source of Variation     ETA Sqd trality      Power

      FACTA                      .940 140.563       1.000
- - - - - - - - - - - - - - - - - - - - - - - - - - - - - - -

Tests involving 'FACTB' Within-Subject Effect.

      Mauchly sphericity test, W =         .06404
      Chi-square approx. =        21.22272 with 5 D. F.
      Significance =                       .001

      Greenhouse-Geisser Epsilon =         .45525
      Huynh-Feldt Epsilon =                .62827
      Lower-bound Epsilon =                .33333

AVERAGED Tests of Significance that follow multivariate tests are equivalent to
univariate or split-plot or mixed-model approach to repeated measures.
Epsilons may be used to adjust d.f. for the AVERAGED results.
- - - - - - - - - - - - - - - - - - - - - - - - - - - - - - -

Tests involving 'FACTB' Within-Subject Effect.

AVERAGED Tests of Significance for B using UNIQUE sums of squares
      Source of Variation        SS       DF       MS        F   Sig of F

      WITHIN CELLS             4075.88     27    150.96
      FACTB                   36962.42      3  12320.81    81.62    .000
      FACTA BY FACTB          23905.71      6   3984.28    26.39    .000
- - - - - - - - - - - - - - - - - - - - - - - - - - - - - - -
Effect Size Measures and Observed Power at the .0500 Level
                              Partial Noncen-
      Source of Variation     ETA Sqd trality      Power

      FACTB                      .901 244.852       1.000
      FACTA BY FACTB             .854 158.360       1.000
```

FIG. 8.3.   Output from a one between-, one within-factor ANOVA.

This output is very similar to the one-factor within-subjects ANOVA, except that, in this case, you are also interested in the between-subjects factor's effects. Because "OMEANS" was specified, the means for each level of Factor B at each level of Factor A and the means for the entire sample are given. Note, however, that the marginal means for the between-subjects factor (the final column of the means as arrayed in Table 8.1) were not provided by "MANOVA" and need to be manually calculated.

TABLE 8.1
Marginal and Cell Means for a One Between-, One Within-Subjects Factor ANOVA

	b1	b2	b3	b4	Average
Facta 1	124.50	41.25	28.5	13.75	51.938
Facta 2	118.0	21.0	13.5	14.0	41.625
Facta 3	116.75	122.25	126.25	125.0	122.562
Average	119.667	61.50	56.083	50.917	

Following the "OMEANS" printout is the F test for the between-subjects factor. Factor A is significant, $F(2, 9) = 70.28$, $p = .001$, partial eta squared = .940. Remember that eta squared is interpreted as the proportion of variance in the dependent variable explained by that effect controlling all other effects in the design. The remainder of the output is concerned with the within-subjects factor. Sphericity tests are shown first (the multivariate output was suppressed with the keyword "AVONLY"). Note here that sphericity is violated ($p = .001$) and, thus, in reality you would need to make one of the corrections discussed in chapter 6. Following the sphericity tests are the F tests for the main effect of Factor B, $F(3, 27) = 81.62$, $p = .001$, partial eta squared = .901, and the interaction between Factor A and Factor B, $F(6, 27) = 26.39$, $p = .001$, partial eta squared = .854. Normally, because there is a significant interaction, you would turn next to exploring that interaction, but to demonstrate contrasts for main effects, main effect contrasts will be described first. Typically, main effect contrasts are only undertaken when the interaction is not significant in an analysis.

MAIN EFFECT CONTRASTS

Between-Subjects Factor(s)

First, contrasts on the between-subjects factor are illustrated. The program in Fig. 8.4 compares the average of the nicotine and group therapy conditions (a1 and a2) to the control group (a3) for Factor A (i.e., the average of the mean of 51.938 and 41.625 [i.e., 46.782] vs. the mean of 122.562). Keep in mind that, although effect size and power are not requested here, that is only for space reasons and these two statistics should be requested.

```
1.    MANOVA b1 b2 b3 b4 BY facta (1,3)

2.    /WSFACTORS=factb(4)

3o.   /PRINT=SIGNIF (AVONLY)

4.    /CONTRAST(facta)=SPECIAL (1 1 1, –1 –1 2, 0 1 -1)

5.    /DESIGN=facta(1) facta(2).
```

FIG. 8.4.   Syntax commands for main effect contrasts on the between-subjects factor in a one between-, one within-factor ANOVA.

The contrasts on the between-subjects factor in a mixed-design ANOVA are set up analogously to the way they are set up for a between-subjects factor design. Note that the second contrast named previously (0 1 −1) is merely included to fill out the square matrix for "SPECIAL" rather than because there is true interest in it, and it happens to be nonorthogonal. This is not a problem on the between-subjects factor, but both it and the desired contrast have to be specified on the "DESIGN" subcommand (i.e., you must specify 'DESIGN=facta(1) facta(2)', rather than simply 'DESIGN= facta(1)'). If either contrast is omitted, the result SPSS produces for nonorthogonal, as well as orthogonal, cases will be numerically incorrect. Figure 8.5 shows the relevant section of printout.

```
Tests of Between-Subjects Effects.

AVERAGED Tests of Significance for B using UNIQUE sums of squares
Source of Variation         SS        DF      MS          F   Sig of F

WITHIN+RESIDUAL          3976.63       9     441.85
FACTA(1)               61256.51       1   61256.51     138.64      .000
FACTA(2)               52407.03       1   52407.03     118.61      .000
```

FIG. 8.5.   Output for main effect contrasts on the between-subjects factor in a one between-, one within-factor ANOVA.

The syntax in Fig. 8.4 will also automatically produce the tests for the interaction contrasts, but these will be discussed later, in the next section.

Within-Subjects Factor(s)

To conduct a main effect contrast on the within-subjects factor in a mixed design, consideration needs to be given to whether the contrasts are orthogonal or not, just as in the case of only within-subjects factors designs. If the contrasts are all orthogonal, either the "CONTRAST" method or the "TRANSFORM" method may be used. If they are nonorthogonal, however, only the latter produces correct answers. In the next example, a set of orthogonal contrasts is considered, in order to exemplify both methods and compare their printouts. (The first contrast, for example, compares the means 119.667 and 50.917.) The syntax for the "CONTRAST/WSDESIGN" method is in Fig. 8.6.

```
1.    MANOVA b1 b2 b3 b4 BY facta(1,3)

2.    /WSFACTORS=factb(4)

3.    /CONTRAST(factb)=SPECIAL (1 1 1 1, 1 0 0 -1, 0 1 -1 0, 1 -1 -1 1)

4.    /WSDESIGN=factb(1) factb(2) factb(3)

5o.   /DESIGN.
```

FIG. 8.6.   Syntax commands for main effect contrasts on the within-subjects factor in a one between-, one within-factor ANOVA using the CONTRAST subcommand.

Note that the "DESIGN" subcommand (line 5) could have been omitted with no difference in output. In Fig. 8.7 the salient printout is shown.

```
Tests of Between-Subjects Effects.

AVERAGED Tests of Significance for B using UNIQUE sums of squares
Source of Variation         SS         DF        MS          F   Sig of F

WITHIN+RESIDUAL          3976.63       9      441.85
FACTA                   62107.29       2    31053.65       70.28    .000
- - - - - - - - - - - - - - - - - - - - - - - - - - - - - - - - - - - - -

Tests involving 'FACTB(1)' Within-Subject Effect.

AVERAGED Tests of Significance for B using UNIQUE sums of squares
Source of Variation         SS         DF        MS          F   Sig of F

WITHIN+RESIDUAL          1031.87       9      114.65
FACTB(1)                28359.38       1    28359.38      247.35    .000
FACTA BY FACTB(1)       17829.25       2     8914.62       77.75    .000
- - - - - - - - - - - - - - - - - - - - - - - - - - - - - - - - - - - - -

Tests involving 'FACTB(2)' Within-Subject Effect.

AVERAGED Tests of Significance for B using UNIQUE sums of squares
Source of Variation         SS         DF        MS          F   Sig of F

WITHIN+RESIDUAL           570.88       9       63.43
FACTB(2)                  176.04       1      176.04        2.78    .130
FACTA BY FACTB(2)         293.58       2      146.79        2.31    .155
- - - - - - - - - - - - - - - - - - - - - - - - - - - - - - - - - - - - -

Tests involving 'FACTB(3)' Within-Subject Effect.

AVERAGED Tests of Significance for B using UNIQUE sums of squares
Source of Variation         SS         DF        MS          F   Sig of F

WITHIN+RESIDUAL          2473.13       9      274.79
FACTB(3)                 8427.00       1     8427.00       30.67    .000
FACTA BY FACTB(3)        5782.87       2     2891.44       10.52    .004
```

FIG. 8.7.   Output for main effect contrasts on the within-subjects factor in a one between-, one within-factor ANOVA using the CONTRAST subcommand.

For example, the first contrast, the average of the first time point versus the average of the fourth time point, is significant, $F(1, 9) = 247.35$, $p = .001$. Note that the output also automatically includes tests for the "FACTA" main effect and for interaction contrasts, such as "FACTA BY FACTB (3)". The latter will be discussed later.

Because the contrasts are orthogonal, equivalent (but not identical looking) results are produced by syntax that uses the "TRANSFORM" method. Such syntax is in Fig. 8.8.

```
1.    MANOVA b1 b2 b3 b4 BY facta (1,3)

2.    /TRANSFORM(b1 to b4)=SPECIAL(1 1 1 1, 1 0 0 -1, 0 1 -1 0, 1 -1 -1 1)

3o.   /NOPRINT=SIGNIF(MULTIV)

4d.   /RENAME=skip b1vb4 b2vb3 b14vb23

5.    /DESIGN=CONSTANT facta.
```

FIG. 8.8.   Syntax command for main effect contrasts on the within-subjects factor in a one between-, one within-factor ANOVA using the TRANSFORM subcommand.

The "RENAME" subcommand (line 4) gives mnemonic names for the three contrasts (and the name 'skip' for the row of ones). For example, 'b14vb23' indicates that the average of Conditions 1 and 4 of Factor B are to be contrasted with the average of Conditions 2 and 3. Note that it is also necessary in this method to include a "DESIGN" subcommand (line 5) that specifies the new keyword "CONSTANT" (this will cause SPSS to give you the F tests for the individual contrasts) as well as 'facta'. The multivariate output is suppressed using the "NOPRINT" subcommand. The salient parts of the printout are in Fig. 8.9.

```
EFFECT .. FACTA
Univariate F-tests with (2,9) D. F.


Variable   Hypoth. SS   Error SS  Hypoth. MS   Error MS        F  Sig. of F

SKIP       248429.167  15906.5000 124214.583 1767.38889  70.28141      .000
B1VB4       35658.5000  2063.75000  17829.2500  229.30556  77.75324      .000
B2VB3         587.16667  1141.75000   293.58333  126.86111   2.31421      .155
B14VB23     23131.5000  9892.50000  11565.7500 1099.16667  10.52229      .004

- - - - - - - - - - - - - - - - - - - - - - - - - - - - - - - - - - - - - -

EFFECT .. CONSTANT
Univariate F-tests with (1,9) D. F.


Variable   Hypoth. SS   Error SS  Hypoth. MS   Error MS        F  Sig. of F

SKIP       996480.333  15906.5000 996480.333 1767.38889 563.81498      .000
B1VB4       56718.7500  2063.75000  56718.7500  229.30556 247.35009      .000
B2VB3         352.08333  1141.75000   352.08333  126.86111   2.77534      .130
B14VB23     33708.0000  9892.50000  33708.0000 1099.16667  30.66687      .000
```

FIG. 8.9. Output from main effect contrasts on the within-subjects factor in a one between-, one within-factor ANOVA using the TRANSFORM subcommand.

Note that the results for the main effect contrasts that provide equivalent F values (i.e., 247.35, 2.77, and 30.67, for the first, second, and third contrasts, respectively) to those on the printout for the "CONTRAST" subcommand method are found here under "EFFECT .. CONSTANT" (which is why line 5 needed to have the specification shown). The F tests under "EFFECT .. FACTA" are actually interaction contrasts, to be discussed in more detail later.

If main effect contrasts are desired on both factors, they may be obtained simultaneously by combining the two sets of syntax. For example, Fig. 8.10 contains syntax that obtains contrasts on both main effects and uses the "CONTRAST" method (and therefore assumes orthogonal contrasts on the within-subjects factor).

```
1.    MANOVA b1 b2 b3 b4 BY facta(1,3)

2.    /WSFACTORS=factb(4)

3o.   /PRINT=SIGNIF(AVONLY)

4.    /CONTRAST(facta)=SPECIAL(1 1 1, -1 -1 2, 0 1 -1)

5.    /CONTRAST(factb)=SPECIAL(1 1 1 1, 1 0 0 -1, 0 1 -1 0, 1 -1 -1 1)

6.    /WSDESIGN=factb(1) factb(2) factb(3)

7.    /DESIGN=facta(1) facta(2).
```

FIG. 8.10. Syntax commands for main effect contrasts on both factors in a one between-, one within-factor ANOVA using the CONTRAST subcommand.

The order in which the contrasts are specified is unimportant, but to obtain the correct significance tests, you must include all contrasts on the "WSDESIGN" and "DESIGN" subcommands, and the "WSDESIGN" subcommand must precede the "DESIGN" subcommand (i.e., lines 6 and 7 must be in the order presented). The printout is in Fig. 8.11, which gives the Fs of 138.64 and 118.61, respectively, for the two between-subjects factor contrasts, as in Fig. 8.5, and 247.35, 2.78, and 30.67, respectively, for the three within-subjects factor contrasts, as in Fig. 8.7.

```
Tests of Between-Subjects Effects.

AVERAGED Tests of Significance for B using UNIQUE sums of squares
Source of Variation              SS       DF         MS          F  Sig of F

WITHIN+RESIDUAL               3976.63      9        441.85
FACTA(1)                     61256.51      1      61256.51     138.64   .000
FACTA(2)                     52407.03      1      52407.03     118.61   .000
- - - - - - - - - - - - - - - - - - - - - - - - - - - - - - - - - - - - - -

Tests involving 'FACTB(1)' Within-Subject Effect.

AVERAGED Tests of Significance for B using UNIQUE sums of squares
Source of Variation              SS       DF         MS          F  Sig of F

WITHIN+RESIDUAL               1031.87      9        114.65
FACTB(1)                     28359.37      1      28359.37     247.35   .000
FACTA(1) BY FACTB(1)         17787.00      1      17787.00     155.14   .000
FACTA(2) BY FACTB(1)         12600.06      1      12600.06     109.90   .000
- - - - - - - - - - - - - - - - - - - - - - - - - - - - - - - - - - - - - -

Tests involving 'FACTB(2)' Within-Subject Effect.

AVERAGED Tests of Significance for B using UNIQUE sums of squares
Source of Variation              SS       DF         MS          F  Sig of F

WITHIN+RESIDUAL                570.88      9         63.43
FACTB(2)                       176.04      1        176.04       2.78   .130
FACTA(1) BY FACTB(2)           266.02      1        266.02       4.19   .071
FACTA(2) BY FACTB(2)           132.25      1        132.25       2.08   .183
- - - - - - - - - - - - - - - - - - - - - - - - - - - - - - - - - - - - - -

Tests involving 'FACTB(3)' Within-Subject Effect.

AVERAGED Tests of Significance for B using UNIQUE sums of squares
Source of Variation              SS       DF         MS          F  Sig of F

WITHIN+RESIDUAL               2473.13      9        274.79
FACTB(3)                      8427.00      1       8427.00      30.67   .000
FACTA(1) BY FACTB(3)          5355.09      1       5355.09      19.49   .002
FACTA(2) BY FACTB(3)          5434.03      1       5434.03      19.78   .002
```

FIG. 8.11. Output from main effect contrasts on both factors in a one between-, one within-factor ANOVA using the CONTRAST subcommand.

In addition to the main effect contrasts specified, the interaction contrasts, such as "FACTA(1) BY FACTB(3)", are also obtained automatically and will be discussed in the next section.

Alternatively, the "TRANSFORM" method on the within-subjects factors may be combined with the contrasts on the between-subjects factors, as seen in Fig. 8.12.

```
1.     MANOVA b1 b2 b3 b4 BY facta(1,3)

2o.    /NOPRINT=SIGNIF(MULTIV)

3.     /CONTRAST(facta)=SPECIAL(1 1 1, -1 -1 2, 0 1 -1)

4.     /TRANSFORM(b1 to b4)=SPECIAL(1 1 1 1, 1 0 0 -1, 0 1 -1 0, 1 -1 -1 1)

5d.    /RENAME=amain b1vb4 b2vb3 b14vb23

6.     /DESIGN=CONSTANT facta(1) facta(2).
```

FIG. 8.12. Syntax commands for main effect contrasts on both factors in a one between-, one within-factor ANOVA using the TRANSFORM subcommand.

A small (and optional but useful) change to be noted in line 5 in Fig. 8.12 is that the row of ones has been "RENAME"d not 'ones' but rather 'amain', because its results are not to be ignored in the combined printout. Note also the "DESIGN" subcommand in line 6, which specifies both the contrasts and "CONSTANT". Note that, if you did not specify that you wanted all of the contrasts on Factor A, then you would have to add in "ERROR=WITHIN" to get the correct significance tests.

In Fig. 8.13 is the relevant portion of output produced by the previous syntax, whose results are numerically equivalent to those in 8.11 (note the shaded F values), but emerge in a very different format.

```
EFFECT .. FACTA(2)
Univariate F-tests with (1,9) D. F.


Variable   Hypoth. SS   Error SS  Hypoth. MS    Error MS          F   Sig. of F

AMAIN      209628.125 15906.5000  209628.125  1767.38889  118.60894        .000
B1VB4       25200.1250 2063.75000  25200.1250   229.30556  109.89758        .000
B2VB3         264.50000 1141.75000    264.50000   126.86111    2.08496        .183
B14VB23     21736.1250 9892.50000  21736.1250  1099.16667   19.77509        .002
- - - - - - - - - - - - - - - - - - - - - - - - - - - - - - - - - - - - - - -
EFFECT .. FACTA(1)
Univariate F-tests with (1,9) D. F.


Variable   Hypoth. SS   Error SS  Hypoth. MS    Error MS          F   Sig. of F

AMAIN      245026.042 15906.5000  245026.042  1767.38889  138.63731        .000
B1VB4       35574.0000 2063.75000  35574.0000   229.30556  155.13798        .000
B2VB3         532.04167 1141.75000    532.04167   126.86111    4.19389        .071
B14VB23     21420.3750 9892.50000  21420.3750  1099.16667   19.48783        .002
- - - - - - - - - - - - - - - - - - - - - - - - - - - - - - - - - - - - - - -
EFFECT .. CONSTANT
Univariate F-tests with (1,9) D. F.


Variable   Hypoth. SS   Error SS  Hypoth. MS    Error MS          F   Sig. of F

AMAIN      996480.333 15906.5000  996480.333  1767.38889  563.81498        .000
B1VB4       56718.7500 2063.75000  56718.7500   229.30556  247.35009        .000
B2VB3         352.08333 1141.75000    352.08333   126.86111    2.77534        .130
B14VB23     33708.0000 9892.50000  33708.0000  1099.16667   30.66687        .000
```

FIG. 8.13. Output from main effect contrasts on both factors in a one between-, one within-factor ANOVA using the TRANSFORM subcommand.

Note that all of the results concerning the second set of Factor A contrasts is first, followed by all of the output concerning the first set of Factor A contrasts. You will note that the effect labeled "AMAIN" is actually the test of the contrast on Factor A ($F = 118.61$ for the second contrast and 138.64 for the first contrast). The significance tests for the Factor B contrasts are found in the section titled "EFFECT .. CONSTANT".

INTERACTION CONTRASTS

As noted, all the syntax discussed in the previous section, designed to produce main effect contrasts, also automatically produced the results for interaction contrasts. When contrasts were specified only on the between-subjects factor, or only on the within-subjects factor, the contrasts of the $A_{Comp} \times B$ type were automatically produced. An example of a contrast only on the between-subjects factor is "FACTA(1) BY FACTB" (which would have been produced by the syntax in Fig. 8.4, but was edited out here), and an example of a contrast only on the within-subjects factor is "FACTA BY FACTB(3)" (which is found to have an F value of 10.52 in Fig. 8.7; note that this same F value is obtained in the "TRANSFORM" printout, Fig. 8.9, under "FACTA, B14VB23", but there the F value is more precise, 10.52229). When contrasts are specified on both factors, the interaction contrasts automatically produced are instead of the $A_{Comp} \times B_{Comp}$ type. An example is "FACTA(2) BY FACTB(1)" from Fig. 8.11, with an F value of 109.90. In Fig. 8.13, in the corresponding "TRANS-FORM" printout, the value is found using the mnemonic name for "FACTB(1)", "B1VB4", under "FACTA(2)". There the F value is more exact, 109.89758.

SIMPLE EFFECTS

As discussed in several places in this book, if the interaction is significant, as in the present example, it is generally appropriate to test the simple effects of one factor at one or more levels of the other factor. In previous designs, this has been handled with a specification of the form 'facta WITHIN factb(2)', either on the "DESIGN" subcommand (between-subjects designs) or on the "WSDESIGN" subcommand (within-subjects designs). The syntax and (especially) the output to test simple effects in mixed designs are a bit more complicated. First, testing the simple effects of the between-subjects factor, Factor A, at each of the levels of the within-subjects factor is discussed. The syntax is in Fig. 8.14.

```
1.   MANOVA b1 b2 b3 b4 BY facta(1,3)

2.     /WSFACTORS=factb(4)

3.     /WSDESIGN=MWITHIN factb(1), MWITHIN factb(2), MWITHIN

4.       factb(3), MWITHIN factb(4)

5o.  /DESIGN=facta.
```

FIG. 8.14. Syntax commands to test the simple effects of the between-subjects factor at all levels of the within-subects factor in a one between-, one within-factor ANOVA.

Note the new twist, which is the keyword "MWITHIN" instead of "WITHIN" on the "WSDESIGN" subcommand. Line 5 is actually optional, because 'facta' is the default "DESIGN" specification when it is the only between-subjects factor. The printout is in Fig. 8.15.

```
Tests involving 'MWITHIN FACTB(1)' Within-Subject Effect.

Tests of Significance for T1 using UNIQUE sums of squares
Source of Variation            SS        DF        MS         F  Sig of F

WITHIN+RESIDUAL             339.50        9      37.72
MWITHIN FACTB(1)        171841.33        1  171841.33  4555.44      .000
FACTA BY MWITHIN FACTB(1)  129.17        2      64.58     1.71      .234
- - - - - - - - - - - - - - - - - - - - - - - - - - - - - - - - - - - -

Tests involving 'MWITHIN FACTB(2)' Within-Subject Effect.

Tests of Significance for T2 using UNIQUE sums of squares
Source of Variation            SS        DF        MS         F  Sig of F

WITHIN+RESIDUAL            5043.50        9     560.39
MWITHIN FACTB(2)         45387.00        1   45387.00    80.99      .000
FACTA BY MWITHIN FACTB(2) 22963.50       2   11481.75    20.49      .000
- - - - - - - - - - - - - - - - - - - - - - - - - - - - - - - - - - - -

Tests involving 'MWITHIN FACTB(3)' Within-Subject Effect.

Tests of Significance for T3 using UNIQUE sums of squares
Source of Variation            SS        DF        MS         F  Sig of F

WITHIN+RESIDUAL            1648.75        9     183.19
MWITHIN FACTB(3)         37744.08        1   37744.08   206.03      .000
FACTA BY MWITHIN FACTB(3) 29990.17       2   14995.08    81.85      .000
- - - - - - - - - - - - - - - - - - - - - - - - - - - - - - - - - - - -

Tests involving 'MWITHIN FACTB(4)' Within-Subject Effect.

Tests of Significance for T4 using UNIQUE sums of squares
Source of Variation            SS        DF        MS         F  Sig of F

WITHIN+RESIDUAL            1020.75        9     113.42
MWITHIN FACTB(4)         31110.08        1   31110.08   274.30      .000
FACTA BY MWITHIN FACTB(4) 32930.17       2   16465.08   145.17      .000
```

FIG. 8.15. Output for the simple effects of Factor A at all levels of Factor B in a one between-, one within-factor ANOVA.

The tests of simple effects are oddly labeled by MANOVA in mixed designs. Instead of "FACTA WITHIN FACTB(3)", for example, it labels the test "FACTA BY MWITHIN FACTB(3)" (and, although cleaned up here, it "word wraps" the last six characters of the foregoing onto the next line). However, it properly tests the mean differences (in this instance, between the 28.5, the 13.5, and the 126.25). The result would be reported as $F(2, 9) = 81.85, p = .001$. Incidentally, the same result would be obtained by the syntax 'MANOVA b3 BY facta(1,3)'.

Previously, the simple effects of the between-subjects factor were tested. The syntax to instead test the simple effects of the within-subjects factor at each of the levels of the between-subjects factor is in Fig. 8.16.

```
1.      MANOVA b1 b2 b3 b4 BY facta (1,3)

2.        /WSFACTORS=factb (4)

3o.       /PRINT = SIGNIF (AVONLY)

4o.       /WSDESIGN=factb

5.        /DESIGN = MWITHIN facta(1), MWITHIN facta(2), MWITHIN facta(3).
```

FIG. 8.16.   Syntax commands to conduct the simple effects of the within-subjects factor at all levels of the between-subjects factor in a one between-, one within-factor ANOVA.

Note that, although the syntax is largely analogous to that in Fig. 8.14, line 3 is added to suppress the multivariate output. Note also that, if you did not specify that you wanted the simple effects of Factor B at all levels of Factor A, then you would have to add in "ERROR=WITHIN" to get the correct significance tests.

In fact, Keppel (1991) argued (in distinction to some other writers, e.g., Winer, Brown, & Michels, 1991) that, when testing simple effects and simple contrasts on a within-subjects factor, the proper error term is not the one SPSS uses at all, which he called the "pooled error term" (p. 383). He recommended using instead one specific to that test or contrast. The only way to get SPSS to use the error term suggested by Keppel is to select the subset of data used for the contrast or simple effect test and treat it like an overall analysis. For example, to obtain the simple effects of Factor B at the first level of Factor A, you would just select (with a "SELECT IF"[1] subcommand or the equivalent PAC sequence) the participants that were in the first condition of Factor A (and ignore the rest of the data) and run an overall one-way within-subjects ANOVA.[2] It should be noted that, in most cases, the pooled error term that SPSS uses will be similar to the specific error term.

In Fig. 8.16, the keyword "MWITHIN" is used on the "DESIGN" subcommand (line 6), whereas the "WSDESIGN" specifies the default design, 'factb' (and the "WSDESIGN" on line 4 is therefore not actually needed). Thus, if you want the simple effects of the between-subjects factor (i.e., Factor A, see Fig. 8.14), the "MWITHIN" statement goes on the "WSDESIGN" statement, whereas, if you want the simple effects of the within-subjects factor (see Fig. 8.16), the "MWITHIN" goes on the "DESIGN" statement. The relevant section of output produced by the syntax in Fig. 8.16 is in Fig. 8.17.

```
Tests involving 'FACTB' Within-Subject Effect.

AVERAGED Tests of Significance for B using UNIQUE sums of squares
Source of Variation           SS       DF        MS         F  Sig of F

WITHIN+RESIDUAL            4075.88      27     150.96
MWITHIN FACTA(1) BY       29403.69       3    9801.23     64.93     .000
FACTB
MWITHIN FACTA(2) BY       31250.75       3   10416.92     69.01     .000
FACTB
```

FIG. 8.17.   Output for the simple effects of the within-subjects factor at each of the levels of the between-subjects factor in a one between-, one within-subjects factor ANOVA.

The output seen in Fig. 8.17 is even more oddly labeled. Instead of "FACTB WITHIN FACTA(2)", for example, it is labeled as "MWITHIN FACTA(2) BY FACTB".

---

[1]Alternatively, if simple effects are desired at each level of the between-subjects factor (rather than at only one or two of them) you may use the split file syntax described in chapter 2, namely 'SORT CASES BY facta.' 'SPLIT FILE SEPARATE BY facta'.

[2]With the syntax 'MANOVA b1 b2 b3 b4 /WSFACTOR=factb (4)'.

SIMPLE COMPARISONS

Simple comparisons are a quite easy extension building on your knowledge of contrasts and the use of the "MWITHIN" keyword. To illustrate a simple comparison on the between-subjects factor, assume you are interested in whether there is a difference between a2 and a3 at the fourth level of Factor B (see Fig. 8.18).

```
1.   MANOVA b1 b2 b3 b4 BY facta(1,3)

2.   /WSFACTORS=factb(4)

3o.  /PRINT=SIGNIF(AVONLY)

4.   /CONTRAST(facta)=SPECIAL(1 1 1, 2 -1 -1, 0 1 -1)

5.   /WSDESIGN=MWITHIN factb(4)

6.   /DESIGN=facta(1) facta(2).
```

FIG. 8.18.   Syntax commands to conduct a simple comparison on Factor A at the fourth level of Factor B in a one between-, one within-factor ANOVA.

The "CONTRAST" subcommand (line 4) is set up exactly as in any between-subjects contrast. On the "WSDESIGN" subcommand (line 6), tell SPSS at which level of the within-subjects factor to conduct the contrast, using the "MWITHIN" keyword, in this case, the fourth level of Factor B. The between-subjects contrast of interest is specified on the "DESIGN" subcommand, line 6. Here the interest is in the first contrast on Factor A. Here, because your contrasts are orthogonal, you could have used the "ERROR=WITHIN" subcommand and simply specified 'facta(1)' on the "DESIGN" subcommand. If your contrasts are nonorthogonal, you must specify all of them on the "DESIGN" subcommand or your significance tests will be incorrect. The output is in Fig. 8.19.

```
Tests involving 'MWITHIN FACTB(4)' Within-Subject Effect.

AVERAGED Tests of Significance for B using UNIQUE sums of squares
Source of Variation              SS        DF        MS          F    Sig of F

WITHIN+RESIDUAL              1020.75        9      113.42
MWITHIN FACTB(4)           31110.08        1    31110.08     274.30       .000
FACTA(1) BY MWITHIN FACTB(4) 8288.17       1     8288.17      73.08       .000
FACTA(2) BY MWITHIN FACTB(4) 24642.00      1    24642.00     217.27       .000
```

FIG. 8.19.   Output for the simple comparison on Factor A at the fourth level of Factor B in a one between-, one within-factor ANOVA.

The test of interest is the "FACTA (1) BY MWITHIN FACTB (4)" and it is significant, $F(1, 9) = 217.27$, thus there is a difference between how much the group therapy group and the control group reported smoking at the last time point, that is, a difference between the means of 14.00 and 125.0.

To illustrate a simple comparison on the within-subjects factor (with a pooled error term), assume you are interested in whether there is a difference between the first and last time at the third level of Factor A (i.e., between the 116.75 and the 125.50). The syntax to conduct this analysis using the "CONTRAST" method is illustrated in Fig. 8.20.

```
1.   MANOVA b1 b2 b3 b4 BY facta (1,3)

2.   /WSFACTORS=factb(4)

3o.  /PRINT=SIGNIF(AVONLY)

4.   /CONTRAST(factb)=SPECIAL(1 1 1 1, -1 0 0 1, -1 2 0 -1, -1 0 2 -1)

5.   /ERROR=WITHIN

6.   /WSDESIGN=factb(1)

7.   /DESIGN=MWITHIN facta(3).
```

FIG. 8.20.   Syntax commands to conduct a simple comparison on Factor B at the third level of Factor A using the CONTRAST method in a one between-, one within-factor ANOVA.

Similar to the commands in Fig. 8.18, the simple comparison is set up in the same way as on the between-subjects factor, but now the contrast is on the within-subjects factor and you follow the setup for that type of contrast (see line 4). The "DESIGN" statement (line 7) reflects the fact that you want the contrast to be evaluated at the third level of Factor A. The "ERROR=WITHIN" subcommand must be included because not all degrees of freedom were specified on the "DESIGN" subcommand. Because this is a mixed design, the keyword "MWITHIN" is used. On the "WSDESIGN" subcommand (line 6), specify which contrast you wish to test. In this case, you are looking at the first contrast. For contrasts on within-subjects factors, only the specific contrast desired needs to be specified. The relevant output is in Fig. 8.21.

```
Tests involving 'FACTB(1)' Within-Subject Effect.

AVERAGED Tests of Significance for B using UNIQUE sums of squares
Source of Variation                    SS       DF       MS        F   Sig of F

WITHIN CELLS                        1031.87      9     114.65
MWITHIN FACTA(3) BY FACTB(1)         136.12      1     136.12     1.19     .304
```

FIG. 8.21. Output for the simple comparison on Factor B at the third level of Factor A using the CONTRAST method in a one between-, one within-subjects factor ANOVA.

Once again, note the odd label: Instead of "FACTA(3) WITHIN FACTB(1)", the test is labeled "MWITHIN FACTA(3) BY FACTB(1)". The output shows that for the control group there is not a significant difference between the amount they smoked at the first time point and the amount they smoked at the last, $F(1, 9) = 1.19$, $p = .304$.[3]

Keep in mind that, in order to use the "CONTRAST" method with a within-subjects factor, the contrasts must be orthogonal. If the contrasts of interest are nonorthogonal, use the "TRANSFORM" method instead, as in Fig. 8.22.

```
1.    MANOVA b1 b2 b3 b4 BY facta (1,3)

2o.   /NOPRINT=SIGNIF (MULTIV)

3.    /TRANSFORM(b1 to b4)=SPECIAL(1 1 1 1, -1 0 0 1, 0 1 -1 0, -1 -1 -1 3)

4d.   /RENAME=ones b1vb4 b2vb3 b123vb4

5.    /ERROR=WITHIN

6.    /DESIGN=MWITHIN facta(3).
```

FIG. 8.22.   Syntax commands to conduct a simple comparison on Factor B at the third level of Factor A using the TRANSFORM method in a one between-, one within-factor ANOVA.

Relevant results are reprinted in Fig. 8.23. Note that the relevant test ("B1VB4") has the same result, $F(1, 9) = 1.19$, as in Fig. 8.21.

```
EFFECT .. MWITHIN FACTA(3)
Univariate F-tests with (1,9) D. F.

Variable    Hypoth. SS   Error SS Hypoth. MS    Error MS            F  Sig. of F

ONES        961380.250 15906.5000 961380.250 1767.38889   543.95513      .000
B1VB4          272.25000 2063.75000  272.25000  229.30556     1.18728      .304
B2VB3           64.00000 1141.75000   64.00000  126.86111      .50449      .496
B123VB4        380.25000 6488.50000  380.25000  720.94444      .52743      .486
```

FIG. 8.23. Output for the simple comparison on Factor B at the third level of Factor A using the TRANSFORM method in a one between-, one within-subjects factor ANOVA.

---

[3]If the separate error term method is preferred, select only participants in Group 3 using "SELECT IF" or equivalent other command, then conduct a one-way within-subjects analysis, with a contrast specified, for example:

```
MANOVA b1 b2 b3 b4
   /WSFACTORS=factb(4)
   /PRINT=SIGNIF(AVONLY)
   /CONTRAST(factb)=SPECIAL(1 1 1 1, -1 0 0 1, 0 1 -1 0, 1 -1 -1 1)
   /WSDESIGN=factb(1).
```

POST HOCS AND TREND ANALYSIS

You can also run main effect contrasts and simple comparisons using any of the canned routines available in "MANOVA", such as "POLYNOMIAL", that will invoke trend analysis. To conduct post hoc analyses, either on marginal means (i.e., main effect contrasts) or cell means within a given row or column (i.e., simple comparisons), use the canned routine "SIMPLE" repeatedly and then correct the output manually for significance, as described in previous chapters, especially chapter 3. Remember that, to use a canned routine in conjunction with "CONTRAST" on the within-subjects factor, the contrasts must be orthogonal.

PAC

A mixed design ANOVA is run from the General Linear Model–Repeated Measures menu. You will see the same screen pop up that you saw in a regular within-subjects design (see Fig. 8.24).

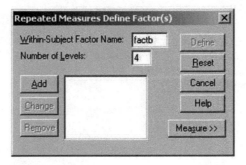

FIG. 8.24.   Dialogue box to name the within-subjects factor in a mixed ANOVA.

After naming your within-subjects factor and number of levels, click Add then click Define. At the next screen you would define your within-subjects variables as before, but would now also choose between-subjects factors, as in Fig. 8.25.

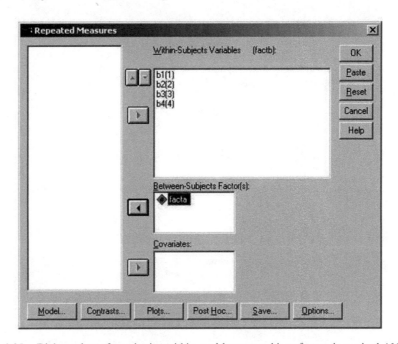

FIG. 8.25.   Dialogue box after selecting within- and between-subjects factors in a mixed ANOVA.

Simply highlight the between-subjects variable(s) and click the darkened right arrow to send them to the Between-Subjects Factor(s) box. All options and caveats that applied to the previous designs apply here. More complex analyses such as main effect contrasts, interaction contrasts, simple effects, simple comparisons, and post hocs are available with syntax (see chap. 13; see also chap. 6 for post hocs on the within-subjects factor).

9 Three- (or Greater) Factor Mixed Designs

In chapter 8 you learned how to analyze a two-factor mixed design that had one between-subjects and one within-subjects factor. In this chapter, this analysis is extended to mixed designs that have three or more factors. These designs are often called *higher order mixed designs*. In this chapter, only abbreviated output is presented, because most of the printout will be very similar to that seen in previous chapters.

Higher order mixed designs are specified by the number of between- and within-subjects factors they have, for example, four between, two within. Generally, higher order mixed designs would follow the conventions of adding extra between-subjects or within-subjects factors, as was discussed previously (in chaps. 4 and 7, respectively). Two categories of three-factor mixed designs are covered in this chapter: a one between-, two within-subjects design and a two between-, one within-subjects design. The syntax to run the general analyses for these designs is in Figs. 9.1 and 9.2, respectively.

```
1.    MANOVA b1c1 b1c2 b1c3 b2c1 b2c2 b2c3 b3c1 b3c2 b3c3 BY facta (1,3)

2.        /WSFACTORS=factb(3) factc(3)

3o.       /PRINT=SIGNIF(AVONLY)

4d.       /OMEANS.
```

FIG. 9.1.   Syntax commands to conduct a three-factor mixed ANOVA with two within- and one between-subjects factors.

```
1.    MANOVA c1 c2 c3 c4 BY facta(1,3) factb(1,3)

2.        /WSFACTORS=factc(4)

3o.       /PRINT=SIGNIF(AVONLY)

4d.       /OMEANS=TABLES(facta, factb, facta*factb).
```

FIG. 9.2.   Syntax commands to conduct a three-factor mixed ANOVA with one within- and two between-subjects factors.

These designs are simply a combination of the two-factor and mixed designs seen previously. The "OMEANS" subcommands must be written the way they are because "MANOVA" will print out values that average over between-subjects factors, but not within-subjects factors. The output for these designs is identical to the two-factor mixed design, except there would either be an added between-subjects factor effect (with all its interactions) or a within-subjects factor effect (with all its interactions). You should also request power and effect size analyses for all of the designs in this chapter the same way they had been requested before. Namely, you would use the "POWER" and "PRINT=SIGNIF(EFSIZE)" subcommands.

SIMPLE TWO-WAY INTERACTIONS

In addition to analyzing main effects and interactions, more complex simple effects and contrasts can be examined with these designs, just as with the other three-way designs discussed in chapters 5 and 7. When working with a three-way design, one of the first types of more specialized analyses encountered is that of simple two-way interactions. For example, in a three-factor mixed design with two within-subjects factors, there could be interest in the interaction between the between-subjects factor (Factor A) and one of the within-subjects factors (e.g., Factor C) at a specific level of the other within-subjects factor (Factor B). Figure 9.3 offers an example of a program that would yield this simple two-way interaction.

```
1.    MANOVA b1c1 b1c2 b1c3 b2c1 b2c2 b2c3 b3c1 b3c2 b3c3 BY facta(1,3)

2.    /WSFACTORS=factb(3) factc(3)

3o.   /PRINT=SIGNIF (AVONLY)

4d.   /OMEANS

5.    /WSDESIGN=factc WITHIN factb(1), factc WITHIN factb(2), factc

6.       WITHIN  factb(3)

7o.   /DESIGN=facta.
```

FIG. 9.3.   Syntax commands to conduct a simple interaction of Factor A and Factor C at each level of the other within-subjects factor (Factor B) in a three-factor mixed ANOVA.

The "WSDESIGN" and "DESIGN" subcommands (in lines 5–7) work in concert to produce the desired tests. The "WSDESIGN" in line 5 tells "MANOVA" to examine Factor C effects within the different levels of Factor B. The "DESIGN" subcommand in line 7 specifies which between-subjects factor you are interested in (because Factor A is the only between-subjects factor here, it is the default and line 7 can be omitted). These two subcommands will produce the Factor A × Factor C two-ways within levels of Factor B. The tests will be labeled, for example, "FACTA BY FACTC WITHIN FACTB(1)".

To provide a more general rule, it is necessary to note that, in the preceding example, the two interacting factors (Factor A and Factor C) were of opposite between-versus-within types (i.e., Factor A was a between factor, whereas Factor C was a within factor). Syntax analogous to that of Fig. 9.3 is appropriate for such an instance. When instead the two factors in the interaction are of the same between-versus-within type (e.g., in the current design, the interaction of Factor B and Factor C, both within factors, within levels of Factor A), the specification would be:

```
o   /WSDESIGN=factb, factc, factb BY factc
    /DESIGN=MWITHIN facta(1), MWITHIN facta(2), MWITHIN facta(3).
```

The "WSDESIGN" subcommand is actually optional here. Remember that, if you do not specify all of the degrees of freedom on the "DESIGN" subcommand, for example, 'DESIGN=

MWITHIN facta(1)', you need to include "ERROR=WITHIN". You can also suppress the multivariate output as before. In such an instance, because you are using "MWITHIN", the output will be oddly labeled, for example, such things as "MWITHIN FACTA(2) BY FACTB BY FACTC" instead of "FACTB BY FACTC WITHIN FACTA(2)" (for the simple two-ways); "MWITHIN FACTA(2) BY FACTC", instead of "FACTC WITHIN FACTA(2)" for simple effects. Table 9.1 gives syntax specifications for "DESIGN" and "WSDESIGN" subcommands and output labels for all the possibilities for mixed three-way designs.

TABLE 9.1
Syntax Specification for DESIGN and WSDESIGN Subcommands and Output Labels
for All Possible Mixed Three-Way Designs for Simple Two-Way Interactions

| Type of Design | Desired Simple Two-Way | Specification for | | Output Labeled |
		DESIGN	WSDESIGN	
A between, B and C within	A × B within C	a[a]	b WITHIN c(1), etc.	A BY B WITHIN C(1), etc.
	A × C within B	a[a]	c WITHIN b(1), etc.	A BY C WITHIN B(1), etc.
	B × C within A	MWITHIN a(1), etc.	b, c, b BY c[a]	MWITHIN A(1) BY B BY C, etc.
A and B between, C within	A × B within C	a, b, a BY b[a]	MWITHIN c(1), etc.	A BY B BY MWITHIN C(1), etc.
	A × C within B	a WITHIN b(1), etc.	c[a]	A WITHIN B(1) BY C, etc.
	B × C within A	b WITHIN a(1), etc.	c[a]	B WITHIN A(1) BY C, etc.

[a]Default specification for that subcommand, therefore subcommand can be safely omitted.

SIMPLE SIMPLE EFFECTS

As explained in chapter 5, simple simple effects examine the effect of one factor, restricting attention to specific levels of both of the other factors. To obtain simple simple effects, again, use a combination of "WSDESIGN" and "DESIGN" subcommands, involving "MWITHIN". When it is desired to examine within both factors of the same between-versus-within type, the required specification is of the form 'MWITHIN factb(1) WITHIN factc(2)'. Table 9.2 provides all the possibilities for the three-way mixed design.

TABLE 9.2
Syntax Specification for DESIGN and WSDESIGN Subcommands and Output Labels
for All Possible Mixed Three-Way Designs for Simple Simple Effects

| Type of Design | Desired Simple Simple | Specification for | | Output Labeled |
		DESIGN	WSDESIGN	
A between, B and C within	A within B and C	a[a]	MWITHIN b(1) WITHIN c(1), MWITHIN b(1) WITHIN c(2), etc.	A BY MWITHIN B(1) WITHIN C(1), etc.
	B within A and C	MWITHIN a(1), etc.	b WITHIN c(1), etc.	MWITHIN A(1) BY B WITHIN C(1), etc.
	C within A and B	MWITHIN a(1), etc.	c WITHIN b(1), etc.	MWITHIN A(1) BY C WITHIN B(1), etc.
A and B between, C within	A within B and C	a WITHIN b(1), etc.	MWITHIN c(1), etc.	A WITHIN B(1) BY MWITHIN C(1), etc.
	B within A and C	b WITHIN a(1), etc.	MWITHIN c(1), etc.	B WITHIN A(1) BY MWITHIN C(1), etc.
	C within A and B	MWITHIN a(1) WITHIN b(1), MWITHIN a(1) WITHIN b(2), etc.	c[a]	MWITHIN A(1) WITHIN B(1) BY C

[a]Default specification for that subcommand, therefore subcommand can be safely omitted.

Note that it may be important to specify "ERROR=WITHIN" (if you are unsure, include it, it cannot hurt you) and "PRINT=SIGNIF(AVONLY)" in some of the previous designs. Also note that the analysis invoked by such syntax uses the pooled error term method.

MAIN EFFECT CONTRASTS AND INTERACTION CONTRASTS

Main effect contrasts are produced in the same manner as described in previous chapters. For between-subjects factors, the rules are as follows:

1. Specify the contrasts with the "CONTRAST" subcommand.
2. Run the contrasts with "DESIGN" subcommands.
3. Unless the contrasts are orthogonal, be sure to specify all of them on the "DESIGN" subcommand. For example, if Factor A has five levels, there are four contrasts. The "DESIGN" specification would be 'a(1), a(2), a(3), a(4)' even if you do not wish to examine all of them; for orthogonal contrasts you can use "ERROR=WITHIN".
4. If contrasts are desired simultaneously on more than one between-subjects factor, employ a "CONTRAST" subcommand for each factor and include all the contrasts on the "DESIGN" subcommand. For example, if both Factor A with three levels and Factor B with four levels are between-subjects factors, the specification for the DESIGN statement would contain at least 'a(1) a(2) b(1) b(2) b(3)', if not also their interactions.

For within-subjects factors, how to request main effect contrasts depends on whether the contrasts are orthogonal or not. For nonorthogonal contrasts, use the "TRANSFORM" method, but for orthogonal contrasts use either the "TRANSFORM" or the "CONTRAST" method. These were described in detail in previous chapters.

Specifying main effect contrasts will automatically also produce some of the interaction contrasts. For example, if Factor A is the only between-subjects factor and contrasts are requested only on Factor A, the following interaction contrasts are also produced: $A_{Comp} \times B$, $A_{Comp} \times C$, $A_{Comp} \times B \times C$ (in other words, with all the factors of the opposite between-versus-within type, plus with the interactions of the factors of the opposite between-versus-within type). To obtain any additional desired interaction contrasts, they need to be explicitly specified. For example, if both Factor A and Factor B are between-subjects factors and contrasts are requested on both using "CONTRAST" statements, their interaction contrast must be requested on the "DESIGN" subcommand with a specification of the form 'facta(3) BY factb(2)'. In this instance, the interaction contrast $A_{Comp3} \times B_{Comp2} \times C$ (i.e., that interaction contrast in interaction with the factor[s] of the opposite between-versus-within type) will also be automatically produced. For two or more within-subjects factors using nonorthogonal contrasts, the rather complex "TRANSFORM" methods of chapter 7 must be used instead of the "CONTRAST" method. In order to obtain triple interaction contrasts, that is, those of the form $A_{Comp} \times B_{Comp} \times C_{Comp}$, the relevant contrast must be requested on each factor. For example, in the Factor A and Factor B between, Factor C within design, the interaction contrast between Factor A and Factor B must be requested on the "DESIGN" statement and the contrast on Factor C specified on the "WSDESIGN" statement (assuming the Factor C contrasts were orthogonal). Then the $A_{Comp} \times B_{Comp} \times C_{Comp}$ interaction will be produced automatically, without specifically requesting it.

For nonorthogonal contrasts on the within-subjects factors, use the "TRANSFORM" method. Syntax is shown in Fig. 9.4 for the example of a Factor A × Factor B × Factor C design with three levels of each factor, and Factor A between and Factor B and Factor C within.

```
1.    MANOVA b1c1 b1c2 b1c3 b2c1 b2c2 b2c3 b3c1 b3c2 b3c3 BY facta(1,3)

2.      /TRANSFORM(b1c1 TO b3c3)=SPECIAL

3.      (1 1 1   1 1 1     1  1  1,

4.        1 1 1   0  0  0    -1 -1 -1

5.        1 1 1   -1 -1 -1    0  0  0

6.        0 1 -1   0  1 -1     0  1 -1

7.        1 0 -1   1  0 -1     1  0 -1

8.        0 1 -1   0  0  0     0 -1  1

9.        1 0 -1   0  0  0    -1  0  1

10.       0 1 -1   0 -1  1     0  0  0

11.       1 0 -1  -1  0  1     0  0  0)

12d.    /RENAME=foraonly b1vb3@b1 b1vb2@b2 c2vc3@c1 c1vc3@c2

13.        ib1xc1 ib1xc2 ib2xc1 ib2xc2

14o.    /NOPRINT=SIGNIF(MULTIV)

15.     /CONTRAST(facta)=SIMPLE(2)

16.     /DESIGN=CONSTANT, facta(1), facta(2).
```

FIG. 9.4. Syntax commands to conduct main effect and interaction contrasts in a one between-, two within-factor ANOVA.

Lines 2 through 11 define the nonorthogonal contrasts on Factor B and Factor C, as well as the four Factor B × Factor C interaction contrasts; then they all are given mnemonic names on the "RE-NAME" subcommand (lines 12–13). The initial row of ones is "RENAME"d 'foraonly', which is more mnemonic than 'ones' (as it was called in chap. 7), as shown later. Then lines 15 and 16 request testing the nonorthogonal "SIMPLE" contrasts on Factor A, as well as "CONSTANT". Note also the usual use of line 14 to suppress the multivariate output. Also note that you must specify all of the contrasts on Factor A on the "DESIGN" subcommand because "SIMPLE" contrasts are nonorthogonal. The relevant portions of the resulting printout are in Fig. 9.5.

```
EFFECT .. A(2) (Cont.)
Univariate F-tests with (1,93) D. F.

Variable    Hypoth. SS   Error SS Hypoth. MS   Error MS        F  Sig. of F

FORAONLY       .06250 2651.34375     .06250   28.50907    .00219      .963
B1VB3@B1       .39062 1558.96875     .39062   16.76310    .02330      .879
B1VB2@B2      9.00000 1427.62500    9.00000   15.35081    .58629      .446
C2VC3@C1     72.25000 1642.62500   72.25000   17.66263   4.09056      .046
C1VC3@C2    150.06250 1504.65625  150.06250   16.17910   9.27508      .003
IB1XC1         .01562  963.56250     .01562   10.36089    .00151      .969
IB1XC2        1.26562  620.71875    1.26562    6.67440    .18962      .664
IB2XC1       26.26563 1252.59375   26.26563   13.46875   1.95012      .166
IB2XC2         .01563 1123.59375     .01563   12.08165    .00129      .971
- - - - - - - - - - - - - - - - - - - - - - - - - - - - - - - - - - -
EFFECT .. A(1) (Cont.)
Univariate F-tests with (1,93) D. F.

Variable    Hypoth. SS   Error SS Hypoth. MS   Error MS        F  Sig. of F

FORAONLY       .01563 2651.34375     .01563   28.50907    .00055      .981
B1VB3@B1     16.00000 1558.96875   16.00000   16.76310    .95448      .331
B1VB2@B2       .00000 1427.62500     .00000   15.35081    .00000     1.000
C2VC3@C1    121.00000 1642.62500  121.00000   17.66263   6.85062      .010
C1VC3@C2      7.56250 1504.65625    7.56250   16.17910    .46742      .496
IB1XC1        3.06250  963.56250    3.06250   10.36089    .29558      .588
IB1XC2        9.00000  620.71875    9.00000    6.67440   1.34844      .249
IB2XC1       10.56250 1252.59375   10.56250   13.46875    .78422      .378
IB2XC2         .76563 1123.59375     .76563   12.08165    .06337      .802
- - - - - - - - - - - - - - - - - - - - - - - - - - - - - - - - - - -
```

FIG. 9.5. *(Continues)*

```
EFFECT .. CONSTANT (Cont.)
Univariate F-tests with (1,93) D. F.

Variable   Hypoth. SS   Error SS  Hypoth. MS    Error MS          F  Sig. of F

FORAONLY   114747.510 2651.34375 114747.510    28.50907 4024.94715      .000
B1VB3@B1     147.51042 1558.96875  147.51042    16.76310    8.79971      .004
B1VB2@B2        .37500 1427.62500     .37500    15.35081     .02443      .876
C2VC3@C1     145.04167 1642.62500  145.04167    17.66263    8.21178      .005
C1VC3@C2      75.26042 1504.65625   75.26042    16.17910    4.65171      .034
IB1XC1       442.04167  963.56250  442.04167    10.36089   42.66446      .000
IB1XC2        90.09375  620.71875   90.09375     6.67440   13.49841      .000
IB2XC1        17.51042 1252.59375   17.51042    13.46875    1.30008      .257
IB2XC2        52.51042 1123.59375   52.51042    12.08165    4.34629      .040
```

FIG. 9.5. Output for main effect and interaction contrasts in a one between-, two within-factor ANOVA.

Rearranging this output gives the *F* values found in Table 9.3 for all the contrasts.

TABLE 9.3
Rearranged *F* Tests for Main Effects and Interaction Contrasts
in a One Between-, Two Within-Factor ANOVA

Contrast	F Value
A(1)	.00055
A(2)	.00219
B(1)	8.79971
B(2)	.02443
C(1)	8.21178
C(2)	4.65171
A(1) × B(1)	.95448
A(1) × B(2)	.00000
A(2) × B(1)	.02330
A(2) × B(2)	.58629
A(1) × C(1)	6.85062
A(1) × C(2)	.46742
A(2) × C(1)	4.09056
A(2) × C(2)	9.27508
B(1) × C(1)	42.66446
B(1) × C(2)	13.49841
B(2) × C(1)	1.30008
B(2) × C(2)	4.34629
A(1) × B(1) × C(1)	.29558
A(1) × B(1) × C(2)	1.34844
A(1) × B(2) × C(1)	.78422
A(1) × B(2) × C(2)	.06337
A(2) × B(1) × C(1)	.00151
A(2) × B(1) × C(2)	.18962
A(2) × B(2) × C(1)	1.95012
A(2) × B(2) × C(2)	.00129

SIMPLE CONTRASTS: SIMPLE COMPARISONS, SIMPLE SIMPLE COMPARISONS, AND SIMPLE INTERACTION CONTRASTS

The analyses of the three types of simple contrasts (i.e., simple comparisons, simple simple comparisons, and simple interaction contrasts) are discussed next. Recall that simple comparisons examine a contrast on one of the factors within levels of one of the other factors; simple simple comparisons examine a contrast on one of the factors within certain levels of both of the other factors; and simple interaction contrasts are interaction contrasts between two of the factors within certain levels of the third factor. (The reader who desires a more extensive review of these analyses, together with the relevant means being compared, is directed to chap. 5.) In general, simple contrasts are accomplished by specifying "WITHIN" or "MWITHIN" on the factor(s) within levels of which the simple contrast is desired, while specifying a contrast (either with "CONTRAST" or with "TRANSFORM") on the factor(s) desired.

For example, consider the Factor A between, Factor B and Factor C within design. If a simple comparison on Factor A within levels of Factor B is desired, specify the contrast on Factor A (with the "CONTRAST" subcommand and the "DESIGN" subcommand specifying all the Factor A contrasts) and specify the desired levels of Factor B within which the simple comparison is desired via the "WSDESIGN" statement, using "MWITHIN", as in the first row of Table 9.4. If instead the reverse simple comparison (i.e., a simple comparison on Factor B within levels of Factor A) is desired (and assuming the contrasts on Factor B are all orthogonal, qualifying the analysis for the "CONTRAST" method), reverse the specifications on the "DESIGN" and "WSDESIGN" subcommands, as in row 2 of Table 9.4. Note that, if you leave off a level of the between-subjects factor on the "DESIGN" subcommand, you must use "ERROR=WITHIN". The remaining rows of Table 9.4 give specifications for every category of simple contrasts (when the within-subjects contrasts are orthogonal) and display the often odd labels that MANOVA assigns to the results.

TABLE 9.4
Syntax Specification for DESIGN and WSDESIGN Subcommands and Output Labels
for All Possible Mixed Three-Way Designs for Simple Comparisons, Simple Simple Comparisons,
and Simple Interaction Contrasts When the Within-Subjects Contrasts are Orthogonal

	A between, B and C within		
	Specification for		
Contrast	DESIGN	WSDESIGN	Output Labeled
A_{Comp} within B[a]	a(1), a(2), etc.	MWITHIN b(1), MWITHIN b(2), etc.	A(1) BY MWITHIN B(1), etc.
B_{Comp} within A[a]	MWITHIN a(1), MWITHIN a(2), etc.	b(1), b(2), etc.	MWITHIN A(1) BY B(1), etc.
C_{Comp} within B[a]	a[b]	c(1) WITHIN b(1), c(2) WITHIN b(1), etc.	C(1) WITHIN B(1), etc.
A_{Comp} within B and C[c]	a(1), a(2), etc.	MWITHIN b(1) WITHIN c(1), MWITHIN b(2) WITHIN c(1), etc.	A(1) BY MWITHIN B(1) WITHIN C(1), etc.
C_{Comp} within A and B[c]	MWITHIN a(1), MWITHIN a(2), etc.	c(1) WITHIN b(1), etc.	MWITHIN A(1) BY C(1) WITHIN B(1), etc.
$A_{Comp} \times C_{Comp}$ within B[d]	a(1), a(2), etc.	c(1) WITHIN b(1), etc.	A(1) BY C(1) WITHIN B(1), etc.
$B_{Comp} \times C_{Comp}$ within A[d]	MWITHIN a(1), MWITHIN a(2), etc.	b(1) BY c(1), etc.	MWITHIN A(1) BY B(1) BY C(1), etc.
	A and B between, C within		
A_{Comp} within B[a]	a(1) WITHIN b(1), etc.	c[b]	A(1) WITHIN B(1), etc.
A_{Comp} within C[a]	a(1), a(2), etc.	MWITHIN c(1), etc.	A(1) BY MWITHIN C(1), etc.
C_{Comp} within A[a]	MWITHIN a(1), MWITHIN a(2), etc.	c(1), c(2), etc.	MWITHIN A(1) BY C(1), etc.
A_{Comp} within B and C[c]	a(1) WITHIN b(1), etc.	MWITHIN c(1), etc.	A(1) WITHIN B(1) BY MWITHIN C(1), etc.
C_{Comp} within A and B[c]	MWITHIN a(1) WITHIN b(1)	c(1), c(2), etc.	MWITHIN A(1) WITHIN B(1) BY C(1), etc.
$A_{Comp} \times B_{Comp}$ within C[d]	a(1) BY b(1), etc.	MWITHIN c(1), etc.	A(1) BY B(1) BY MWITHIN C(1), etc.
$A_{Comp} \times C_{Comp}$ within B[d]	a(1) WITHIN b(1), etc.	c(1), c(2), etc.	A(1) WITHIN B(1) BY C(1), etc.

[a]Simple Comparison. [b]Default specification for that subcommand, therefore subcommand can be safely omitted. [c]Simple simple comparison. [d]Simple interaction contrast.

When the simple contrasts desired are nonorthogonal contrasts on the within-subjects factor, the "TRANSFORM" method must be used instead. The "DESIGN" specification will contain

"WITHIN", "MWITHIN", or "BY" keywords as needed; if all degrees of freedom are not specified, use "ERROR=WITHIN". Table 9.5 presents the "DESIGN" specifications and output labels for all the categories of simple contrasts.

TABLE 9.5
Syntax Specification for the DESIGN Subcommand and Output Labels for All Possible
Mixed Three-Way Designs for Simple Comparisons, Simple Simple Comparisons,
and Simple Interaction Contrasts When the Within-Subjects Contrasts are Nonorthogonal

Type of Design	Simple Contrast	DESIGN	Variable
A between, B and C within	B_{Comp} within A[a]	MWITHIN a(1), MWITHIN a(2), etc.	B1VB3@B1, B1VB2@B2, etc.
	C_{Comp} within B[a]	CONSTANT	C1VC2WB1, C3VC2WB1, etc.
	C_{Comp} within A and B[b]	MWITHIN a(1), MWITHIN a(2), etc.	C1VC2WB1, C3VC2WB1, etc.
	$A_{Comp} \times C_{Comp}$ within B[c]	a(1), a(2), etc.	C1VC2WB1, C3VC2WB1, etc.
	$B_{Comp} \times C_{Comp}$ within A[c]	MWITHIN a(1), MWITHIN a(2), etc.	IB1XC1, IB1XC2, etc.
A and B between, C within	C_{Comp} within A[a]	MWITHIN a(1), MWITHIN a(2), etc.	C1VC3, C2VC3
	C_{Comp} within A and B[b]	MWITHIN a(1) WITHIN b(1), MWITHIN a(2) WITHIN b(1), etc.	C1VC3, C2VC3
	$A_{Comp} \times C_{Comp}$ within B[c]	a(1) WITHIN b(1), etc.	C1VC3, C2VC3

[a]Simple comparison. [b]Simple simple comparison. [c]Simple interaction contrast.

In considering Table 9.5, for the one between, two within design, the first and fifth rows are based on the set of TRANSFORMs found in Fig. 9.4. For the darkened entry in row 1 of the one between, two within design denoted "B1VB3@B1", the "DESIGN" specification would be 'MWITHIN facta(1), MWITHIN facta(2)', and so on. A portion of the printout is in Fig. 9.6. The darkened result is where the F and p values for B_{Comp1} within A(1) are found, corresponding to the darkened area in row 1 of Table 9.5.

```
EFFECT .. MWITHIN A(1)  (Cont.)
Univariate F-tests with (1,93) D. F.

Variable    Hypoth. SS    Error SS  Hypoth. MS    Error MS          F  Sig. of F

FORAONLY   38157.0313  2651.34375  38157.0313    28.50907  1338.41714      .000
B1VB3@B1      12.50000  1558.96875    12.50000    16.76310      .74569      .390
B1VB2@B2       1.12500  1427.62500     1.12500    15.35081      .07329      .787
C2VC3@C1      55.12500  1642.62500    55.12500    17.66263     3.12100      .081
C1VC3@C2      11.28125  1504.65625    11.28125    16.17910      .69727      .406
IB1XC1       108.78125   963.56250   108.78125    10.36089    10.49922      .002
IB1XC2         4.50000   620.71875     4.50000     6.67440      .67422      .414
IB2XC1         3.12500  1252.59375     3.12500    13.46875      .23202      .631
IB2XC2        24.50000  1123.59375    24.50000    12.08165     2.02787      .158
```

FIG. 9.6.   Output for 'b1vb3@b1' at the first level of Factor A.

For rows 2 through 4 of Table 9.5, it is assumed the "TRANSFORM" is the following:

```
/TRANSFORM(b1c1 TO b1c3/b2c1 TO b2c3/b3c1 TO
   b3c3)=SIMPLE(2)
/RENAME=onesb1 c1vc2wb1 c3vc2wb1 onesb2 c1vc2wb2 c3vc2wb2
   onesb3 c1vc2wb3 c3vc2wb3
```

For the darkened entry in row 2 of the one between, two within design denoted "C1VC2WB1", the "DESIGN" specification would be "CONSTANT". A portion of the printout is seen in Fig. 9.7. The darkened result is where the F and p values for C_{Comp1} within B(1) are found, corresponding to the darkened area in row 2 of Table 9.5.

```
EFFECT .. CONSTANT (Cont.)
Univariate F-tests with (1,93) D. F.

Variable   Hypoth. SS   Error SS Hypoth. MS   Error MS         F  Sig. of F

ONESB1     4488.78125  609.18750 4488.78125    6.55040  685.26793      .000
C1VC2WB1      3.78125  612.68750    3.78125    6.58804     .57396      .451
C3VC2WB1      7.03125  605.40625    7.03125    6.50974    1.08011      .301
ONESB2     4925.28125  925.31250 4925.28125    9.94960  495.02320      .000
C1VC2WB2      1.12500  516.75000    1.12500    5.55645     .20247      .654
C3VC2WB2      3.12500  653.06250    3.12500    7.02218     .44502      .506
ONESB3     3444.50000  961.71875 3444.50000   10.34106  333.08959      .000
C1VC2WB3     10.12500  320.59375   10.12500    3.44724    2.93713      .090
C3VC2WB3    247.53125  375.84375  247.53125    4.04133   61.24994      .000
```

FIG. 9.7. Output for nonorthogonal simple comparisons in a one between-, two within-factor ANOVA.

Finally, note that, for the two between, one within design, where only Factor C is within, it is assumed that the following are the "TRANSFORM/RENAME" specifications:

/TRANSFORM(c1 to c3)=SPECIAL (1 1 1, 1 0 –1, 0 1 –1)
/RENAME=skip c1vc3 c2vc3

For the row of Table 9.5 with the darkened entry for the two between, one within design denoted "C1VC3", the "DESIGN" specification would be 'MWITHIN a(1) WITHIN b(1), MWITHIN a(2) WITHIN b(1)', and so on (adding all desired levels of Factor A and Factor B). A portion of the printout is in Fig. 9.8. The darkened result is where the F and p values for C_{Compl} within A(1) within B(1) are found, corresponding to the darkened area in the bottom portion of Table 9.5.

```
EFFECT .. MWITHIN A(1) WITHIN B(1) (Cont.)
Univariate F-tests with (1,27) D. F.

Variable   Hypoth. SS   Error SS Hypoth. MS   Error MS         F  Sig. of F

SKIP        784.00000  256.75000  784.00000    9.50926   82.44596      .000
C1VC3         1.00000  101.25000    1.00000    3.75000     .26667      .610
C2VC3        36.00000  121.75000   36.00000    4.50926    7.98357      .009
```

FIG. 9.8. Output for nonorthogonal simple simple comparisons in a two between-, one within-factor ANOVA.

PAC

Whenever a design contains a within-subjects factor, the analysis is under the General Linear Model–Repeated Measures menu. Additional between- or within-subjects factors may easily be added in (see chaps. 4, 5, 6, and 8) to obtain basic analyses for three or greater factor mixed designs. Because marginal means are given for a within-subjects factor with PAC, you may wish to run the overall analysis from here and then switch to MANOVA for more complex analyses. The more complex analyses (e.g., simple two-ways, simple contrasts, etc.) need to be obtained with syntax. However, it is recommended that "MANOVA" syntax be used for all analyses not available by PAC as the latter syntax is cumbersome (see chap. 13) and mistakes could be easily made.

10 Analysis of Covariance

Analysis of covariance (ANCOVA) is another variant of analysis of variance in which the analyst enters into the analysis a variable(s) other than the dependent variable on which participants are also measured, called a *covariate*. ANCOVA has two major advantages over ANOVA. First, it provides a way to statistically equate groups that have somewhat different values on the covariate. Second, and most important, using the covariate can reduce unexplained variability, thereby increasing power to detect an effect of the independent variable. Additionally, not adjusting for a covariate may lead to the wrong conclusions. Specifically, random assignment does not guarantee that the groups are the same on the dependent variable before the experiment begins. If you are studying ways to decrease depression, for example, you may have a group of participants that were more depressed to begin with than the other groups. If you do not covary out pretest depression, it will look like there was not a treatment effect at the end of the experiment even if the treatment was efficacious, because their scores were already higher than everyone else's. In ANCOVA, a participant's response on the dependent variable is adjusted for the value of the covariate by calculating what that response would have been if all participants had had the same value for the covariate. Subsequent aspects of the analysis then use this adjusted dependent variable. Removing the covariate error variance from both the denominator and numerator of the F ratio generally increases the F ratio, making for a more powerful F test.

In ANCOVA, the regression line relating the covariate to the dependent variable is estimated and then used to predict a participant's response on the dependent variable. The deviations from this predicted response are then used to compute the variances for the F test, in this way taking into account the covariate's association with the dependent variable. The use of a covariate can be expected to increase F values when the covariate is similarly distributed among the levels of the independent variable, because in this case correcting for the covariate decreases the error term. It can either increase or decrease the F value when the covariate is distributed differently over the levels of the independent variable. There are some questions about the interpretability of the results when there are large differences in the covariate among the levels of the independent variable.

This chapter presents syntax first for one-factor completely randomized designs in which one and then more than one covariate is discussed. Next, two-factor completely randomized designs are presented, followed by designs that include a within-subjects factor (or repeated measures), including mixed designs.

The first program presented is for a one-factor completely randomized design with a single covariate. The data are from Stevens (2002, p. 358). One dependent variable has been left out and one participant has been dropped to achieve an equal N design. There are 14 participants in each of two groups. Assume that the between-subjects factor is named 'facta', the dependent variable is called 'score', and the variable name of the covariate is 'cov'.

1.	MANOVA score BY facta(1,2) WITH cov
2d.	/OMEANS
3d.	/PMEANS
4d.	/POWER
5d.	/PRINT=SIGNIF(EFSIZE)
6o.	/DESIGN.

FIG. 10.1.   Syntax commands to conduct a one-factor between-subjects design with a covariate.

The syntax for this program, in Fig. 10.1, is almost identical to the syntax for a regular one-factor between-subjects design. The most important difference between an ANOVA and an ANCOVA program is that, in ANCOVA, after listing the dependent variable and the between-subjects factor(s) on the "MANOVA" command, you add the keyword "WITH" followed by the name of the covariate. Second, means are now requested with both "OMEANS" and "PMEANS" (which are both optional, but highly recommended). In the ANCOVA case, "OMEANS" gives the mean, standard deviation, N, and 95% confidence interval for each group for both the dependent variable and the covariate. "PMEANS" gives the actual (observed) means for the dependent variable (note that this part is redundant with "OMEANS"), as well as the predicted (or adjusted) means (i.e., what the means for that group are predicted to be if the group's mean on the covariate had been equal to the overall covariate mean). Basically, it is determined what the mean score for each group would be if the covariate were the same for all groups. The "DESIGN" subcommand is optional here and for other programs presented in this chapter, unless noted otherwise. As usual, the options of power and effect were also requested. Although in subsequent programs effect size and power analyses are not requested, this is only to save space and it is recommended that the researcher always obtain these analyses.

First, in Fig. 10.2, is the output generated by the "OMEANS" subcommand, which is somewhat familiar, but note that the means on the covariate are also provided. Notice that Group 1's mean on the covariate is slightly above the overall mean, whereas Group 2's mean is slightly below. Next, as usual, comes the actual test of significance in an ANOVA summary table. The error term is found in the line headed "WITHIN CELLS". The main effect of Factor A is in the "FACTA" line. Here it is significant, $F(1, 25) = 7.13$, $p = .013$ and 22.20% of the variance in the dependent variable is accounted for by Factor A. The row labeled "REGRESSION" is new; it gives a test that the average slope of the covariate on the dependent variable is 0 across the levels of Factor A. The test is significant, $F(1, 25) = 51.39$, $p = .001$, thus the common slope is significantly different from zero. You can also think of this test as the test of the significance of the correlation between the dependent variable and the covariate (see later discussion) or as the amount of variability attributed to the covariate. It is labeled as "REGRESSION" because this is the same sum of squares you would obtain if you ran a regression predicting the dependent variable from the covariate.

After the power and effect size estimates, the estimate of the correlation between the covariate and the dependent variable is given next in a table that bears the title "Regression analysis for WITHIN CELLS error term". This table presents the slope of the relationship (the value under "B", here, 1.23039) between the covariate (on the x axis) and the dependent variable (on the y axis), as computed from raw scores. This is called the *common slope* and MANOVA uses this to calculate the adjusted means for each cell. The same table offers a "BETA" value, which refers to the same relationship as "B," but is computed with standardized scores. In the one covariate case, "BETA" is equivalent to the correlation between the covariate and the dependent variable. Here, that correlation is .81074. A t test of this correlation is also given in the table and is seen to have a significance value of .001, exactly the same as for the test of "REGRESSION" in the ANOVA table. This is because the two tests are alternate versions of an identical test.

Finally, the output generated by the "PMEANS" subcommand, the observed and adjusted means, is printed. Note, for example, that Group 2's adjusted mean is 14.18, slightly greater than its

```
Cell Means and Standard Deviations
Variable .. SCORE
        FACTOR              CODE              Mean  Std. Dev.           N

   FACTA                      1             12.286     2.998           14
   FACTA                      2             13.786     4.560           14
For entire sample                          13.036     3.863           28
- - - - - - - - - - - - - - - - - - - - - - - - - - - - - - - - - - - - -
Variable .. COV
        FACTOR              CODE              Mean  Std. Dev.           N

   FACTA                      1             11.357     2.098           14
   FACTA                      2             10.714     2.972           14
For entire sample                          11.036     2.546           28
- - - - - - - - - - - - - - - - - - - - - - - - - - - - - - - - - - - - -

Tests of Significance for SCORE using UNIQUE sums of squares
Source of Variation         SS         DF         MS          F  Sig of F

WITHIN CELLS             126.72         25       5.07
REGRESSION               260.49          1     260.49      51.39      .000
FACTA                     36.13          1      36.13       7.13      .013

(Model)                  276.24          2     138.12      27.25      .000
(Total)                  402.96         27      14.92

R-Squared =              .686
Adjusted R-Squared =     .660
- - - - - - - - - - - - - - - - - - - - - - - - - - - - - - - - - - - - -
Effect Size Measures and Observed Power at the .0500 Level
                            Partial Noncen-
Source of Variation      ETA Sqd trality       Power

Regression                 .673  51.389       1.000
FACTA                      .222   7.128        .726
- - - - - - - - - - - - - - - - - - - - - - - - - - - - - - - - - - - - -
Regression analysis for WITHIN CELLS error term
--- Individual Univariate .9500 confidence intervals
--- two-tailed observed power taken at .0500 level
Dependent variable .. SCORE

COVARIATE              B         Beta    Std. Err.    t-Value   Sig. of t

COV               1.23039      .81074        .172      7.169        .000

COVARIATE   Lower -95% CL- Upper    ETA Sq.    Noncent.      Power

COV               .877       1.584      .673      51.389      1.000
- - - - - - - - - - - - - - - - - - - - - - - - - - - - - - - - - - - - -
Adjusted and Estimated Means
Variable .. SCORE
   CELL      Obs. Mean   Adj. Mean   Est. Mean  Raw Resid. Std. Resid.

    1         12.286      11.890      12.286       .000       .000
    2         13.786      14.181      13.786       .000       .000
```

FIG. 10.2.   Output for a one-factor between-subjects design with one covariate.

observed mean of 13.78. The adjusted mean is greater because that group's mean on the covariate is 10.71, which is lower than the overall mean of 11.03, and the covariate and dependent variable are positively related. The results suggest that, if Group 2 had had a higher mean on the covariate, as high, say, as the overall mean, it would have likely had a higher mean on the dependent variable.

TESTING THE HOMOGENEITY OF REGRESSION ASSUMPTION

An important assumption of ANCOVA is that the regression slope (of the covariate on the dependent variable) is the same (homogeneous) across the various groups, or levels, of Factor A. This assumption, if violated, might mean abandoning a typical ANCOVA in favor of alternate techniques. A test of the assumption is possible with the syntax in Fig. 10.3.

```
1.   MANOVA score BY facta(1,2) WITH cov

2.      /ANALYSIS=score

3.      /DESIGN=facta, cov, facta BY cov.
```

FIG. 10.3.   Syntax commands to test the homogeneity of regression assumption in ANCOVA.

Line 2 introduces the "ANALYSIS" subcommand, a statement that tells MANOVA which dependent variables and covariates to really use in the analysis, overriding what is specified on the "MANOVA" command itself. Here, it tells MANOVA not to perform the typical ANCOVA with 'score' as the dependent variable and 'cov' as the covariate, but rather to still use 'score' as the dependent variable but not include a covariate (in the regular ANCOVA case, the "ANALYSIS" subcommand defaults to 'score WITH cov'). Line 3 requests the significance tests needed. Note that, although "DESIGN" would default to 'facta' in this instance, you are overriding that, and asking also for the tests for the covariate and, most importantly, the covariate × group interaction (which is actually the test of homogeneity desired). The relevant portion of printout is in Fig. 10.4.

```
Tests of Significance for SCORE using UNIQUE sums of squares
 Source of Variation        SS       DF        MS         F  Sig of F

WITHIN+RESIDUAL          124.20       24      5.17
FACTA                       .10        1       .10       .02    .892
COV                      215.34        1    215.34     41.61    .000
FACTA BY COV               2.53        1      2.53       .49    .491

(Model)                  278.77        3     92.92     17.96    .000
(Total)                  402.96       27     14.92

R-Squared =      .692
```

FIG. 10.4. Output for testing the homogeneity of regression assumption in ANCOVA.

If this test is statistically significant, you need to abandon the assumption of homogeneity of regression slopes. Because the results show that the "FACTA BY COV" interaction is not significant, $F(1, 24) = .49$, $p = .491$, you conclude instead that the assumption of homogeneity of regression slopes remains tenable.

MULTIPLE COVARIATES

It is possible to measure and adjust for more than one covariate. For example, had a second covariate (e.g., 'cov2') been available in a design like the preceding one, the "WITH" keyword in line 1 would have been followed by 'cov cov2'. In the printout, the primary change is that degrees of freedom for "REGRESSION" would be increased to 2 and degrees of freedom "WITHIN CELLS" would be decreased by 1 to 24. Otherwise, interpretations remain as before. In addition, some new or changed-format printout would emerge (see Fig. 10.5).

```
Correlations between Covariates and Predicted Dependent Variable
             COVARIATE

VARIABLE        COV        COV2

SCORE          .625        .233
- - - - - - - - - - - - - - - - - - - - - - - - - - - - - - - - - -
Squared Correlations between Covariates and Predicted Dependent Variable

VARIABLE   AVER. R-SQ

COV          .391
COV2         .054
- - - - - - - - - - - - - - - - - - - - - - - - - - - - - - - - - -
Regression analysis for WITHIN CELLS error term
--- Individual Univariate .9500 confidence intervals
Dependent variable .. SCORE

COVARIATE          B        Beta   Std. Err.   t-Value   Sig. of t

COV          1.24642      .53883      .406      3.068      .006
COV2          .34983      .10148      .607       .577      .571

COVARIATE   Lower -95%  CL- Upper

COV              .396      2.097
COV2            -.920      1.619
```

FIG. 10.5. Output for a one-factor between-subjects design with two covariates.

The printout yields correlations and squared correlations of each covariate with the dependent variable and the "Regression analysis" portion of the printout is now that of "multiple regression." To test the homogeneity of regression assumption with, say, three covariates (called 'cov', 'cov2', and 'cov3') requires syntax like that of Fig. 10.3 with 'cov cov2 cov3' after the "WITH" and the "DESIGN" specification of 'CONTIN(cov,cov2,cov3), facta, facta BY CONTIN(cov, cov2,cov3)'. "CONTIN" tells MANOVA to combine multiple continuous variables into a single test. The final effect, 'facta BY CONTIN(cov, cov2,cov3)', yields the test of the homogeneity of regression assumption.

Contrasts

Planned contrasts may be conducted[1] on the adjusted means by adding a "CONTRAST" sub-command, which specifies which groups are to be compared, together with a specification on the "DESIGN" subcommand that requests each contrast to be tested. Remember to request all the contrasts, even if you do not wish to examine all of them. Syntax is presented in Fig. 10.6 to compare the first group's to the last group's adjusted mean in a three-group design.

1.	MANOVA score BY facta(1,3) WITH cov
2.	/CONTRAST(facta)=SPECIAL(1 1 1, 1 0 −1, -1 2 −1)
3.	/DESIGN=facta(1), facta(2).

FIG. 10.6. Syntax commands to test planned contrasts in an ANCOVA with one covariate.

Post Hocs

Post hocs in ANCOVA, analogous to Tukey tests, require a number of manual calculations. First, the output of the ANCOVA, in terms of adjusted means and "MS WITHIN CELLS", should be computed as described in Keppel (1991, pp. 314–316). It should be noted that formula 14-13 (Keppel, pp. 314–316) also requires values of what Keppel refers to as "$MS_{A(X)}$" and "$SS_{S/A(X)}$." These quantities result from a separate ANOVA in which the covariate is treated as the dependent variable (with the usual independent variable; in the example, Factor A). $MS_{A(X)}$ is the mean square for "FACTA" and $SS_{S/A(X)}$ is the sum of squares for "WITHIN CELLS" in such an analysis. Second, special tables (the Bryant-Paulson tables; Bryant & Paulson, 1976), not commonly available, are needed. (See Huitema, 1980, chap. 5, for a description of the method, additional discussion, and tables.)

MULTIPLE BETWEEN-SUBJECTS FACTORS

The program for a two-factor completely randomized design with a covariate is almost identical to that for a regular two-factor between-subjects design. The only differences are the added specification of the covariate using "WITH" on the "MANOVA" command and the request for adjusted means with "PMEANS", with the same specification as for the "OMEANS" subcommand. Fig. 10.7 illustrates such a program.

---

[1]Keppel (1991) provided a special formula (formula 14-13) as the error term to test planned contrasts; MANOVA provides results that differ numerically from that formula. Instead, MANOVA's test conforms to the formula Winer (1971, p. 779) proposed, discussed in Keppel (1991, p. 315, fn. 9) and in Keppel (1982, p. 502). In his 1982 edition, Keppel suggested that the method of Winer is "often recommended," but involves more work and, citing Snedecor (1956), he regards the extra work as not worth the greater accuracy in most problems. Because MANOVA calculates the more accurate Winer method automatically, it is recommended here.

```
1.    MANOVA score BY facta(1,2) factb(1,2) WITH cov

2d.   /OMEANS=TABLES(facta,factb,facta BY factb)

3d.   /PMEANS=TABLES(facta,factb,facta BY factb)

4o.   /DESIGN.
```

FIG. 10.7.   Syntax commands to conduct a two-factor between- subjects design with a covariate.

The output for this program would be similar to that in Fig. 10.2, except there would now be a test for Factor B, in addition to the Factor A × Factor B interaction. There would also be extended printout of cell and marginal means, both actual or observed and adjusted means.

It should be clear from examining Figs. 10.1 and 10.4 that an ANCOVA program can be altered to accommodate virtually any number of between-subjects factors by simply specifying more factors on the "MANOVA" command and with additional sets of means selected on "OMEANS" and "PMEANS" subcommands. All the specialized planned analyses that pertain to these designs, such as (for two-factor designs) main effect contrasts, simple effects, simple comparisons, interaction contrasts, as well as (for three or more factors) simple two-way interactions, simple simple effects, simple simple comparisons, and simple interaction contrasts can also be computed by MANOVA simply by using the "DESIGN" specifications introduced in chapters 3 through 5, along with specification of the covariate(s) after the "WITH" on the "MANOVA" command.

ANCOVAs IN DESIGNS WITH WITHIN-SUBJECTS FACTORS

An ANCOVA is also possible in designs with one or more within-subjects factors, including mixed designs, which contain both within-subjects and between-subjects factors. There are two possibilities for such covariate(s). One is the *varying* covariate, in which the participant has one (or more) covariate(s) for each level of the within-subjects factor. An example is when the dependent variable is how much time the participant takes to respond to each stimulus and the covariate is the participant's rating of the attractiveness of each stimulus. The second possibility is the *constant* covariate, in which each participant has a covariate(s) that applies to that participant (rather than to each level of the within-subjects factor). An example is when the GPA of each participant is considered a covariate. Because the constant covariate adjusts all of the participants' scores, the constant covariate would be of no use for designs that comprise only within-subjects factors. Rather, constant covariates are useful only if the design also contains one or more between-subjects factors, for example, mixed designs. In contrast, a varying covariate might be employed in designs involving only within-subjects factors, such as one- and two-factor within-subjects designs, as well as in mixed designs, because the varying covariate provides an adjustment to each of the individual scores. First, the analysis of the constant covariate is considered.

Constant Covariate

The syntax to conduct an ANCOVA in the mixed design with a constant covariate involves the usual specification of the between-subjects and within-subjects factors, but enclosing the covariate named after the "WITH" in parentheses. For example, syntax to analyze the data of Huitema's (1980) example (p. 225), which is a 2 × 3 mixed design, is in Fig. 10.8.

```
1.    MANOVA b1 b2 b3 BY facta(1,2) WITH (cov)

2.    /WSFACTORS=factb(3)

3d.   /OMEANS

4o.   /DESIGN.
```

FIG. 10.8.   Syntax commands to conduct an ANCOVA for a one between-, one within-subjects design with a constant covariate.

The relevant portions of output for this design are in Fig. 10.9.

```
Cell Means and Standard Deviations
 Variable .. B1
      FACTOR               CODE                Mean  Std. Dev.           N

   FACTA                    1                  7.800   1.304             5
   FACTA                    2                  4.400   2.074             5
   For entire sample                           6.100   2.424            10
- - - - - - - - - - - - - - - - - - - - - - - - - - - - - - - - - - - - -
 Variable .. B2
      FACTOR               CODE                Mean  Std. Dev.           N

   FACTA                    1                  6.200   1.304             5
   FACTA                    2                  4.200   1.643             5
   For entire sample                           5.200   1.751            10
- - - - - - - - - - - - - - - - - - - - - - - - - - - - - - - - - - - - -
 Variable .. B3
      FACTOR               CODE                Mean  Std. Dev.           N

   FACTA                    1                  6.800    .837             5
   FACTA                    2                  3.800   1.483             5
   For entire sample                           5.300   1.947            10
- - - - - - - - - - - - - - - - - - - - - - - - - - - - - - - - - - - - -
 Variable .. COV
      FACTOR               CODE                Mean  Std. Dev.           N

   FACTA                    1                  5.200   1.304             5
   FACTA                    2                  5.800   2.168             5
   For entire sample                           5.500   1.716            10
 Variable .. COV
      FACTOR               CODE                Mean  Std. Dev.           N

   FACTA                    1                  5.200   1.304             5
   FACTA                    2                  5.800   2.168             5
   For entire sample                           5.500   1.716            10
- - - - - - - - - - - - - - - - - - - - - - - - - - - - - - - - - - - - -


Tests of Between-Subjects Effects.

Tests of Significance for T1 using UNIQUE sums of squares
Source of Variation          SS       DF        MS          F   Sig of F

WITHIN CELLS               4.52        7       .65
REGRESSION                38.82        1     38.82       60.17    .000
FACTA                     75.43        1     75.43      116.91    .000
- - - - - - - - - - - - - - - - - - - - - - - - - - - - - - - - - - - - -
Regression analysis for WITHIN CELLS error term
--- Individual Univariate .9500 confidence intervals
Dependent variable .. T1

COVARIATE               B        Beta   Std. Err.    t-Value   Sig. of t

TCOV               .71094     .62724       .092        7.757    .000

COVARIATE    Lower -95%  CL- Upper

TCOV               .494       .928
- - - - - - - - - - - - - - - - - - - - - - - - - - - - - - - - - - - - -

Tests involving 'FACTB' Within-Subject Effect.

AVERAGED Tests of Significance for B using UNIQUE sums of squares
Source of Variation          SS       DF        MS          F   Sig of F

WITHIN CELLS               9.87       16       .62
FACTB                      4.87        2      2.43        3.95    .040
FACTA BY FACTB             2.60        2      1.30        2.11    .154
```

FIG. 10.9.   Output for an ANCOVA for a one between-, one within-subjects design with a constant covariate.

Note that, in the second to last portion of Fig. 10.9, the covariate is automatically given the odd name "TCOV". Note also that, in the syntax, the "PMEANS" subcommand was omitted, because the results it gives are misleading and incorrect in within-subjects situations. Fortunately, the regression analysis "B" coefficient may be used to manually calculate the adjusted means. The formula is:

$$\overline{Y}_{AB}' = \overline{Y}_{AB} - B_{BS}(\overline{X}_A - \overline{X}_T)$$

where $\overline{Y}_{AB}'$ is the adjusted cell mean, $\overline{Y}_{AB}$ is the observed cell mean, $\overline{X}_A$ is the observed A marginal mean on the covariate, $\overline{X}_T$ is the overall mean on the covariate, and B_{BS} is the "B" coefficient. These are all found on the printout and are as follows: $B_{BS} = .71094$, $\overline{X}_A$ for Group 1 = 5.2, $\overline{X}_A$ for Group 2

= 5.8 (it should be noted that the means on the covariate "COV" with the preceding two values inexplicably appear two separate times in the "OMEANS" section of the printout), $\overline{X}_T = 5.5$ (found as the "For entire sample" mean), and the $\overline{Y}_{AB}$ are in Table 10.1.

TABLE 10.1
Observed Cell Means (i.e., $\overline{Y}_{AB}$) for the Two-Factor Mixed ANOVA With a Constant Covariate

	b1	b2	b3
facta 1	7.8	6.2	6.8
facta 2	4.4	4.2	3.8

For example, for the upper left cell, the calculations are:

$$\overline{Y}'_{AB} = \overline{Y}_{AB} - B_{BS}(\overline{X}_A - \overline{X}_T) = 7.8 - .71094\,(5.2 - 5.5) = 8.01.$$

The entire set of adjusted cell means, calculated in analogous fashion (with marginals computed as the means of the relevant cell means), are in Table 10.2.

TABLE 10.2
Calculated Adjusted Means for the Two-Factor Mixed ANOVA With a Constant Covariate

	b1	b2	b3	Average
facta 1	8.01	6.41	7.01	7.14
facta 2	4.19	3.99	3.59	3.92
Average	6.10	5.20	5.30	

Varying Covariate

First, an example of a design without any between-subjects factors is given, namely, a one-way within-subjects case. First, you specify the variables containing the scores for various levels of the within-subjects factor; then, after the "WITH", specify the variables that are the covariates for the respective dependent variables. An example, with two levels of the within-subjects factor, is found in Tabachnick and Fidell (2001, p. 417).

```
1.    MANOVA a1 a2 WITH cv1 cv2

2.        /WSFACTOR=facta(2)

3d.       /OMEANS

4o.       /DESIGN.
```

FIG. 10.10. Syntax commands to conduct an ANCOVA for a within-subjects design with a varying covariate.

The abbreviated output that results from this syntax is in Fig. 10.11.

```
Cell Means and Standard Deviations
Variable .. A1
                                    Mean  Std. Dev.            N
    For entire sample              10.333    2.784             9
- - - - - - - - - - - - - - - - - - - - - - - - - - - - - -
    Variable .. A2
                                    Mean  Std. Dev.            N
    For entire sample              15.111    4.428             9
- - - - - - - - - - - - - - - - - - - - - - - - - - - - - -
    Variable .. CV1
                                    Mean  Std. Dev.            N
    For entire sample               7.667    3.742             9
- - - - - - - - - - - - - - - - - - - - - - - - - - - - - -
    Variable .. CV2
                                    Mean  Std. Dev.            N
    For entire sample               7.444    2.789             9
- - - - - - - - - - - - - - - - - - - - - - - - - - - - - -


Tests involving 'FACTA' Within-Subject Effect.

Tests of Significance for T2 using UNIQUE sums of squares
Source of Variation         SS       DF       MS        F  Sig of F

WITHIN CELLS              26.08        7      3.73
REGRESSION                 .70        1       .70      .19     .677
FACTA                    99.16        1     99.16    26.62     .001
- - - - - - - - - - - - - - - - - - - - - - - - - - - - - -
Regression analysis for WITHIN CELLS error term
--- Individual Univariate .9500 confidence intervals
Dependent variable .. T2

COVARIATE            B        Beta    Std. Err.    t-Value   Sig. of t

T4            -.21805    -.16198        .502       -.434        .677

COVARIATE    Lower -95% CL- Upper

T4            -1.405        .969
```

FIG. 10.11.   Output for an ANCOVA for a within-subjects design with a varying covariate.

The F for "FACTA" is significant, $F(1, 7) = 26.62$, $p = .001$. Note that "PMEANS" was not specified, meaning that adjusted means are not printed out. This is because MANOVA does not calculate them properly. However, as in the earlier example, these means can be constructed by manual calculation based on the printout. Here, the relevant formula is:

$$\overline{Y}_A' = \overline{Y}_A - B_{WS}(\overline{X}_A - \overline{X}_T)$$

where $\overline{Y}_A'$ is the adjusted mean, $\overline{Y}_A$ is the observed mean, $\overline{X}_A$ is the observed A mean on the covariate, $\overline{X}_T$ is the overall mean on the covariate, and B_{WS} is the B-coefficient (this time with the subscript $_{WS}$, indicating "within subjects"). Most of the values are found on the printout: $B_{WS} = -.21805$, $\overline{X}_A$ for Level 1 = 7.667, $\overline{X}_A$ for Level 2 = 7.444. The $\overline{Y}_A$ values are 10.333 and 15.111, respectively. $\overline{X}_T$ is not given, but can be found by averaging the two $\overline{X}_A$ values, obtaining 7.555. Thus, the two adjusted means are 10.34 and 15.09, respectively.

Although in the preceding example MANOVA printed out all the relevant figures to enable manual calculation of the adjusted means, unfortunately, it will not do so when there are more than two levels of the factor, at least not with commands given here. Specifically, it will not give the value for B_{WS}. An alternative method to handle such designs, and to obtain B_{WS}, involves using the one-line-per-level setup, as opposed to the one-line-per-subject setup that has been used up to this point. Because the one-line-per-level setup requires some additional concepts, discussion of it is postponed until chapter 11.

Another design possibility where you might see a varying covariate is the mixed design, which contains both between- and within-subjects factors. An example of a program for a two-factor mixed design with a varying covariate using data from Winer, Brown, and Michels (1991, p. 833) is in Fig. 10.12.

```
1.    MANOVA b1 b2  BY facta(1,3) WITH cv1 cv2

2.    /WSFACTOR=factb(2)

3d.   /OMEANS

4o.   /DESIGN.
```

FIG. 10.12. Syntax commands to conduct an ANCOVA for a mixed design with a varying covariate.

Note that the "MANOVA" command is altered in the expected fashion, by adding the names of both levels of the within-subject factor before the "BY" and adding the covariates that pertain to each of those scores, respectively, after the "WITH". Line 2 adds the "WSFACTORS" sub-command necessary for within-subjects factors. Figure 10.13 provides edited printout.

```
Cell Means and Standard Deviations
 Variable .. B1
       FACTOR            CODE                  Mean  Std. Dev.            N

 FACTA                   1                   11.667    4.041              3
 FACTA                   2                    9.000    3.000              3
 FACTA                   3                   13.000    2.646              3
 For entire sample                           11.222    3.346              9
- - - - - - - - - - - - - - - - - - - - - - - - - - - - - - - - - - - - - -
 Variable .. B2
       FACTOR            CODE                  Mean  Std. Dev.            N

 FACTA                   1                   18.000    4.000              3
 FACTA                   2                   10.667    3.055              3
 FACTA                   3                   16.667    6.110              3
 For entire sample                           15.111    5.207              9
- - - - - - - - - - - - - - - - - - - - - - - - - - - - - - - - - - - - - -
 Variable .. CV1
       FACTOR            CODE                  Mean  Std. Dev.            N

 FACTA                   1                    6.333    4.163              3
 FACTA                   2                    6.667    4.163              3
 FACTA                   3                    8.000    1.000              3
 For entire sample                            7.000    3.082              9
- - - - - - - - - - - - - - - - - - - - - - - - - - - - - - - - - - - - - -
 Variable .. CV2
       FACTOR            CODE                  Mean  Std. Dev.            N

 FACTA                   1                    9.000    5.000              3
 FACTA                   2                    6.333    4.619              3
 FACTA                   3                    8.667    4.163              3
 For entire sample                            8.000    4.183              9
- - - - - - - - - - - - - - - - - - - - - - - - - - - - - - - - - - - - - -

Tests of Between-Subjects Effects.

 Tests of Significance for T1 using UNIQUE sums of squares
 Source of Variation              SS       DF       MS          F    Sig of F

 WITHIN CELLS                  44.37        5      8.87
 REGRESSION                   132.63        1    132.63      14.95       .012
 FACTA                         54.26        2     27.13       3.06       .136
- - - - - - - - - - - - - - - - - - - - - - - - - - - - - - - - - - - - - -
 Regression analysis for WITHIN CELLS error term
 --- Individual Univariate .9500 confidence intervals
 Dependent variable .. T1

 COVARIATE              B        Beta   Std. Err.    t-Value   Sig. of t
 T3                 .84747     .71106        .219      3.866        .012

- - - - - - - - - - - - - - - - - - - - - - - - - - - - - - - - - - - - - -

Tests involving 'FACTB' Within-Subject Effect.

 Tests of Significance for T2 using UNIQUE sums of squares
 Source of Variation              SS       DF       MS          F    Sig of F

 WITHIN CELLS                   3.00        5       .60
 REGRESSION                    10.00        1     10.00      16.68       .010
 FACTB                         31.55        1     31.55      52.61       .001
 FACTA BY FACTB                 2.34        2      1.17       1.95       .236
- - - - - - - - - - - - - - - - - - - - - - - - - - - - - - - - - - - - - -
Regression analysis for WITHIN CELLS error term
```

FIG. 10.13. *(Continues)*

```
--- Individual Univariate .9500 confidence intervals
Dependent variable .. T2

COVARIATE         B       Beta    Std. Err.   t-Value   Sig. of t
T4            .84524    .71382       .207      4.084       .010
```

FIG. 10.13.   Output for an ANCOVA with a varying covariate, mixed design.

As can be seen in Fig. 10.13, whereas neither the interaction nor the "FACTA" (between-subjects factor) main effect is significant, $F(2, 5) = 1.95$, $p = .236$ and $F(2, 5) = 3.06$, $p = .136$, respectively, the "FACTB" (within-subjects factor) main effect is highly significant, $F(1, 5) = 52.61$, $p = .001$. Note that there is a separate "REGRESSION" effect tested for the between-subjects and within-subjects portion of the design and each is significant.

Again, in this example, as is true for any design with a varying covariate, adjusted means should not be requested with "PMEANS" because MANOVA does not compute them correctly. Again, in this case (which has two levels of the within-subjects factor), all the relevant values to manually compute adjusted means are present in the printout. The appropriate formula for the two-factor mixed design is:

$$\overline{Y}'_{AB} = \overline{Y}_{AB} - B_{BS}(\overline{X}_A - \overline{X}_T) - B_{WS}(\overline{X}_{AB} - \overline{X}_A)$$

where $\overline{Y}'_{AB}$ is the adjusted cell mean, $\overline{Y}_{AB}$ is the observed cell mean, $\overline{X}_{AB}$ is the observed cell mean on the covariate, $\overline{X}_A$ is the observed A marginal mean on the covariate, $\overline{X}_T$ is the overall mean on the covariate, B_{BS} is the between-subjects "B" coefficient, and B_{WS} is the within-subjects "B" coefficient. B_{BS}, the between-subjects coefficient, is found as the "B" coefficient from "T3" to "T1", which in the example is .84747, whereas B_{WS} is found as the "B" from "T4" to "T2" and, here, is .84524. You also obtain the cell means for the dependent variable and cell and marginal means for the covariate (see Table 10.3).

TABLE 10.3
Means on the Dependent Variable and Covariate for the Two-Factor Mixed ANOVA

	Dependent Variable		Covariate		
	b1	b2	b1	b2	Average
facta 1	11.667	18.000	6.333	9.000	7.667
facta 2	9.000	10.667	6.667	6.333	6.500
facta 3	13.000	16.667	8.000	8.667	8.334
Average					7.500

TABLE 10.4
Adjusted Cell and Marginal Means for the Two-Factor Mixed ANOVA

	b1	b2	Average
facta 1	12.653	16.732	14.692
facta 2	9.706	11.656	10.681
facta 3	12.576	15.679	14.127
	11.645	14.689	13.167

The entire set of adjusted cell means (with marginals computed as the means of the relevant cell means) is in Table 10.4. For example, the calculation for the upper left cell would be:

$$\overline{Y}'_{AB} = \overline{Y}_{AB} - B_{BS}(\overline{X}_A - \overline{X}_T) - B_{WS}(\overline{X}_{AB} - \overline{X}_A)$$
$$= 11.667 - .84747\,(7.667 - 7.5) - .84524\,(6.333 - 7.667) = 12.653.$$

MANOVA printed out all the relevant figures to enable manual calculation of the adjusted means in the preceding example because there were only two levels of the within-subjects factor. Had the within-subjects factor contained three or more levels, the value for B_{ws} could not have been computed with the previous commands and setup. Again, however, the alternative one-line-per-level setup could have been employed to obtain this value (see chap. 11 for details on how to obtain these values).

PAC

For between-subjects designs, an ANCOVA is run from the General Linear Model–Univariate menu. Everything stays the same for setting up the analyses, except that now you select your covariates and put them in the Covariate(s) box, as shown in Fig. 10.14.

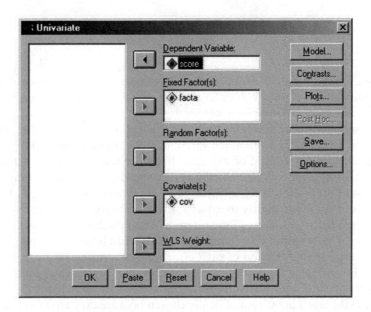

FIG. 10.14.   Dialogue box for ANCOVA.

All other options and caveats remain the same. Adjusted means are the means printed out when you get the means for Factor A using the Options menu. You cannot obtain the unadjusted means if the covariate is in the design. The General Linear Model (GLM) statistical approach to within-subjects factors, with both varying and constant covariates, is different from MANOVA's. According to Tabachnik and Fidell (2001, p. 415), GLM should be avoided in this instance.

11 Designs With Random Factors

Up until this point, all of the analyses have been concerned with independent variables that may be considered *fixed* factors. A different type of factor is called a *random* factor. A random factor is one in which you have sampled some levels of the factor but think there are many more (actually, virtually infinitely more) levels that exist to which you wish to generalize. In comparison, a fixed factor is one in which all the levels of the variables that exist in reality and to which you wish to generalize are included in the study. For example, if gender was a factor in a study with two levels (men and women), those are all that exist in reality and that you wish to generalize to, so it is a fixed factor. Most of the factors in the social sciences are fixed factors (Keppel, 1991). Researchers typically use random factors primarily to expand generalizability of the research results. Often the effect of the random factor per se is of little interest. When random factors are included in the design, the error term for each *F* ratio may change. MANOVA can handle both random and fixed factors by permitting explicit specification of each effect's error term on the "DESIGN" subcommand.

For example, consider a two-factor between-subjects design in which Factor A is frequency of feedback with three levels: frequent, infrequent, or none (control). Clearly this factor is fixed, because the levels are very specifically chosen because they are of inherent interest. Suppose that each of 10 experimenters delivers each of these three treatments to five participants and a goal of the study is to evaluate the extent to which feedback has an effect over all experimenters. Thus, Factor B would be Experimenter, with 10 levels. But here you would likely treat Factor B as a random factor, because those 10 experimenters included are regarded as merely representatives of a virtually infinite class of experimenters to which you wish to generalize. You may not be interested in any main effect differences between these individuals per se and you are willing to regard them as a random sample of experimenters.

In a two-factor between-subjects design, in which Factor A is fixed and Factor B is random, Factor B and the interaction are tested as usual, using "WITHIN CELLS" as the denominator of the *F* ratio (i.e., the error term). Factor A is tested with the interaction as its error term (see Keppel, 1973, pp. 340–341). To force MANOVA to use the appropriate error terms, the "DESIGN" subcommand should have the following specification:

/DESIGN=facta VS 1, factb VS WITHIN, facta BY factb=1 VS WITHIN.

Turning to the middle specification first, 'factb VS WITHIN', you are indicating that you want the main effect of Factor B to be tested against ("VS") the error term "WITHIN" (CELLS; this is the default in a two-factor design, so the "VS WITHIN" could be safely omitted). The third specification ('facta BY factb=1 VS WITHIN') instructs MANOVA that the interaction should also be tested against within cells (the "VS WITHIN" part), but the 'facta BY factb' interaction effect becomes a special error term, namely, error term number 1 (the '=1' part). Finally, the first specification ('facta VS 1') instructs MANOVA that special error term number 1 (namely the 'facta BY factb' interaction) is to be its error term. The printout from such an example is in Fig. 11.1.

```
Tests of Significance for DV using UNIQUE sums of squares
   Source of Variation          SS        DF        MS        F   Sig of F

WITHIN CELLS                 555.20       120      4.63
FACTB                         69.36         9      7.71     1.67     .105
FACTA BY FACTB (ERROR 1)     159.96        18      8.89     1.92     .020
- - - - - - - - - - - - - - - - - - - - - - - - - - - - - - - - - - - - -
Error 1                      159.96        18      8.89
FACTA                         10.57         2      5.29      .59     .562
```

FIG. 11.1. Output for a one fixed-, one random-factor ANOVA.

The altered layout of the output makes it clear that "FACTB" and "FACTA BY FACTB" both use "WITHIN CELLS" as the error term, but that "FACTA" is tested with the interaction "FACTA BY FACTB", also called "Error 1". The results show that Factor A is not significant, $F(2,18) = .59$, $p = .562$. Factor B has a nonsignificant main effect, $F(9, 120) = 1.67$, $p = .105$, but, as mentioned earlier, there is little inherent interest in this effect. Note carefully the degrees of freedom in the preceding statements. Larger designs with more random factors have special considerations for error terms (see Keppel, 1982, appendix C-4), but all can be handled essentially in this way.

RANDOM FACTORS NESTED IN FIXED FACTORS

Random factors are sometimes arranged so as to be "nested" within the fixed factors. An example is from Keppel (1991, p. 564). In this experiment, a researcher is interested in how people solve problems. The dependent variable is amount of time it takes to solve a problem ('dv'). There are two types of problems being investigated, either disjunctive or conjunctive (Factor A, fixed factor). Instead of using just one problem, however, the researcher decides to use several of each type to increase the generalizability of the experiment. She decides to use four different problems of each problem type (Factor B, random factor). Each participant solved one problem and two different participants were randomly assigned to each problem (there were $2 \times 4 = 8$ different problems, so 16 participants in all). In this design, 'problem' is nested within 'problem type' (random Factor B nested within fixed Factor A, symbolized as "B/A"). The data are in Fig. 11.2.

a1: Disjunctive				a2: Conjunctive		
problems	dv			problems	dv	
b1	3, 2			b5	10, 10	
b2	1, 1			b6	3, 3	
b3	5, 3			b7	6, 6	
b4	5, 9			b8	4, 3	

FIG. 11.2. Data for a two-factor nested design in which Factor B is nested within Factor A. From *Design and Analysis: A Researcher's Handbook* (p. 564), by G. Keppel, 1991, Upper Saddle River, NJ, Pearson Education. Copyright 1991 by Pearson Education, Inc. Reprinted with permission.

The analysis of this design is similar to that of a two-factor between-subjects design. Although technically there are eight levels of Factor B (4 problems × 2 types = 8), there are only four levels within any given level of Factor A and that is what SPSS needs to know. Thus, the "MANOVA" command would specify 'time BY facta(1,2) factb(1,4)', as in an ordinary two-factor between-subjects design. As Keppel (1991) showed, in this kind of design, the error term for the Factor A effect is the "Factor B within Factor A" effect, the error term for which, in turn, is "WITHIN CELLS". Thus, the "DESIGN" subcommand here would be:

/DESIGN=facta VS 1, factb WITHIN facta = 1 VS WITHIN.

As described earlier, 'factb WITHIN facta = 1 VS WITHIN' instructs MANOVA that the 'factb within facta' effect should be tested against within cells and that it also becomes itself a special error term, namely number 1. Furthermore, 'facta VS 1' instructs MANOVA that special error term number 1 is to be the error term for Factor A. The output from this syntax is in Fig. 11.3.

```
Tests of Significance for TIME using UNIQUE sums of squares
  Source of Variation                   SS        DF        MS        F  Sig of F

WITHIN CELLS                          11.00        8      1.38
FACTB WITHIN FACTA (ERROR 1)         100.75        6     16.79     12.21     .001
- - - - - - - - - - - - - - - - - - - - - - - - - - - - - - - - - - - - - - - -
Error 1                              100.75        6     16.79
FACTA                                 16.00        1     16.00       .95     .367
```

FIG. 11.3.   Output for the main effects of Factors A and B in a nested design.

There is a significant effect for B/A, $F(6, 8) = 12.21$, $p = .001$, which tells you that there is a difference between the problems used. The F for Factor A, however, is nonsignificant, $F(1, 6) = .95$, $p = .367$, thus, problem type has no effect. It is interesting to note that, if you had used the error term that ignores the fact that Factor B is nested (namely "WITHIN"), the F for Factor A would have been 11.64 and significant, thus leading to the wrong conclusion. For a more complete discussion of the issues in nested designs, including more complex designs, the reader is referred to Keppel (1982, 1991).

SUBJECTS AS RANDOM FACTORS IN WITHIN-SUBJECTS DESIGNS: THE ONE-LINE-PER-LEVEL SETUP

It may have occurred to you that, if experimenters should be treated as a random factor, perhaps participants should be as well. In fact, analysts virtually always treat participants as randomly chosen from a potentially infinite population, though this fact was not made explicit earlier in this book. The fact that participants may truly be considered another factor (always a random factor) in within-subjects and mixed designs assumes more importance now as an alternative data setup and syntax are presented. This alternative setup and syntax is always available. In most applications, however, it is slightly more difficult to program, and is therefore a slightly inferior alternative to the methods taught in previous chapters. There is one (relatively uncommon) instance, however, in which it produces a result that is not available by the standard method, namely, for the varying covariate with more than two levels ANCOVA situation, described in chapter 10. Before explicating this situation, the simplest within-subjects situation, the one-factor within-subjects design, is explained.

The One-Factor Within-Subjects Design

The one-factor within-subjects design was considered in chapter 6. The data set example used there is reprinted in Fig. 11.4.

In chapter 6, these data might have been read into SPSS with a "DATA LIST" command that had the three scores for each participant on the same data line, for example:

	Length of Words		
	a1: Short	a2: Medium	a3: Long
s_1	30	28	34
s_2	14	18	22
s_3	24	20	30
s_4	38	34	44
s_5	26	28	30

FIG. 11.4.   Data from the one-factor within-subjects ANOVA from chapter 6 (identical to Fig. 6.1).

```
DATA LIST /a1 1-2 a2 3-4 a3 5-6.
```

Such a setup is called the one-line-per-subject setup. However, the layout in Fig. 11.4 suggests that each of the data points could be alternatively regarded as the entry of a cell in a two-factor design, in which one factor is 'condition' and the other is 'subject', which, of course, is treated as a random factor. This implies the following alternative "DATA LIST" statement:

```
DATA LIST /dv 1-2 facta 3 subj 4.
```

This setup is the one-line-per-level setup, where each line of data contains the data for one participant (i.e., subject) for one level of the within-subjects factor. Figures 11.5 and 11.6 show how each of the two different setups would look in the Data Editor window of SPSS for Windows.

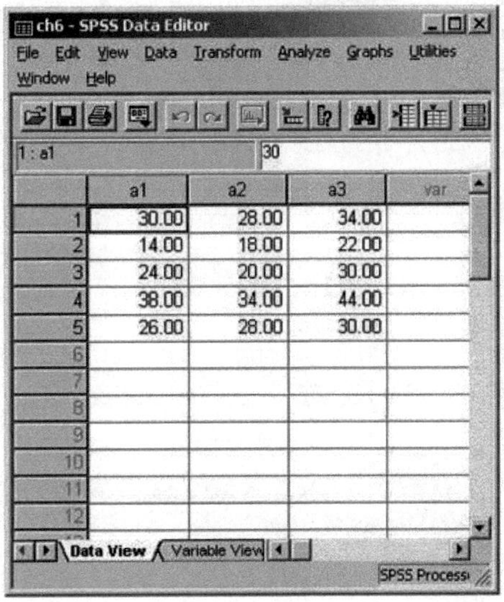

	a1	a2	a3	var
1	30.00	28.00	34.00	
2	14.00	18.00	22.00	
3	24.00	20.00	30.00	
4	38.00	34.00	44.00	
5	26.00	28.00	30.00	
6				
7				
8				
9				
10				
11				
12				

FIG. 11.5. The regular one-line-per-subject setup for the data in Fig. 11.4.

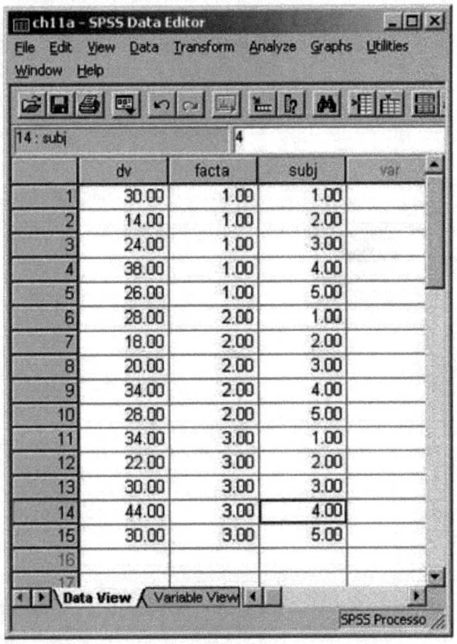

	dv	facta	subj	var
1	30.00	1.00	1.00	
2	14.00	1.00	2.00	
3	24.00	1.00	3.00	
4	38.00	1.00	4.00	
5	26.00	1.00	5.00	
6	28.00	2.00	1.00	
7	18.00	2.00	2.00	
8	20.00	2.00	3.00	
9	34.00	2.00	4.00	
10	28.00	2.00	5.00	
11	34.00	3.00	1.00	
12	22.00	3.00	2.00	
13	30.00	3.00	3.00	
14	44.00	3.00	4.00	
15	30.00	3.00	5.00	
16				

FIG. 11.6. The alternative one-line-per-level setup for the data in Fig. 11.4.

Note that Fig. 11.6 contains, in column 1, all the data from the three columns of Fig. 11.5. The remaining two columns describe which level of 'facta' and which 'subject' the data come from, respectively.

It should be noted parenthetically that, if you already have the data entered in one setup, you do not necessarily have to completely retype it to get it into the other, at least through Windows. Rather, Windows' cut-and-paste capabilities can be used. First, highlight all the cells in the second column with your left mouse button held down. Then, while leaving the cursor in the blackened area, right click, then left click Cut as seen in Fig. 11.7.

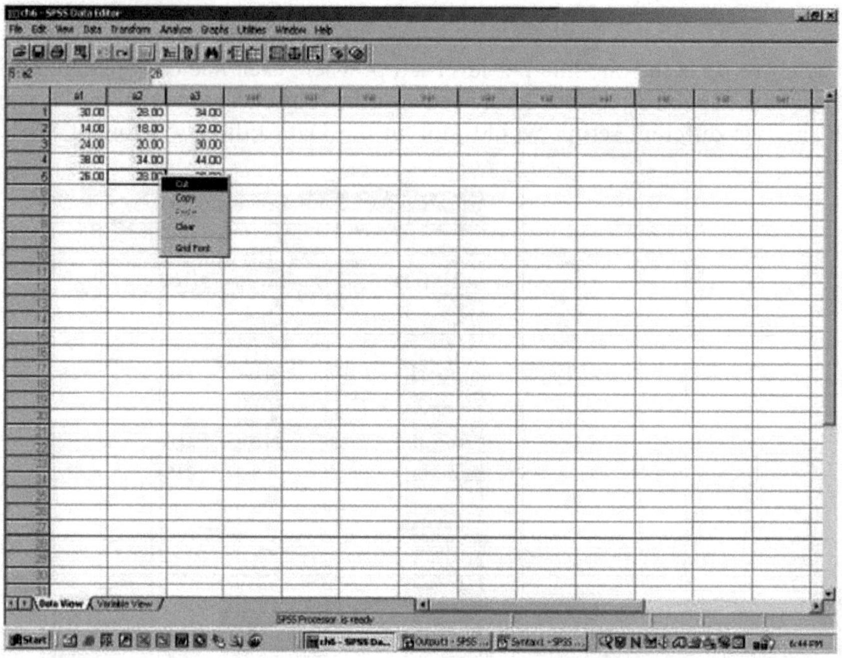

FIG. 11.7.   An example of how to cut data in PAC.

All the data from column 2 will disappear. Then move your cursor to the first blank cell in column 1, then right click and hit Paste as seen in Fig. 11.8.

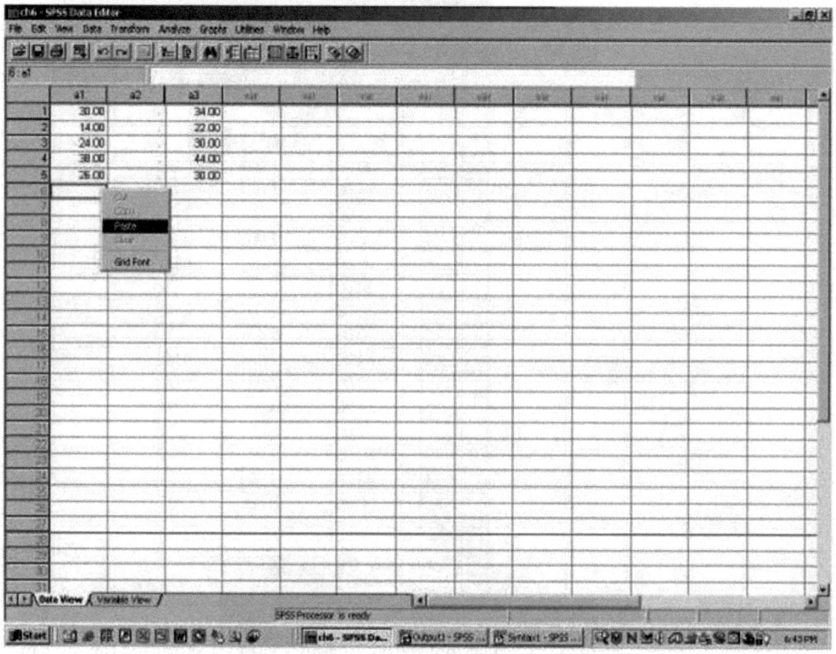

FIG. 11.8.   Pasting the cut data into another column.

The result is in Fig. 11.9.

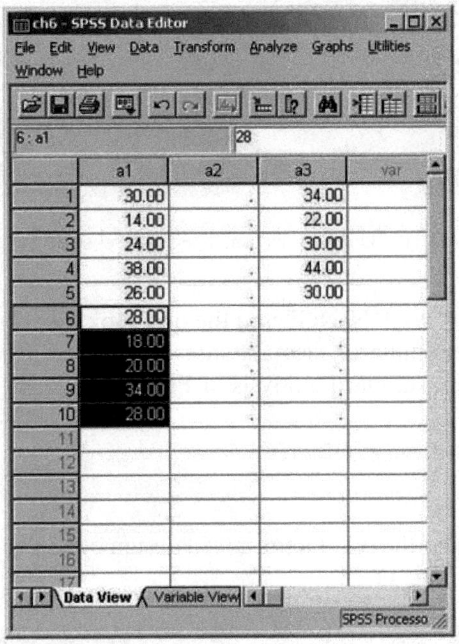

FIG. 11.9.   The result of cutting and pasting the data.

Continue in this fashion until all the data are moved to column 1. Rename all columns as needed on Variable View and type in the level numbers and subject numbers in columns 2 and 3, which can generally be done rapidly.

Keppel (1991, p. 346) showed the actual ANOVA summary table for the one-factor within-subjects design to contain the following entries (with names changed to reflect the current nomenclature):

Source
FACTA
SUBJ
FACTA × SUBJ

Assuming that 'SUBJ' is a random factor and 'FACTA' is fixed, 'FACTA × SUBJ' is the error term for 'FACTA'. This can be programmed in the one-line-per-level setup, using the "DESIGN" subcommand to indicate error terms as earlier, seen in Fig. 11.10.

```
1.    MANOVA dv BY subj(1,5) facta(1,3)

2o.      /OMEANS=TABLES (facta)

3.       /DESIGN=facta VS 1, subj, facta BY subj=1.
```

FIG. 11.10.   Syntax commands for a one-line-per-level setup for a one-factor within-subjects ANOVA.

The output is in Fig. 11.11.

```
* * * * * * * * * * * * * * * * * * * * * * * * * * * * * * * * * * * * *
*                    *                                                   *
*   W A R N I N G    *   Too few degrees of freedom in RESIDUAL         *
*                    *   error term for the following test(s) (DF = 0). *
*                    *                                                   *
* * * * * * * * * * * * * * * * * * * * * * * * * * * * * * * * * * * * *

Tests of Significance for DV using UNIQUE sums of squares
Source of Variation            SS       DF        MS        F   Sig of F

RESIDUAL                      .00        0         .
SUBJ                       696.00        4     174.00        .        .
- - - - - - - - - - - - - - - - - - - - - - - - - - - - - - - - - - -
Error 1                     38.40        8       4.80
FACTA                      121.60        2      60.80     12.67     .003
```

FIG. 11.11.   Output for a one-line-per-level setup for a one-factor within-subjects ANOVA.

Despite the "WARNING" and the odd-looking printout, these results suggest the identical numerator and denominator mean square and degrees of freedom values, *F* value, and significance level as the more standard analysis in Fig. 6.3.

Two-Factor Mixed Design

Similarly, consider the two-factor mixed design of Fig. 8.1, discussed previously in chapter 8 and reprinted here in Fig. 11.12.

a1: Nicotine Patch				a2: Group Therapy				a3: Control			
b: Time				b: Time				b: Time			
b1	b2	b3	b4	b1	b2	b3	b4	b1	b2	b3	b4
120	84	47	20	115	50	30	30	125	127	128	120
119	51	40	14	118	30	22	24	120	122	122	124
123	20	18	21	120	0	0	0	114	122	128	128
135	10	9	0	119	4	2	2	108	118	127	128

FIG. 11.12.   Data from the one between-, one within-factor ANOVA from chapter 8 (identical to Fig. 8.1).

Keppel (1991) suggested that this design may be alternatively conceived as a three-factor design, with the factors being Factor A, Factor B, and Subject. The latter is to be regarded as a random factor, the former two as fixed. Keppel pointed out that, when conceived this way, the ANOVA source column would look as follows (see Keppel, p. 371):

Source
FACTA
SUBJ/FACTA
FACTB
FACTA × FACTB
FACTB × SUBJ/FACTA

In this layout, 'SUBJ/FACTA' (the slash means "within") is the error term for Factor A, whereas 'FACTB × SUBJ/FACTA' is the error term for both Factor B and the Factor A × Factor B interaction. This suggests that, if the data from Fig. 11.12 were entered in the alternate one-line-per-level setup (see Fig. 11.13), the syntax would be as in Fig. 11.14.

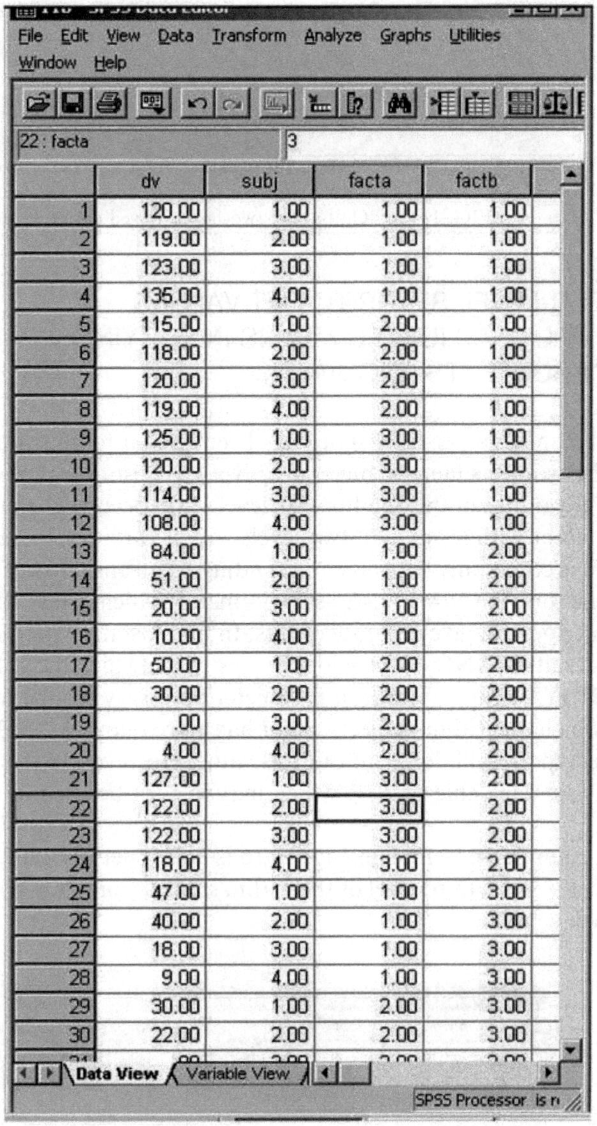

	dv	subj	facta	factb
1	120.00	1.00	1.00	1.00
2	119.00	2.00	1.00	1.00
3	123.00	3.00	1.00	1.00
4	135.00	4.00	1.00	1.00
5	115.00	1.00	2.00	1.00
6	118.00	2.00	2.00	1.00
7	120.00	3.00	2.00	1.00
8	119.00	4.00	2.00	1.00
9	125.00	1.00	3.00	1.00
10	120.00	2.00	3.00	1.00
11	114.00	3.00	3.00	1.00
12	108.00	4.00	3.00	1.00
13	84.00	1.00	1.00	2.00
14	51.00	2.00	1.00	2.00
15	20.00	3.00	1.00	2.00
16	10.00	4.00	1.00	2.00
17	50.00	1.00	2.00	2.00
18	30.00	2.00	2.00	2.00
19	.00	3.00	2.00	2.00
20	4.00	4.00	2.00	2.00
21	127.00	1.00	3.00	2.00
22	122.00	2.00	3.00	2.00
23	122.00	3.00	3.00	2.00
24	118.00	4.00	3.00	2.00
25	47.00	1.00	1.00	3.00
26	40.00	2.00	1.00	3.00
27	18.00	3.00	1.00	3.00
28	9.00	4.00	1.00	3.00
29	30.00	1.00	2.00	3.00
30	22.00	2.00	2.00	3.00

FIG. 11.13. The alternative, one-line-per-level setup for the data in Fig. 11.12.

```
1.   MANOVA dv BY subj(1,4) facta(1,3) factb(1,4)
2o.   /OMEANS=TABLES (facta, factb, facta*factb)
3.    /DESIGN=facta VS 1, subj WITHIN facta=1,
4.     factb VS 2, facta BY factb VS 2, factb BY subj WITHIN facta=2.
```

FIG. 11.14. Syntax commands for two-factor mixed design in one-line-per-level setup.

This syntax informs MANOVA that the Factor A effect is to be tested against error term number 1, which is 'subj WITHIN facta', whereas the Factor B effect and the interaction should both be tested against special error term 2, which is 'factb BY subj WITHIN facta'. The results, in Fig. 11.15, are far different in format, but identical in numeric value to the regular setup and syntax, which were presented previously in Fig. 8.3.

```
Tests of Significance for DV using UNIQUE sums of squares
  Source of Variation          SS      DF        MS         F   Sig of F

  Error 1                   3976.63     9      441.85
  FACTA                    62107.29     2    31053.65     70.28    .000
- - - - - - - - - - - - - - - - - - - - - - - - - - - - - - - - - - - - - - -
  Error 2                   4075.87    27      150.96
  FACTB                    36962.42     3    12320.81     81.62    .000
  FACTA BY FACTB           23905.71     6     3984.28     26.39    .000
```

FIG. 11.15.   Output for two-factor mixed design in one-line-per-level setup.

USING ONE-LINE-PER-LEVEL SETUP TO GET VALUES TO MANUALLY COMPUTE ADJUSTED MEANS IN VARYING COVARIATE WITHIN-SUBJECTS ANCOVA

So far, the one-line-per-level setup has been shown to be simply an alternative method of dealing with within-subjects factors, but probably a less desirable method, because it is a bit more difficult. The real advantage of the one-line-per-level setup occurs when using ANCOVA to analyze a within-subjects factor with more than two levels with a varying covariate. In ANCOVA, as chapter 10 explained, it is commonly desirable to get adjusted means. However, in the case of designs with within-subjects factors, the "PMEANS" subcommand, which will yield adjusted means in between-subjects situations, does not give accurate results. In that instance, manual calculations need to be completed with the results MANOVA provides. In designs in which the within-subjects factor has only two levels, MANOVA prints out B_{WS}, a parameter necessary for the manual calculations. However, in designs in which the within-subjects factor has more than two levels, MANOVA in its normal one-line-per-subject mode will not print out this value. However, in the one-line-per-level setup, MANOVA will print out the value of B_{WS}, which may in turn be used in the manual calculations of adjusted means.

For example, presented in Fig. 11.16 is a data set (modified by adding to the data on p. 833 of Winer et al., 1991 a third level of the within subjects and its accompanying covariate) in the one-line-per-subject setup.

	cv1	dv1	cv2	dv2	cv3	dv3	facta
1	3.00	8.00	4.00	14.00	4.00	6.00	1.00
2	5.00	11.00	9.00	18.00	6.00	5.00	1.00
3	11.00	16.00	14.00	22.00	7.00	7.00	1.00
4	2.00	6.00	1.00	8.00	2.00	11.00	2.00
5	8.00	12.00	9.00	14.00	9.00	14.00	2.00
6	10.00	9.00	9.00	10.00	5.00	12.00	2.00
7	7.00	10.00	4.00	10.00	7.00	5.00	3.00
8	8.00	14.00	10.00	18.00	3.00	8.00	3.00
9	9.00	15.00	12.00	22.00	9.00	7.00	3.00

FIG. 11.16.   Data in a one-line-per-subject setup for an ANCOVA with a varying covariate in which the within-subjects factor has more than two levels. From *Statistical Principles in Experiment Design* (3rd ed., p. 833), by B. J. Winer, D. R. Brown, and K. M. Michels, 1991, New York: McGraw-Hill. Copyright 1991 by McGraw-Hill. Adapated with permission.

Note that there are three levels of the within-subjects factor 'factb' (dv1, dv2, dv3), each with a varying covariate (cv1, cv2, cv3), and three levels of Factor A, a between-subjects factor. The syntax in Fig. 11.17 would analyze the design as specified in chapter 10.

```
1.  MANOVA dv1 dv2 dv3 BY facta(1,3) WITH cv1 cv2 cv3
2.     /WSFACTOR=factb(3)
3.     /OMEANS
4.     /DESIGN.
```

FIG. 11.17. Syntax commands for a one-line-per-subject setup for an ANCOVA with a varying covariate in which the within-subjects factor has more than two levels.

This would yield the "B" coefficient for between subjects, B_{BS}, but not the "B" coefficient for within subjects, B_{WS}; both are necessary to compute the adjusted means. However, the alternate one-line-per-level setup for the preceding data, shown in Fig. 11.18, can get both "B" coefficients.

ancova mixed varying cv one line per level setup - SPSS D...

	cv	dv	facta	factb	subj
1	3.00	8.00	1.00	1.00	1.00
2	5.00	11.00	1.00	1.00	2.00
3	11.00	16.00	1.00	1.00	3.00
4	2.00	6.00	2.00	1.00	1.00
5	8.00	12.00	2.00	1.00	2.00
6	10.00	9.00	2.00	1.00	3.00
7	7.00	10.00	3.00	1.00	1.00
8	8.00	14.00	3.00	1.00	2.00
9	9.00	15.00	3.00	1.00	3.00
10	4.00	14.00	1.00	2.00	1.00
11	9.00	18.00	1.00	2.00	2.00
12	14.00	22.00	1.00	2.00	3.00
13	1.00	8.00	2.00	2.00	1.00
14	9.00	14.00	2.00	2.00	2.00
15	9.00	10.00	2.00	2.00	3.00
16	4.00	10.00	3.00	2.00	1.00
17	10.00	18.00	3.00	2.00	2.00
18	12.00	22.00	3.00	2.00	3.00
19	4.00	6.00	1.00	3.00	1.00
20	6.00	5.00	1.00	3.00	2.00
21	7.00	7.00	1.00	3.00	3.00
22	2.00	11.00	2.00	3.00	1.00
23	9.00	14.00	2.00	3.00	2.00
24	5.00	12.00	2.00	3.00	3.00
25	7.00	5.00	3.00	3.00	1.00
26	3.00	8.00	3.00	3.00	2.00
27	9.00	7.00	3.00	3.00	3.00

FIG. 11.18. Data from Fig. 11.16 in a one-line-per-level setup for an ANCOVA with a varying covariate in which the within-subjects factor has more than two levels.

The syntax for such an analysis is in Fig. 11.19.

```
1.   MANOVA dv BY subj(1,3) facta(1,3) factb(1,3) WITH cv
2o.    /OMEANS=TABLES(CONSTANT, facta, factb, facta *factb)
3.     /DESIGN=facta VS 1, subj WITHIN facta=1, factb VS 2,
4.       facta BY factb vs 2, factb BY subj WITHIN facta=2.
```

FIG. 11.19. Syntax commands for the one-line-per-level setup for an ANCOVA with a varying covariate in which the within-subjects factor has more than two levels.

Note that the syntax looks very similar to that of Fig. 11.14. The primary difference (besides the different number of levels) is the inclusion of 'WITH cv' on line 1 and the inclusion of "CONSTANT" on the "OMEANS" subcommand in line 2. Recalling that the formula for the adjusted means is

$$\overline{Y}_{AB}' = \overline{Y}_{AB} - B_{BS}(\overline{X}_A - \overline{X}_T) - B_{WS}(\overline{X}_{AB} - \overline{X}_A)$$

the "CONSTANT" specification causes MANOVA to print out $\overline{X}_T$. In Fig. 11.20 is the printout, edited to retain only the results of interest here.

```
Combined Observed Grand Means
   Variable .. CV
        GMEAN
                    WGT.      6.92593
- - - - - - - - - - - - - - - - - - - - - - - - - - - - -
   Variable .. CV
      FACTA
         1          WGT.      7.00000
         2          WGT.      6.11111
         3          WGT.      7.66667
- - - - - - - - - - - - - - - - - - - - - - - - - - - - -
Combined Observed Means for FACTA BY FACTB
  Variable .. DV
                    FACTA         1           2           3
        FACTB
          1         WGT.     11.66667     9.00000    13.00000
          2         WGT.     18.00000    10.66667    16.66667
          3         WGT.      6.00000    12.33333     6.66667
- - - - - - - - - - - - - - - - - - - - - - - - - - - - -
  Variable .. CV
                    FACTA         1           2           3
        FACTB
          1         WGT.      6.33333     6.66667     8.00000
          2         WGT.      9.00000     6.33333     8.66667
          3         WGT.      5.66667     5.33333     6.33333
- - - - - - - - - - - - - - - - - - - - - - - - - - - - -

Tests of Significance for DV using UNIQUE sums of squares
  Source of Variation         SS       DF        MS        F   Sig of F

  Error 1                   44.54       5       8.91
  REGRESSION               109.90       1     109.90    12.34    .017
  FACTA                      1.32       2        .66      .07    .930
- - - - - - - - - - - - - - - - - - - - - - - - - - - - -
  Error 2                   30.06      11       2.73
  REGRESSION                16.83       1      16.83     6.16    .031
  FACTB                    103.00       2      51.50    18.85    .000
  FACTB BY FACTA           150.40       4      37.60    13.76    .000
- - - - - - - - - - - - - - - - - - - - - - - - - - - - -
Regression analysis for Error 1 error term
--- Individual Univariate .9500 confidence intervals
Dependent variable .. DV

COVARIATE               B        Beta    Std. Err.   t-Value   Sig. of t
CV                  .76143     .52799        .217     3.512        .017

COVARIATE     Lower -95%  CL- Upper
CV                  .204       1.319
- - - - - - - - - - - - - - - - - - - - - - - - - - - - -
Regression analysis for Error 2 error term
--- Individual Univariate .9500 confidence intervals
Dependent variable .. DV

COVARIATE               B        Beta    Std. Err.   t-Value   Sig. of t
CV                  .54280     .37639        .219     2.481        .031

COVARIATE     Lower -95%  CL- Upper
CV                  .061       1.024
```

FIG. 11.20.   Output for the one-line-per-level setup for an ANCOVA with a varying covariate in which the within-subjects factor has more than two levels.

Based on the printout, you find that $B_{BS} = .76143$ (listed as the "B" in the "Error 1 error term" section) and $B_{WS} = .54280$ (listed as the "B" in the "Error 2 error term" section). You also obtain the cell means for the dependent variable and cell and marginal means for the covariate (see Table 11.1).

TABLE 11.1
Means for the Dependent Variable and Covariate

| | Dependent Variable | | | Covariate | | | |
	b1	b2	b3	b1	b2	b3	Average
facta1	11.667	18.000	6.000	6.333	9.000	5.667	7.000
facta2	9.000	10.667	12.333	6.667	6.333	5.333	6.111
facta3	13.000	16.667	6.667	8.000	8.667	6.333	7.667
Average							6.926

The adjusted cell means, with the adjusted marginal means (computed as the average of the relevant adjusted cell means) are in Table 11.2. For example, the upper left cell can be found by:

$$\overline{Y}'_{AB} = \overline{Y}_{AB} - B_{BS}(\overline{X}_A - \overline{X}_T) - B_{WS}(\overline{X}_{AB} - \overline{X}_A)$$
$$= 11.667 - .76143(7 - 6.926) - .5428(6.333 - 7) = 11.973.$$

TABLE 11.2
Adjusted Means Hand Calculated for an ANCOVA Using the One-Line-per-Level Setup

	b1	b2	b3	Average
facta1	11.973	16.858	6.667	11.833
facta2	9.319	11.167	13.376	11.287
facta3	12.255	15.560	6.827	11.547
Average	11.182	14.528	8.957	11.556

PAC

Designs with random factors, including nested designs, are run from the General Linear Model–Univariate menu (see Fig. 3.15). For a random, non-nested factor it is necessary to do two computer runs to get the correct significance tests for all the effects. Using the data that generated Fig. 11.1 (where FACTA is fixed and FACTB is random), to get the correct results for Factor A and the interaction, after sending FACTA to the Fixed factor(s) box and FACTB to the Random factor(s) box, click Ok. You will see that the F for FACTA is .595 and the F for the interaction is 1.921 (the same results you obtained in Fig. 11.1). To obtain the correct results for Factor B (if you need it, since this effect is usually not of interest), rerun the analysis, but specify both factors as fixed. The F's for FACTB (1.666) and the interaction (1.921) are correct.

For a nested factors design, send the nested factor to the Random factor(s) box (here Factor B is nested in Factor A). In order to obtain the correct significance tests, you have to tell SPSS which effects are in the design. To do this, in the Univariate screen (seen in Fig. 3.15), click on the Model button at the top right-hand corner. A screen like the one in Fig. 11.21 will pop up.

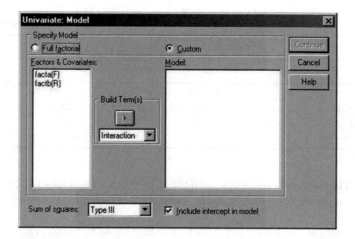

FIG. 11.21.   Dialogue box to change from Full factorial to Custom error term.

When the screen pops up, the Full factorial button will be highlighted. For nested designs like Fig. 11.2, change that to Custom.

By default, the Factor A, Factor B, and interaction effects are included and, because you do not want the Factor B effect, you need to tell this to SPSS. To do this, highlight the 'facta' and send it over to the Model box. You also want the 'B/A' effect, which SPSS will by default label as the 'facta*factb' effect in the output; to obtain it, highlight 'facta' and 'factb' together (highlight 'facta' and, while holding down the Shift key, select 'factb'). Your box should look like the one in Fig. 11.22.

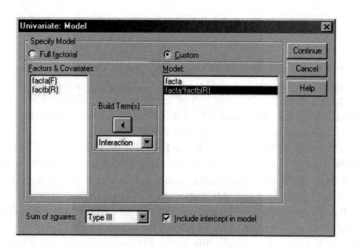

FIG. 11.22.   Dialogue box with the Custom model set.

You can now hit Continue and then OK. As long as you have specified the correct model, SPSS automatically uses the correct error term. If you had hit the Paste button before running, you would see that the "DESIGN" specification was 'DESIGN = facta, facta*factb'. To increase the readability of the output, you could also rewrite the pasted "DESIGN" statement so that it reads 'DESIGN = facta, factb(facta)', which would make it more clear that Factor B is nested within Factor A. For more complex designs, there is some doubt as to whether GLM produces the correct results, so caution is advised. Do not attempt within-subjects designs in which the within-subjects factor is random from PAC GLM.

12   Multivariate Analysis of Variance: Designs With Multiple Dependent Variables Tested Simultaneously

In all of the previous chapters in this book, the examples involved only a single dependent variable. In this chapter, analyses that have more than one dependent variable are considered; such analyses are termed *multivariate*, whereas tests involving but a single dependent variable will here be called *univariate*. An analysis is only considered multivariate when multiple dependent variables are analyzed simultaneously. Although it is possible to analyze the multiple dependent variables univariately, that is, one at a time (say, with multiple sets of "MANOVA" commands), it is far more efficient to analyze all the dependent variables multivariately, that is, all at once. Doing this allows you to test with a single test (the multivariate ANOVA or MANOVA), whether the groups differ on the entire set of dependent variables taken together. Fortunately, MANOVA and GLM also automatically provide each of the univariate tests as well, the ones evaluating whether each specific dependent variable is significant.

Besides being more efficient, there is a more important reason to test all the dependent variables simultaneously. Conducting only the univariate tests could result in a large number of tests, which in turn leads to the possibility of alpha inflation, discussed initially in chapter 3. In essence, with a large number of tests, the chance that any one (or more) of them is significant by chance alone is higher than the alpha you set and desire. The solution for the multiple dependent variables case is to conduct only one test (at least, initially), a multivariate one that tests all the dependent variables at once. The multivariate analysis of variance takes into account not only how many dependent variables you are testing simultaneously (the more dependent variables, the greater the tendency for alpha inflation, so the greater correction MANOVA provides), but also how correlated the various dependent variables are in the analysis (the more uncorrelated the dependent variables are, the greater the chance for alpha inflation, so MANOVA again provides more correction). The present chapter also includes the method of analyzing within-subject designs with multiple dependent variables. Within-subjects designs with multiple dependent variables are commonly called *doubly multivariate* designs.

BASIC ANALYSIS OF VARIANCE COMMANDS

Figure 12.1 shows the data for an example of a multivariate design for a study with three different measures of aggression ('dep1', 'dep2', and 'dep3'), looking at differences across first-, third-, and fifth-grade children (thus there are three dependent variables and one between-subjects factor with three levels).

a1: First grade			a2: Third grade			a3: Fifth grade		
dep1	dep2	dep3	dep1	dep2	dep3	dep1	dep2	dep3
2	2	8	4	6	10	8	6	10
3	4	8	5	6	12	7	8	12
2	4	9	6	7	12	9	8	14
5	5	11	7	8	13	10	9	13

FIG. 12.1.   Data for a multivariate analysis of variance with three dependent viarables (Dep) and one three-level between-subjects factor.

The syntax, presented in Fig. 12.2, is followed by an explanation of the function of the different commands in the program.

```
1.    MANOVA dep1 dep2 dep3 BY facta(1,3)

2d.   /OMEANS

3d.   /POWER

4d.   /PRINT=SIGNIF(EFSIZE) HOMO CELLINFO(COR) ERROR(COR)

5o.   /DESIGN.
```

FIG. 12.2.   Syntax commands to conduct a multivariate ANOVA.

The main command for the multivariate ANOVA appears similar to that for a mixed design. Start with the "MANOVA" command and follow it with the names of each of the dependent variables, which are followed in turn by the keyword "BY" and then by the between-subjects factors. In this case, there are three dependent variables, so there are three scores named on the "MANOVA" command. The difference between a multivariate and mixed design is that, in a basic multivariate design, there is no "WSFACTORS" subcommand. As in other designs, line 2 requests the observed means and in lines 3 and 4 effect size and power analyses have been requested, as has a test of homogeneity of variance. Two new keywords also appear on line 4, namely "CELLINFO(COR)" and "ERROR(COR)", whose output will be explained later. Line 5 is optional because it is the default. The output from this analysis is in Fig. 12.3.

```
Cell Means and Standard Deviations
 Variable .. DEP1
         FACTOR           CODE              Mean   Std. Dev.            N

 FACTA                    1                 3.000    1.414              4
 FACTA                    2                 5.500    1.291              4
 FACTA                    3                 8.500    1.291              4
 For entire sample                          5.667    2.640             12
 - - - - - - - - - - - - - - - - - - - - - - - - - - - - - - - - - - - -
 Variable .. DEP2
         FACTOR           CODE              Mean   Std. Dev.            N

 FACTA                    1                 3.750    1.258              4
 FACTA                    2                 6.750     .957              4
 FACTA                    3                 7.750    1.258              4
 For entire sample                          6.083    2.065             12
 - - - - - - - - - - - - - - - - - - - - - - - - - - - - - - - - - - - -
 Variable .. DEP3
         FACTOR           CODE              Mean   Std. Dev.            N

 FACTA                    1                 9.000    1.414              4
 FACTA                    2                11.750    1.258              4
 FACTA                    3                12.250    1.708              4
 For entire sample                         11.000    2.000             12
 - - - - - - - - - - - - - - - - - - - - - - - - - - - - - - - - - - - -
```

FIG. 12.3.   (Continues)

```
Univariate Homogeneity of Variance Tests

Variable .. DEP1

      Cochrans C(3,3) =                           .37500, P = 1.000 (approx.)
      Bartlett-Box F(2,182) =                     .01462, P =  .985

Variable .. DEP2

      Cochrans C(3,3) =                           .38776, P = 1.000 (approx.)
      Bartlett-Box F(2,182) =                     .12033, P =  .887

Variable .. DEP3

      Cochrans C(3,3) =                           .44872, P =  .839 (approx.)
      Bartlett-Box F(2,182) =                     .12500, P =  .883
- - - - - - - - - - - - - - - - - - - - - - - - - - - - - - - - - - - - - -
Cell Number .. 1
Correlation matrix with Standard Deviations on Diagonal

              DEP1        DEP2        DEP3

DEP1         1.414
DEP2          .749       1.258
DEP3          .833        .749       1.414

Determinant of Covariance matrix of dependent variables =         .75000
LOG(Determinant) =                                               -.28768
- - - - - - - - -
Cell Number .. 2
Correlation matrix with Standard Deviations on Diagonal

              DEP1        DEP2        DEP3

DEP1         1.291
DEP2          .944        .957
DEP3          .923        .761       1.258

Determinant of Covariance matrix of dependent variables =         .00926
LOG(Determinant) =                                              -4.68213
- - - - - - - - - -
Cell Number .. 3
Correlation matrix with Standard Deviations on Diagonal

              DEP1        DEP2        DEP3

DEP1         1.291
DEP2          .513       1.258
DEP3          .529        .814       1.708

Determinant of Covariance matrix of dependent variables =        1.81481
LOG(Determinant) =                                                .59598
- - - - - - - - - -
Determinant of pooled Covariance matrix of dependent vars. =      .84739
LOG(Determinant) =                                               -.16559
- - - - - - - - - - - - - - - - - - - - - - - - - - - - - - - - - - - - - -
Multivariate test for Homogeneity of Dispersion matrices

Boxs M =                        11.63118
F WITH (12,392) DF =                 .47295, P =   .930 (Approx.)
Chi-Square with 12 DF =             6.03098, P =   .915 (Approx.)
- - - - - - - - - - - - - - - - - - - - - - - - - - - - - - - - - - - - - -
WITHIN CELLS Correlations with Std. Devs. on Diagonal

              DEP1        DEP2        DEP3

DEP1         1.333
DEP2          .714       1.167
DEP3          .736        .776       1.472
- - - - - - - - - - - - - - - - - - - - - - - - - - - - - - - - - - - - - -
Statistics for WITHIN CELLS correlations

Log(Determinant) =              -1.82245
Bartlett test of sphericity =   13.06086 with 3 D. F.
Significance =                     .005

F(max) criterion =               1.59184 with (3,9) D. F.
- - - - - - - - - - - - - - - - - - - - - - - - - - - - - - - - - - - - - -
EFFECT .. FACTA
Multivariate Tests of Significance (S = 2, M = 0, N = 2 1/2)

Test Name       Value  Approx. F Hypoth. DF   Error DF  Sig. of F

Pillais        1.24437   4.39149      6.00      16.00      .008
Hotellings     5.40928   5.40928      6.00      12.00      .006
Wilks           .10198   4.97320      6.00      14.00      .006
Roys            .82408
Note.. F statistic for WILKS' Lambda is exact.
- - - - - - - - - - - - - - - - - - - - - - - - - - - - - - - - - - - - - -
```

FIG. 12.3.   *(Continues)*

```
Multivariate Effect Size and Observed Power at .0500 Level

TEST NAME      Effect Size    Noncent.        Power

Pillais                .622      26.349            .91
Hotellings             .730      32.456            .94
Wilks                  .681      29.839            .93
- - - - - - - - - - - - - - - - - - - - - - - - - - - - - - - -
EFFECT .. FACTA (Cont.)
Univariate F-tests with (2,9) D. F.

Variable   Hypoth. SS   Error SS  Hypoth. MS   Error MS        F  Sig. of F

DEP1         60.66667   16.00000   30.33333    1.77778  17.06250      .001
DEP2         34.66667   12.25000   17.33333    1.36111  12.73469      .002
DEP3         24.50000   19.50000   12.25000    2.16667   5.65385      .026


Variable   ETA Square    Noncent.       Power

DEP1          .79130    34.12500      .99439
DEP2          .73890    25.46939      .97168
DEP3          .55682    11.30769      .71651
```

FIG. 12.3.   Output from a multivariate ANOVA.

The means, standard deviations, and Ns for each dependent variable are printed out first for each level of Factor A, in response to the "OMEANS" subcommand. This is followed by the output called for by the "HOMO" specification. In true MANOVA cases (i.e., those in which multiple dependent variables are named on the main command), the keyword "HOMO" without any specifications will automatically generate both the univariate and the multivariate tests of this assumption. The univariate tests were described in chapter 3; there will be one test for each dependent variable. It is generally desirable that these tests be nonsignificant. In this case, all three tests are nonsignificant, with p values of .985, .887, and .883 (by the Bartlett-Box criterion), all comfortably above .05. Next comes the printout that culminates in the multivariate test of homogeneity. This multivariate analog of the univariate test evaluates the equivalence or homogeneity of the variance-covariance matrices over the three cells.

To show what this test is evaluating, the optional "CELLINFO" keyword is included. Although the variance-covariance matrices themselves were not requested (you would add "COV" to the specification for "CELLINFO" in line 4 to obtain these), the closely related (and perhaps more interpretable) correlation matrixes were requested (with the "CELLINFO" specification "COR"). For cell 1 (i.e., Group 1, first graders), for example, the correlation between "DEP1" and "DEP2" is .749; for cell 2, the same correlation is .944; for cell 3, it is .513. Along the diagonals of each matrix are the cells' standard deviations for that dependent variable. For example, in cell 2, the standard deviation for "DEP2" is .957; this value was also displayed in the earlier means printout. Immediately after the correlation matrix printout is the "Determinant of the Covariance matrix" and the "LOG" of that determinant; these values are not informative by themselves, but are used for the multivariate homogeneity test. Then you get the "Determinant of the pooled Covariance matrix" and its "LOG" (also used for the multivariate test) and, finally, the test itself, the Box's M test, which evaluates whether these three matrices (more accurately, the three variance-covariance matrices to which the correlation matrices are closely related) are similar versus significantly different from one another (i.e., homogeneous vs. heterogeneous). The larger the value of Box's M, the more heterogeneity that is present. Box's M may be tested either with an F or a chi-square statistic. Fortunately, they come out nearly identical, with both p values near .92, nonsignificant, which is desirable and suggests that the multivariate homogeneity assumption is likely not violated, so that the main test may proceed.

Next comes the "WITHIN CELLS", or pooled or error, correlation matrix, obtained because of the "PRINT" request "ERROR(COR)". This matrix shows how the dependent variables intercorrelate on average over the three cells. For example, the pooled (over the three cells) correlation of "DEP1" with "DEP2" is .714. The next segment of printout (which was omitted here) presents the test of sphericity, which is unimportant in true multivariate situations and should be ignored (it is important in within-subjects designs, as was discussed in chap. 6).

Next come the main tests of whether the means of the three groups are significantly different. First come the multivariate F tests. Here you are testing whether there is a significant effect of Factor

A across the set of the dependent variables. The four multivariate tests reported (i.e., Pillai's, Hotelling's, Wilks', and Roy's) each approach the analysis from somewhat different perspectives, but in most cases will give similar answers. You can see that, by all of the tests, the multivariate test is significant (all p values are near .007). Most APA journals will accept any one of the variants. If you were choosing to report the Hotelling's criterion, for example, the language might be: "The multivariate test is significant by Hotelling's criterion, $F(6, 12) = 5.41$, $p = .006$". APA (2001) also suggested reporting the variance-covariance matrix along with the cell means and Ns. The multivariate effect size and power statistics are given in the next portion of the printout.

After the multivariate tests come the univariate tests, that is, the tests of whether there is an effect of Factor A on each dependent variable taken one at a time. Although the format of output is slightly different from what was described in earlier chapters, these tests come out identically to what you would have obtained if that dependent variable was the only one named on the "MANOVA" command. For example, for "DEP2", the effect of Factor A is significant, $F(2, 9) = 12.73$, $p = .002$. Finally, you also obtain the univariate (i.e., one dependent variable at a time) effect size and power values, in response to the "POWER" and "PRINT=SIGNIF(EFSIZE)" specifications.

One common convention when there are multiple dependent variables is to examine the multivariate test first. If and only if this test is significant do you have permission to examine the univariate results. It is not uncommon for one or more univariate results to be significant while the multivariate test is not. According to the preceding convention, the univariate results in this instance should be ignored and not reported. Once you have a significant multivariate effect, however, examination of which dependent variables discriminate between the groups is permitted.

MANOVA contains a number of easily obtained optional coefficients that aid the advanced user in understanding the relationship between the factors and the set of dependent variables.[1] Probing of this multivariate effect can be across groups or across variables. There is no agreed-upon order with respect to whether you should examine first which variables all the groups differ on (i.e., the univariate tests) versus which groups differ on the set of variables (i.e., multivariate planned contrasts), so your next step should depend on your theoretical question. If you are looking across variables, you simply report which univariate tests from the main analysis are significant (see Fig. 12.3). An alternative is to examine across groups rather than by variables. Thus, you can ask how the groups differ in multivariate space (i.e., on the set of variables). In other words, you could perform multivariate planned contrasts.

MULTIVARIATE PLANNED CONTRASTS AND POST HOCS

All of the syntax learned in previous chapters to test planned contrasts or post hocs generalizes to the multivariate design. For example, if you are interested in the difference between the first and third levels of Factor A in multivariate space, the syntax would be as follows:

```
MANOVA dep1 dep2 dep3 BY facta(1,3)
    /CONTRAST(facta)=SPECIAL(1 1 1, 1 0 –1, 1 –2 1)
    /DESIGN=facta(1), facta(2).
```

If you only wanted to answer the question of whether there is a difference between the first and third levels of Factor A for the first dependent variable, you would simply ignore the multivariate output from the preceding syntax and look at the univariate output for "DEP1". You could even suppress all the multivariate output with the following subcommand:

```
/NOPRINT=SIGNIF(MULTIV)
```

---

[1]These include Dimension Reduction Analysis and the Roy-Bargman Stepdown Fs—obtain both, for example, with "PRINT=SIGNIF(DIMENR STEPDOWN)")—or the various discriminant printouts—both raw and standardized can be obtained with "DISCRIM(RAW, STAN)", for example. Explanation of the meaning of these coefficients and how they may be used in interpretation of multivariate ANOVA is beyond the scope of this book, but consult Harris (2001), Stevens (2002), or Tabachnik and Fidell (2000), for example, for further information.

One caveat in reading the output is to always make sure you are reading the *F* tests for the effect of interest (SPSS sometimes provides the output for the second contrast before the first).

EXTENSION TO FACTORIAL BETWEEN-SUBJECTS DESIGNS

All of the previous syntax can be expanded to designs that include more than one between-subjects factor by using the syntax appropriate for that design (for example, including more than one factor name after the "BY"). In a factorial multivariate design you would get multivariate and univariate tests for each main effect, as well as for each interaction effect. If you requested specialized tests with "DESIGN" specifications, such as simple interactions or simple simple comparisons, these would generally emerge in both multivariate and univariate form.

MULTIPLE DEPENDENT VARIABLES IN WITHIN-SUBJECT DESIGNS: DOUBLY MULTIVARIATE DESIGNS

A design with both multiple dependent variables and within-subjects factors is said to be doubly multivariate. An example of such a design would be if the researchers discussed earlier collected two of the aggression measures used earlier (i.e., dep1 and dep2), at three times, for example, at the beginning, middle, and end of the school year. Thus, they would have two aggression measures at Time 1, two aggression measures at Time 2, and two aggression measures at Time 3. To distinguish which time the dependent variable is measured at, you need to lengthen the variable names so that they simultaneously reflect which dependent variable it is and when it is measured. Thus, for example, 'dep2t3' refers to dependent variable number 2, measured at Time 3. Note that this means there are six different variables to be named on the "MANOVA" command before the "BY" (two dependent variables times three measurement points or levels of the within-subjects factor). For the example, assume there is still one between-subjects factor of grade level (first, third, or fifth). The question of interest now becomes whether the groups differ over time on the set of dependent variables. Hypothetical data for such a problem are in Fig. 12.4 and the syntax is in Fig. 12.5.

a1: First Grade			a2: Third Grade			a3: Fifth Grade		
			Dependent Variable 1					
Time 1	Time 2	Time 3	Time 1	Time 2	Time 3	Time 1	Time 2	Time 3
dep1t1	dep1t2	dep1t3	dep1t1	dep1t2	dep1t3	dep1t1	dep1t2	dep1t3
1	4	5	3	8	3	7	7	9
4	4	4	4	6	4	9	8	1
3	5	6	7	6	5	8	8	6
2	5	4	8	6	7	7	6	4
			Dependent Variable 2					
Time 1	Time 2	Time 3	Time 1	Time 2	Time 3	Time 1	Time 2	Time 3
dep2t1	dep2t2	dep2t3	dep2t1	dep2t2	dep2t3	dep2t1	dep2t2	dep2t3
3	3	3	5	7	6	5	4	5
3	4	4	6	7	6	6	5	6
5	5	5	9	9	8	6	6	8
5	5	6	10	8	10	7	7	7

FIG. 12.4.   Data for a doubly multivariate ANOVA.

```
1.    MANOVA dep1t1 dep1t2 dep1t3 dep2t1 dep2t2 dep2t3 BY facta(1,3)

2.       /WSFACTORS=factb(3)

3d.      /OMEANS

4.       /MEASURE=dep1 dep2

5.       /PRINT=SIGNIF(UNIV AVERF).
```

FIG. 12.5. Syntax commands to conduct a doubly multivariate ANOVA.

On line 1, all of the names of the first dependent variable should be listed first, the second dependent variable next, and so on, before the "BY". On line 2, the name of the within-subjects factor is given; here it is called 'factb' and you tell MANOVA that there are three levels (each person is measured at the beginning, middle, and end of the school year). You could have multiple within-subjects factors, as well as multiple between-subjects factors. Line 3 is optional. In line 4, a new subcommand, "MEASURES", is introduced. In this subcommand, you are specifying that you have two distinct true dependent variables or measures, to which you are assigning the names 'dep1' and 'dep2', respectively (as always, these names should be chosen so as to be mnemonic). In line 5, you are requesting both the univariate or measure-by-measure printout ("UNIV"), as well as the univariate or averaged F approach ("AVERF") to testing the within-subjects factor (see chap. 6). As you will observe, without additional specification, MANOVA will also conduct the doubly multivariate tests. However, it does not readily simultaneously provide separate tests for each dependent variable of main effects or interactions of the within-subjects factor using the multivariate approach. To obtain these tests, it is easiest to simply write additional "MANOVA" commands with just one set of the dependent variables, leaving off the other set(s).

The doubly multivariate significance test output produced by the preceding syntax is in Fig. 12.6. Because the printout is complicated, its various sections are identified by a boxed number for ease of reference. Although homogeneity of variance tests were not requested here, they should be an important first step in identifying problems. To obtain sphericity tests, it would be necessary to run a "MANOVA" on one set of dependent variables at a time.

```
EFFECT .. FACTA
Multivariate Tests of Significance (S = 2, M = -1/2, N = 3 )

Test Name        Value  Approx. F Hypoth. DF   Error DF  Sig. of F      ┌───┐
                                                                        │ 1 │
Pillais        1.19025   6.61455      4.00      18.00      .002         └───┘
Hotellings     3.11534   5.45185      4.00      14.00      .007
Wilks           .15830   6.05361      4.00      16.00      .004
Roys            .67013
Note.. F statistic for WILKS' Lambda is exact.
- - - - - - - - - - - - - - - - - - - - - - - - - - - - - - - - - - - -
EFFECT .. FACTA (Cont.)                                                 ┌───┐
Univariate F-tests with (2,9) D. F.                                     │ 2 │
                                                                        └───┘
Variable   Hypoth. SS   Error SS Hypoth. MS    Error MS       F  Sig. of F

T1           46.05556   23.16667   23.02778     2.57407  8.94604    .007
T4           66.72222   45.83333   33.36111     5.09259  6.55091    .018
- - - - - - - - - - - - - - - - - - - - - - - - - - - - - - - - - - - -
EFFECT .. CONSTANT
Multivariate Tests of Significance (S = 1, M = 0, N = 3 )               ┌───┐
                                                                        │ 3 │
Test Name        Value   Exact F Hypoth. DF   Error DF  Sig. of F       └───┘

Pillais         .98099 206.41441      2.00       8.00      .000
Hotellings    51.60360 206.41441      2.00       8.00      .000
Wilks           .01901 206.41441      2.00       8.00      .000
Roys            .98099
Note.. F statistics are exact.
```

FIG. 12.6. *(Continues)*

```
- - - - - - - - - - - - - - - - - - - - - - - - - - - - - - - - - - - - - -
EFFECT .. CONSTANT (Cont.)                                           ┌─────┐
Univariate F-tests with (1,9) D. F.                                  │  4  │
                                                                     └─────┘
Variable   Hypoth. SS    Error SS Hypoth. MS   Error MS        F  Sig. of F

T1         1045.44444   23.16667 1045.44444    2.57407  406.14388      .000
T4         1272.11111   45.83333 1272.11111    5.09259  249.79636      .000
- - - - - - - - - - - - - - - - - - - - - - - - - - - - - - - - - - - - - -
Tests involving 'FACTB' Within-Subject Effect.

EFFECT .. FACTA BY FACTB
Multivariate Tests of Significance (S = 2, M = 1/2, N = 2 )         ┌─────┐
                                                                   │  5  │
                                                                   └─────┘
Test Name          Value  Approx. F Hypoth. DF   Error DF Sig. of F

Pillais           .69009    .92193       8.00       14.00     .527
Hotellings       1.20050    .75031       8.00       10.00     .651
Wilks             .40928    .84465       8.00       12.00     .583
Roys              .48534
Note.. F statistic for WILKS' Lambda is exact.
- - - - - - - - - - - - - - - - - - - - - - - - - - - - - - - - - - - - - -
EFFECT .. FACTA BY FACTB (Cont.)                                    ┌─────┐
Univariate F-tests with (2,9) D. F.                                │  6  │
                                                                   └─────┘
Variable   Hypoth. SS   Error SS Hypoth. MS   Error MS        F  Sig. of F

T2         25.33333    31.12500   12.66667    3.45833  3.66265      .069
T3           .44444    22.70833     .22222    2.52315   .08807      .916
T5           .33333     3.00000     .16667     .33333   .50000      .622
T6          1.44444     5.66667     .72222     .62963  1.14706      .360
- - - - - - - - - - - - - - - - - - - - - - - - - - - - - - - - - - - - - -
EFFECT .. FACTB
Multivariate Tests of Significance (S = 1, M = 1 , N = 2 )

Test Name          Value   Exact F Hypoth. DF   Error DF Sig. of F

Pillais           .46381   1.29749      4.00        6.00     .369      ┌─────┐
Hotellings        .86500   1.29749      4.00        6.00     .369      │  7  │
Wilks             .53619   1.29749      4.00        6.00     .369      └─────┘
Roys              .46381
Note.. F statistics are exact.
- - - - - - - - - - - - - - - - - - - - - - - - - - - - - - - - - - - - - -
EFFECT .. FACTB (Cont.)                                            ┌─────┐
Univariate F-tests with (1,9) D. F.                                │  8  │
                                                                   └─────┘
Variable   Hypoth. SS   Error SS Hypoth. MS   Error MS        F  Sig. of F

T2         1.04167     31.12500    1.04167    3.45833   .30120      .596
T3         8.68056     22.70833    8.68056    2.52315  3.44037      .097
T5          .66667      3.00000     .66667     .33333  2.00000      .191
T6          .22222      5.66667     .22222     .62963   .35294      .567
- - - - - - - - - - - - - - - - - - - - - - - - - - - - - - - - - - - - - -
Tests involving 'FACTB' Within-Subject Effect.                     ┌─────┐
                                                                   │  9  │
EFFECT .. FACTA BY FACTB                                           └─────┘
AVERAGED Multivariate Tests of Significance (S = 2, M = 1/2, N = 7 1/2)

Test Name          Value  Approx. F Hypoth. DF   Error DF Sig. of F

Pillais           .51574   1.56364      8.00       36.00     .170
Hotellings        .73443   1.46887      8.00       32.00     .207
Wilks             .54280   1.51857      8.00       34.00     .187
Roys              .34705
Note.. F statistic for WILKS' Lambda is exact.
- - - - - - - - - - - - - - - - - - - - - - - - - - - - - - - - - - - - - -
EFFECT .. FACTA BY FACTB (Cont.)                                  ┌─────┐
Univariate F-tests with (4,18) D. F.                              │ 10  │
                                                                  └─────┘
Variable   Hypoth. SS   Error SS Hypoth. MS   Error MS        F  Sig. of F

DEP1       25.77778    53.83333    6.44444    2.99074  2.15480      .116
DEP2        1.77778     8.66667     .44444     .48148   .92308      .472
- - - - - - - - - - - - - - - - - - - - - - - - - - - - - - - - - - - - - -
EFFECT .. FACTB                                                   ┌─────┐
AVERAGED Multivariate Tests of Significance (S = 2, M = -1/2, N = 7 1/2)│11 │
                                                                  └─────┘
Test Name          Value  Approx. F Hypoth. DF   Error DF Sig. of F

Pillais           .29193   1.53823      4.00       36.00     .212
Hotellings        .39090   1.56360      4.00       32.00     .208
Wilks             .71440   1.55651      4.00       34.00     .208
Roys              .26832
Note.. F statistic for WILKS' Lambda is exact.
- - - - - - - - - - - - - - - - - - - - - - - - - - - - - - - - - - - - - -
EFFECT .. FACTB (Cont.)                                           ┌─────┐
Univariate F-tests with (2,18) D. F.                              │ 12  │
                                                                  └─────┘
Variable   Hypoth. SS   Error SS Hypoth. MS   Error MS        F  Sig. of F

DEP1       9.72222     53.83333    4.86111    2.99074  1.62539      .224
DEP2        .88889      8.66667     .44444     .48148   .92308      .415
```

FIG. 12.6.   Output for a doubly multivariate ANOVA.

The multivariate between-subjects effect (for "FACTA") is first in box 1, showing that "FACTA" (the between-subjects factor) has a significant multivariate main effect by Hotelling's criterion, $F(4, 14) = 5.45$, $p = .007$. Because this effect is significant, most analysts would be interested in the univariate Factor A main effects for the individual dependent variables, which come next, in box 2 (as a result of the "UNIV" specification). Because of a programming quirk, MANOVA does not label them by their assigned names in this portion of printout, instead calling them "T1" (for "DEP1") and "T4" (for "DEP2"). As can be seen, "DEP1", for example, is significant, $F(2, 9) = 8.95$, $p = .007$.

Next, in boxes 3 and 4, come sections of output labeled "CONSTANT", which should be ignored. Four sets of significance tests next evaluate each of the two effects involving the within-subjects factor, "FACTB": the "FACTB" main effect and the "FACTA BY FACTB" interaction (note that they are in the reverse order). In boxes 5 and 7 are the tests that use the multivariate approach to analyzing the within-subjects factor, as well as being multivariate for multiple dependent variables, in other words, the doubly multivariate output. In this analysis in box 5, the interaction is nonsignificant, with Hotelling's criterion $F(8, 10) = .75$, $p = .651$. Box 7 shows that the "FACTB" main effect is also nonsignificant, $F(4, 6) = 1.297$, $p = .369$. In boxes 6 and 8 are univariate printout using the variables named as "T2," "T3," and so on, which can be ignored. Following that, in boxes 9 and 11, are the "AVERAGED Multivariate" F tests (obtained in response to the "AVERF" specification). The averaged tests are equivalent to using the univariate approach for the within-subjects factors, which assume sphericity, but are still multivariate for the multiple dependent variables. In box 9, this singly multivariate output suggests that, by Hotelling's criterion, the interaction is nonsignificant, $F(8, 32) = 1.47$, $p = .207$, and box 11 shows that the "FACTB" main effect is nonsignificant as well by Hotelling's criterion, $F(4, 32) = 1.56$, $p = .208$. Thus, even by this less stringent criterion, neither the Factor B main effect nor the interaction effects are multivariately significant. Boxes 10 and 12 give the univariate (or averaged) F tests for each dependent variable (now properly labeled), for the interaction and "FACTB" main effects, respectively. Most analysts would not even examine these tests, because the multivariate tests were not close to significance by either the doubly multivariate or the averaged tests approach. Were you to look, the effect that comes closest to significance, for example, is the interaction for "DEP1", $F(4, 18) = 2.15$, $p = .116$.

Contrasts in Doubly Multivariate Designs

Specifying Contrasts on the Between-Subjects Factor

Obtaining contrasts on the between-subjects factor in a doubly multivariate design involves adding two subcommands to the syntax in Fig. 12.5: (a) a "CONTRAST" subcommand, with the specification of the type and nature of the contrast desired, for example, "HELMERT", "SIMPLE", "SPECIAL", the latter of which also requires a square matrix following; and (b) a "DESIGN" subcommand, specifying each of the $k - 1$ contrasts to test, such as 'facta(1), facta(2)'. The printout will be an augmented version of Fig. 12.6; for each segment involving "FACTA" in Fig. 12.6, there will be $k - 1$ analogous segments in the augmented version, one for each contrast. For example, the "AVERAGED Multivariate Test" for "FACTA BY FACTB" in Fig. 12.6 (box 9) will have $k - 1$ corresponding counterparts in the augmented printout, one for "FACTA(1) BY FACTB", another for "FACTA(2) BY FACTB", and so on.

Specifying Contrasts on the Within-Subjects Factor

MANOVA can also provide tests for one or more within-subjects factors contrasts in the doubly multivariate design, although its labels for the contrasts on the output are very confusing. Accordingly, it is recommend that the "TRANSFORM/RENAME" method always be used for doubly multivariate designs, whether or not the contrasts are orthogonal. An example is in Fig. 12.7.

```
1.    MANOVA dep1t1 TO dep2t3 BY facta(1,3)

2.      /TRANSFORM(dep1t1 TO dep2t3)=SPECIAL

3.        (1 1 1 0 0 0

4.         1 -2 1 0 0 0

5.         1 0 -1 0 0 0

6.         0 0 0 1 1 1

7.         0 0 0 1 -2 1

8.         0 0 0 1 0 -1)

9.      /RENAME=amaindv1 b13vb2d1 b1vb3dv1 amaindv2 b13vb2d2

10.       b1vb3dv2

11.     /ANALYSIS=amaindv1 amaindv2

12.     /PRINT=SIGNIF(MULTIV)

13.     /NOPRINT=SIGNIF(UNIV)

14.     /DESIGN=CONSTANT facta

15.     /ANALYSIS=b13vb2d1 b13vb2d2

16.     /DESIGN=CONSTANT facta

17.     /ANALYSIS=b1vb3dv1 b1vb3dv2

18.     /DESIGN=CONSTANT facta

19.     /ANALYSIS=amaindv1 TO b1vb3dv2

20.     /PRINT=SIGNIF(UNIV)

21.     /NOPRINT=SIGNIF(MULTIV)

22.     /DESIGN=CONSTANT facta .
```

FIG. 12.7.   Syntax commands to conduct within-subjects contrasts in a doubly multivariate ANOVA.

In lines 3 through 8, the "TRANSFORM" subcommand appears. Because there are six variables to be analyzed (three levels of the within-subjects factor times two true dependent variables), six rows and columns need to be specified. The first row contains all ones for the first dependent variable and all zeroes for the second (i.e., the first three vs. the last three named). The first contrast is defined in the second row, which compares the first and third levels of the within-subjects factor to the second, but only for the first dependent variable. The second contrast on the within-subjects factor is next in the third row, contrasting the first and third levels, again only for the first dependent variable. Rows 4 through 6 repeat each of the preceding contrasts for the second dependent variable (i.e., giving zeroes for the first dependent variable in each case). Lines 9 and 10 "RENAME" the six previous transformed variables for easy recognition in the printout. For example, the third transformed variable (on line 5) is renamed 'b1vb3dv1', mnemonic for Factor B Level 1 versus Level 3, on Dependent Variable 1. (Note that, for the first contrast, the eight-letter variable name restriction forced elimination of the 'v' in 'dv'). The first and fourth transformed variable names refer to lines 3 and 6, respectively, the row of ones for the respective dependent variables. These are "RENAME"d 'amaindv1' and 'amaindv2', respectively (a similar naming convention was introduced in chap. 7, Fig. 7.13). The function of the remaining lines is explained after the relevant printout produced is provided in Fig. 12.8.

```
Order of Variables for Analysis

   Variates    Covariates
    AMAINDV1
    AMAINDV2

    2 Dependent Variables
    0 Covariates
- - - - - - - - - - - - - - - - - - - - - - - - - - - - - - - - - - -
Note..  TRANSFORMED variables are in the variates column.

* * * * * * A n a l y s i s   o f   V a r i a n c e -- design  1 * * * * * *
EFFECT .. FACTA
Multivariate Tests of Significance (S = 2, M = -1/2, N = 3 )

Test Name        Value  Approx. F Hypoth. DF   Error DF  Sig. of F

Pillais        1.19025   6.61455      4.00      18.00      .002
Hotellings     3.11534   5.45185      4.00      14.00      .007
Wilks           .15830   6.05361      4.00      16.00      .004
Roys            .67013
Note.. F statistic for WILKS' Lambda is exact.
- - - - - - - - - - - - - - - - - - - - - - - - - - - - - - - - - - -
EFFECT .. CONSTANT
Multivariate Tests of Significance (S = 1, M = 0, N = 3 )

Test Name        Value   Exact F Hypoth. DF   Error DF  Sig. of F

Pillais         .98099 206.41441      2.00       8.00      .000
Hotellings    51.60360 206.41441      2.00       8.00      .000
Wilks           .01901 206.41441      2.00       8.00      .000
Roys            .98099
Note.. F statistics are exact.

* * * * * * A n a l y s i s   o f   V a r i a n c e -- design  2 * * * * * *

Order of Variables for Analysis

   Variates    Covariates
    B13VB2D1
    B13VB2D2

    2 Dependent Variables
    0 Covariates
- - - - - - - - - - - - - - - - - - - - - - - - - - - - - - - - - - -
Note..  TRANSFORMED variables are in the variates column.

EFFECT .. FACTA
Multivariate Tests of Significance (S = 2, M = -1/2, N = 3 )

Test Name        Value  Approx. F Hypoth. DF   Error DF  Sig. of F

Pillais         .25042    .64410      4.00      18.00      .638
Hotellings      .32508    .56890      4.00      14.00      .689
Wilks           .75248    .61119      4.00      16.00      .661
Roys            .23824
Note.. F statistic for WILKS' Lambda is exact.
- - - - - - - - - - - - - - - - - - - - - - - - - - - - - - - - - - -
EFFECT .. CONSTANT
Multivariate Tests of Significance (S = 1, M = 0, N = 3 )

Test Name        Value   Exact F Hypoth. DF   Error DF  Sig. of F

Pillais         .45546   3.34565      2.00       8.00      .088
Hotellings      .83641   3.34565      2.00       8.00      .088
Wilks           .54454   3.34565      2.00       8.00      .088
Roys            .45546
Note.. F statistics are exact.

* * * * * * A n a l y s i s   o f   V a r i a n c e -- design  3 * * * * * *

Order of Variables for Analysis

   Variates    Covariates
    B1VB3DV1
    B1VB3DV2

    2 Dependent Variables
    0 Covariates
- - - - - - - - - - - - - - - - - - - - - - - - - - - - - - - - - - -
Note..  TRANSFORMED variables are in the variates column.
```

FIG. 12.8.   *(Continues)*

```
EFFECT .. FACTA
Multivariate Tests of Significance (S = 2, M = -1/2, N = 3 )

Test Name          Value  Approx. F Hypoth. DF   Error DF  Sig. of F

Pillais            .54778   1.69740      4.00     18.00      .194
Hotellings         .92394   1.61689      4.00     14.00      .225
Wilks              .49667   1.67581      4.00     16.00      .205
Roys               .44873
Note.. F statistic for WILKS' Lambda is exact.
- - - - - - - - - - - - - - - - - - - - - - - - - - - - - - - - - - -
EFFECT .. CONSTANT
Multivariate Tests of Significance (S = 1, M = 0, N = 3 )

Test Name          Value   Exact F Hypoth. DF   Error DF  Sig. of F

Pillais            .20969   1.06130      2.00      8.00      .390
Hotellings         .26532   1.06130      2.00      8.00      .390
Wilks              .79031   1.06130      2.00      8.00      .390
Roys               .20969

Note.. F statistics are exact.

* * * * * * A n a l y s i s   o f   V a r i a n c e -- design  4 * * * * * *

Order of Variables for Analysis

    Variates    Covariates
    AMAINDV1
    B13VB2D1
    B1VB3DV1
    AMAINDV2
    B13VB2D2
    B1VB3DV2


    6 Dependent Variables
    0 Covariates
- - - - - - - - - - - - - - - - - - - - - - - - - - - - - - - - - - -
Note.. TRANSFORMED variables are in the variates column.

EFFECT .. FACTA
Univariate F-tests with (2,9) D. F.

Variable  Hypoth. SS   Error SS  Hypoth. MS   Error MS       F   Sig. of F

AMAINDV1  138.16667   69.50000   69.08333    7.72222   8.94604    .007
B13VB2D1    2.66667  136.25000    1.33333   15.13889    .08807    .916
B1VB3DV1   50.66667   62.25000   25.33333    6.91667   3.66265    .069
AMAINDV2  200.16667  137.50000  100.08333   15.27778   6.55091    .018
B13VB2D2    8.66667   34.00000    4.33333    3.77778   1.14706    .360
B1VB3DV2     .66667    6.00000     .33333     .66667    .50000    .622
- - - - - - - - - - - - - - - - - - - - - - - - - - - - - - - - - - -
EFFECT .. CONSTANT
Univariate F-tests with (1,9) D. F.

Variable  Hypoth. SS   Error SS  Hypoth. MS   Error MS       F   Sig. of F

AMAINDV1  3136.33333   69.50000 3136.33333    7.72222 406.14388    .000
B13VB2D1    52.08333  136.25000   52.08333   15.13889   3.44037    .097
B1VB3DV1     2.08333   62.25000    2.08333    6.91667    .30120    .596
AMAINDV2  3816.33333  137.50000 3816.33333   15.27778 249.79636    .000
B13VB2D2     1.33333   34.00000    1.33333    3.77778    .35294    .567
B1VB3DV2     1.33333    6.00000    1.33333     .66667   2.00000    .191
```

FIG. 12.8. The output for a within-subjects contrast in a doubly multivariate ANOVA.

Lines 11 through 18 produce the multivariate results and lines 19 through 22 the univariate. Line 11 requests the analysis of only the two Factor A main effect variables together, line 15 requests the first two contrasts, line 17 the second two contrasts, and line 19 requests all the effects. Only the multivariate tests will be printed out by the specification on lines 12 and 13. You will keep getting multivariate output only until that request is altered by lines 20 and 21 (which provide the univariate effects, which reverse what is to be printed and what printout is to be withheld). The "DESIGN" subcommand on line 14 indicates that you want tests for both Factor A and the "CONSTANT", as originally introduced in chapter 7. This subcommand must be repeated (in lines 16, 18, and 22) to trigger each of the requested analyses.

To discuss the remaining results, Table 12.1 contains the F values (or "Approx. F" values) and degrees of freedom for each of the relevant effects extracted from Fig. 12.8.

As requested by the "ANALYSIS" subcommands, the multivariate printout appears first. The F values given in Table 12.1 are Hotelling's. The Factor A multivariate main effect comes from the first analysis requesting analysis of 'amaindv1' and 'amaindv2', for "EFFECT .. FACTA". The sec-

TABLE 12.1
Relevant *F* Values and *df*s Extracted From the Printout in Fig. 12.8

	Multivariate		Univariate DEP1		Univariate DEP2	
	F	*df*	*F*	*df*	*F*	*df*
FactA	5.452*	4,14	8.946*	2,9	6.551*	2,9
FactB(1)	3.346**	2,8	3.440**	1,9	0.353	1,9
FactB(2)	1.061	2,8	0.301	1,9	2.000	1,9
FactA × FactB(1)	0.569	4,14	0.088	2,9	1.147	2,9
FactA × FactB(2)	1.617	4,14	3.663**	2,9	0.500	2,9

*$p < .05$. **$p < .10$.

tion labeled "design 2" contains two multivariate tests relating to Contrast 1 as requested by 'ANALYSIS=b13vb2d1 b13vb2d2', both as a main effect (found under "EFFECT .. CONSTANT") and as an interaction with Factor A (found under "EFFECT .. FACTA"). Similar printout follows in "design 3", the two multivariate tests relating to Contrast 2 as requested by 'ANALYSIS=b1vb3d1 b1vb3d2", both as a main effect (found under "EFFECT .. CONSTANT") and as an interaction with Factor A (found under "EFFECT .. FACTA"). Line 19 requests all the transformed variables to be analyzed and, in combination with lines 20 through 22 alluded to earlier, results in the remaining portion of printout, listed as "design 4", from which all the univariate, individual dependent variables test data are extracted.

Because the multivariate Factor A effect was significant beyond $p < .05$, interpretation of the two Factor A effects for "DEP1" and "DEP2" would be appropriate (and, as indicated in Table 12.1, both are significant). Of the contrasts involving Factor B, however, only the first contrast, and only as a main effect, approached significance (actually, at the $p < .10$ level). Thus, it would be questionable to examine the univariate results for any but the FactB(1) effects in Table 12.1. Thus, the 'FactA × FactB(2)' for "DEP1" *F* value of 3.663, which approaches significance, should probably be ignored. Because the multivariate effect for 'FactB(1)' approaches significance, however, many analysts might interpret the near-significant univariate *F* value of 3.440 found for "DEP1".

PAC

You would access the menu for multivariate tests through Analyze–General Linear Model–Multivariate (see Fig. 3.14) and would obtain the screen in Fig. 12.9.

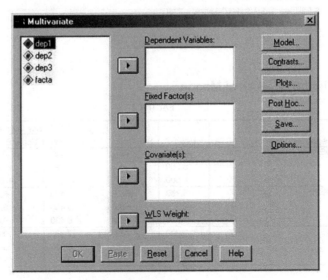

FIG. 12.9. Dialogue box to run a Multivariate ANOVA.

You would send your dependent variables over to the Dependent Variables box and your independent variables to the Fixed Factor(s) box. You could also request means, power, and effect sizes as was done in earlier chapters. Selected output from this analysis is in Fig. 12.10.

General Linear Model

Multivariate Tests[d]

Effect		Value	F	Hypothesis df	Error df	Sig.	Partial Eta Squared	Noncent. Parameter	Observed Power[a]
Intercept	Pillai's Trace	.988	184.697[b]	3.000	7.000	.000	.988	554.090	1.000
	Wilks' Lambda	.012	184.697[b]	3.000	7.000	.000	.988	554.090	1.000
	Hotelling's Trace	79.156	184.697[b]	3.000	7.000	.000	.988	554.090	1.000
	Roy's Largest Root	79.156	184.697[b]	3.000	7.000	.000	.988	554.090	1.000
FACTA	Pillai's Trace	1.244	4.391	6.000	16.000	.008	.622	26.349	.912
	Wilks' Lambda	.102	4.973[b]	6.000	14.000	.006	.681	29.839	.932
	Hotelling's Trace	5.409	5.409	6.000	12.000	.006	.730	32.456	.936
	Roy's Largest Root	4.684	12.491[c]	3.000	8.000	.002	.824	37.474	.985

a. Computed using alpha = .05

b. Exact statistic

c. The statistic is an upper bound on F that yields a lower bound on the significance level.

d. Design: Intercept+FACTA

Tests of Between-Subjects Effects

Source	Dependent Variable	Type III Sum of Squares	df	Mean Square	F	Sig.	Partial Eta Squared	Noncent. Parameter	Observed Power[a]
Corrected Model	DEP1	60.667[b]	2	30.333	17.063	.001	.791	34.125	.994
	DEP2	34.667[c]	2	17.333	12.735	.002	.739	25.469	.972
	DEP3	24.500[d]	2	12.250	5.654	.026	.557	11.308	.717
Intercept	DEP1	385.333	1	385.333	216.750	.000	.960	216.750	1.000
	DEP2	444.083	1	444.083	326.265	.000	.973	326.265	1.000
	DEP3	1452.000	1	1452.000	670.154	.000	.987	670.154	1.000
FACTA	DEP1	60.667	2	30.333	17.062	.001	.791	34.125	.994
	DEP2	34.667	2	17.333	12.735	.002	.739	25.469	.972
	DEP3	24.500	2	12.250	5.654	.026	.557	11.308	.717
Error	DEP1	16.000	9	1.778					
	DEP2	12.250	9	1.361					
	DEP3	19.500	9	2.167					
Total	DEP1	462.000	12						
	DEP2	491.000	12						
	DEP3	1496.000	12						
Corrected Total	DEP1	76.667	11						
	DEP2	46.917	11						
	DEP3	44.000	11						

a. Computed using alpha = .05

b. R Squared = .791 (Adjusted R Squared = .745)

c. R Squared = .739 (Adjusted R Squared = .681)

d. R Squared = .557 (Adjusted R Squared = .458)

Estimated Marginal Means

FACTA

Dependent Variable	FACTA	Mean	Std. Error	95% Confidence Interval	
				Lower Bound	Upper Bound
DEP1	1.00	3.000	.667	1.492	4.508
	2.00	5.500	.667	3.992	7.008
	3.00	8.500	.667	6.992	10.008
DEP2	1.00	3.750	.583	2.430	5.070
	2.00	6.750	.583	5.430	8.070
	3.00	7.750	.583	6.430	9.070
DEP3	1.00	9.000	.736	7.335	10.665
	2.00	11.750	.736	10.085	13.415
	3.00	12.250	.736	10.585	13.915

FIG. 12.10.   PAC output from a multivariate ANOVA.

The multivariate output is first. You would ignore the output for the intercept and look at the output for the between-subjects factor, "FACTA". The only difference between this output and that from MANOVA concerns Roy's test. GLM outputs the root rather than the test value outputted in MANOVA (to convert to the test value take the root and divide by [1 + the root]), however, the *F* and *p* values for Roy's test are printed out here, thus the test value is not really necessary. The univariate output follows the multivariate; again, you would ignore everything except for the output associated with the between-subjects factor(s). The means are presented last. You could request canned contrasts or post hocs on the between-subjects factor as you did in a simple between-subjects design. See chapter 13 to conduct user-defined contrasts.

A doubly multivariate design is run from the Analyze–General Linear Model–Repeated Measures menu (see Fig. 12.11). In addition to defining the within-subjects factor, you need to click on the Measure button on the right side of the menu so that you will be able to tell SPSS that there are multiple dependent variables.

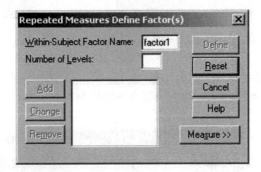

FIG. 12.11.   Dialogue box to define the within-subjects factor for a doubly multivariate ANOVA.

Once you click on that, you will obtain the screen seen in Fig. 12.12.

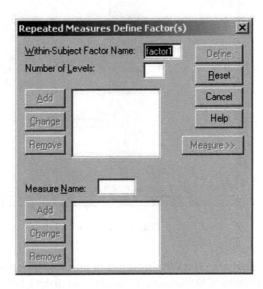

FIG. 12.12.   Blank dialogue box after clicking on the Measure button.

In the preceding example, 'factb' was the within-subjects factor; it had three levels and there were two dependent variables. You would define Factor B just as you did in chapter 6. For each dependent variable, you would name the variable in the Measure Name box and then hit the Add button. Because you have two dependent variables, here you would do this two times. Figure 12.13 shows how the screen would appear just before you click Add for the second time.

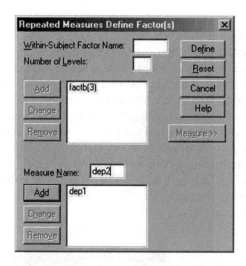

FIG. 12.13. Dialogue box with the within-subjects factor and dependent variables named.

After you have finished defining the within-subjects factor(s) and the dependent variables, you would hit the Define button, which would bring up the next screen, seen in Fig. 12.14.

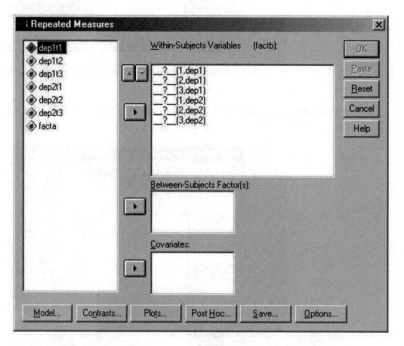

FIG. 12.14. Dialogue box to set up the doubly multivariate ANOVA.

You can see that in the Within-Subjects Variables window at the right, you will be putting in the three measurements of Dependent Variable 1 (in order), followed by the three measurements of Dependent Variable 2. Doing this would give you the screen seen in Fig. 12.15 (including the between-subjects factor).

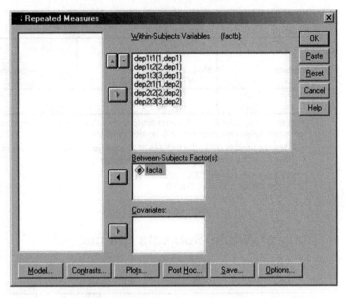

FIG. 12.15. Dialogue box with the doubly multivariate ANOVA set up.

You can obtain the means, effect sizes, and power as in previous mixed designs. The output from this analysis is in Fig. 12.16.

General Linear Model

Multivariate Tests[d]

Effect			Value	F	Hypothesis df	Error df	Sig.	Eta Sqrd	Non-cent. Parameter	Observed Power[a]
Between Subjects	Intercept	Pillai's Trace	.981	206.414[b]	2.000	8.000	.000	.981	412.8	1.000
		Wilks' Lambda	.019	206.414[b]	2.000	8.000	.000	.981	412.8	1.000
		Hotelling's Trace	51.604	206.414[b]	2.000	8.000	.000	.981	412.8	1.000
		Roy's Largest Root	51.604	206.414[b]	2.000	8.000	.000	.981	412.8	1.000
	FACTA	Pillai's Trace	1.190	6.615	4.000	18.0	.002	.595	26.46	.966
		Wilks' Lambda	.158	6.054[b]	4.000	16.0	.004	.602	24.21	.942
		Hotelling's Trace	3.115	5.452	4.000	14.0	.007	.609	21.81	.903
		Roy's Largest Root	2.031	9.142[c]	2.000	9.000	.007	.670	18.28	.903
Within Subjects	FACTB	Pillai's Trace	.464	1.297[b]	4.000	6.000	.369	.464	5.190	.216
		Wilks' Lambda	.536	1.297[b]	4.000	6.000	.369	.464	5.190	.216
		Hotelling's Trace	.865	1.297[b]	4.000	6.000	.369	.464	5.190	.216
		Roy's Largest Root	.865	1.297[b]	4.000	6.000	.369	.464	5.190	.216
	FACTB * FACTA	Pillai's Trace	.690	.922	8.000	14.0	.527	.345	7.375	.274
		Wilks' Lambda	.409	.845[b]	8.000	12.0	.583	.360	6.757	.236
		Hotelling's Trace	1.200	.750	8.000	10.0	.651	.375	6.002	.196
		Roy's Largest Root	.943	1.650[c]	4.000	7.000	.264	.485	6.601	.290

a. Computed using alpha = .05

b. Exact statistic

c. The statistic is an upper bound on F that yields a lower bound on the significance level.

d. Design: Intercept+FACTA
   Within Subjects Design: FACTB

FIG. 12.16. *(Continues)*

Mauchly's Test of Sphericity[b]

Within Subjects Effect	Measure	Mauchly's W	Approx. Chi-Square	df	Sig.	Epsilon[a]		
						Greenhouse-Geisser	Huynh-Feldt	Lower-bound
FACTB	DEP1	.902	.823	2	.662	.911	1.000	.500
	DEP2	.901	.835	2	.658	.910	1.000	.500

Tests the null hypothesis that the error covariance matrix of the orthonormalized transformed dependent variables is proportional to an identity matrix.

a. May be used to adjust the degrees of freedom for the averaged tests of significance. Corrected tests are displayed in the Tests of Within-Subjects Effects table.

b. Design: Intercept+FACTA
Within Subjects Design: FACTB

Tests of Within-Subjects Effects

Multivariate[d,e]

Within Subjects Effect		Value	F	Hypothesis df	Error df	Sig.	Eta Sqrd	Noncent. Parameter	Observed Power[a]
FACTB	Pillai's Trace	.292	1.538	4.000	36.00	.212	.146	6.153	.427
	Wilks' Lambda	.714	1.557[b]	4.000	34.00	.208	.155	6.226	.428
	Hotelling's Trace	.391	1.564	4.000	32.00	.208	.163	6.254	.427
	Roy's Largest Root	.367	3.300[c]	2.000	18.00	.060	.268	6.601	.551
FACTB * FACTA	Pillai's Trace	.516	1.564	8.000	36.00	.170	.258	12.509	.599
	Wilks' Lambda	.543	1.519[b]	8.000	34.00	.187	.263	12.149	.578
	Hotelling's Trace	.734	1.469	8.000	32.00	.207	.269	11.751	.554
	Roy's Largest Root	.532	2.392[c]	4.000	18.00	.089	.347	9.567	.567

a. Computed using alpha = .05

b. Exact statistic

c. The statistic is an upper bound on F that yields a lower bound on the significance level.

d. Design: Intercept+FACTA
Within Subjects Design: FACTB

e. Tests are based on averaged variables.

FIG. 12.16. *(Continues)*

Univariate Tests

Source	Measure		Type III Sum of Squares	df	Mean Square	F	Sig.	Eta Sqrd	Noncent. Parameter	Observed Power[a]
FACTB	DEP1	Sphericity Assumed	9.722	2	4.861	1.625	.224	.153	3.251	.298
		Greenhouse-Geisser	9.722	1.822	5.336	1.625	.227	.153	2.961	.283
		Huynh-Feldt	9.722	2.000	4.861	1.625	.224	.153	3.251	.298
		Lower-bound	9.722	1.000	9.722	1.625	.234	.153	1.625	.208
	DEP2	Sphericity Assumed	.889	2	.444	.923	.415	.093	1.846	.185
		Greenhouse-Geisser	.889	1.820	.488	.923	.408	.093	1.680	.177
		Huynh-Feldt	.889	2.000	.444	.923	.415	.093	1.846	.185
		Lower-bound	.889	1.000	.889	.923	.362	.093	.923	.138
FACTB * FACTA	DEP1	Sphericity Assumed	25.778	4	6.444	2.155	.116	.324	8.619	.518
		Greenhouse-Geisser	25.778	3.644	7.075	2.155	.124	.324	7.851	.488
		Huynh-Feldt	25.778	4.000	6.444	2.155	.116	.324	8.619	.518
		Lower-bound	25.778	2.000	12.889	2.155	.172	.324	4.310	.330
	DEP2	Sphericity Assumed	1.778	4	.444	.923	.472	.170	3.692	.235
		Greenhouse-Geisser	1.778	3.639	.488	.923	.467	.170	3.359	.223
		Huynh-Feldt	1.778	4.000	.444	.923	.472	.170	3.692	.235
		Lower-bound	1.778	2.000	.889	.923	.432	.170	1.846	.163
Error (FACTB)	DEP1	Sphericity Assumed	53.833	18	2.991					
		Greenhouse-Geisser	53.833	16.40	3.283					
		Huynh-Feldt	53.833	18.00	2.991					
		Lower-bound	53.833	9.000	5.981					
	DEP2	Sphericity Assumed	8.667	18	.481					
		Greenhouse-Geisser	8.667	16.38	.529					
		Huynh-Feldt	8.667	18.00	.481					
		Lower-bound	8.667	9.000	.963					

a. Computed using alpha = .05

Tests of Between-Subjects Effects

Transformed Variable: Average

Source	Measure	Type III Sum of Squares	df	Mean Square	F	Sig.	Eta Squared	Noncent. Parameter	Observed Power[a]
Intercept	DEP1	1045.444	1	1045.444	406.14	.000	.978	406.144	1.000
	DEP2	1272.111	1	1272.111	249.80	.000	.965	249.796	1.000
FACTA	DEP1	46.056	2	23.028	8.946	.007	.665	17.892	.896
	DEP2	66.722	2	33.361	6.551	.018	.593	13.102	.781
Error	DEP1	23.167	9	2.574					
	DEP2	45.833	9	5.093					

a. Computed using alpha = .05

FIG. 12.16. *(Continues)*

Estimated Marginal Means

1. FACTA

Measure	FACTA	Mean	Std. Error	95% Confidence Interval	
				Lower Bound	Upper Bound
DEP1	1.00	3.917	.463	2.869	4.964
	2.00	5.583	.463	4.536	6.631
	3.00	6.667	.463	5.619	7.714
DEP2	1.00	4.250	.651	2.776	5.724
	2.00	7.583	.651	6.110	9.057
	3.00	6.000	.651	4.526	7.474

2. FACTB

Measure	FACTB	Mean	Std. Error	95% Confidence Interval	
				Lower Bound	Upper Bound
DEP1	1	5.250	.479	4.167	6.333
	2	6.083	.250	5.518	6.649
	3	4.833	.649	3.365	6.302
DEP2	1	5.833	.461	4.789	6.877
	2	5.833	.312	5.128	6.539
	3	6.167	.441	5.169	7.164

3. FACTA * FACTB

Measure	FACTA	FACTB	Mean	Std. Error	95% Confidence Interval	
					Lower Bound	Upper Bound
DEP1	1.00	1	2.500	.829	.624	4.376
		2	4.500	.433	3.520	5.480
		3	4.750	1.124	2.207	7.293
	2.00	1	5.500	.829	3.624	7.376
		2	6.500	.433	5.520	7.480
		3	4.750	1.124	2.207	7.293
	3.00	1	7.750	.829	5.874	9.626
		2	7.250	.433	6.270	8.230
		3	5.000	1.124	2.457	7.543
DEP2	1.00	1	4.000	.799	2.192	5.808
		2	4.250	.540	3.028	5.472
		3	4.500	.764	2.772	6.228
	2.00	1	7.500	.799	5.692	9.308
		2	7.750	.540	6.528	8.972
		3	7.500	.764	5.772	9.228
	3.00	1	6.000	.799	4.192	7.808
		2	5.500	.540	4.278	6.722
		3	6.500	.764	4.772	8.228

FIG. 12.16.   PAC output for a doubly multivariate design.

First is the multivariate output, which includes the doubly multivariate tests of the "FACTB" main effect and the interaction. As noted when MANOVA was used (box 1, p. 151), the Factor A multivariate main effect is clearly significant, by Hotelling's criterion, $F(4, 14) = 5.45$, $p = .007$, permitting examination of each of the two univariate Factor A main effects later. Neither the Factor B main effect, $F(4, 6) = 1.297$, $p = .369$ (box 7 of MANOVA), nor the interaction, $F(8, 10) = .75$, $p = .651$ (cf. box 5 of MANOVA), however, is significant. In view of the doubly multivariate test results, further exploration of the Factor A main effect is clearly warranted, whereas exploration of the Factor B effect and the interaction for the two dependent variables may be questionable. Next appears Mauchly's sphericity test for the two dependent variables, which, because both are nonsignificant, suggests that sphericity of the within-subjects factor is a tenable assumption for both "DEP1" and "DEP2".

Next comes the other tests of the within-subjects factors, the ones that are not doubly multivariate, but instead use the univariate approach for the within-subjects factor and are singly multivariate for multiple dependent variables. The output is comparable to that of MANOVA's labeled "AVERAGED Multivariate Tests of Significance" (i.e., boxes 11 and 9). Because the sphericity assumptions appear tenable for both dependent variables, these tests may be preferred to the doubly multivariate tests discussed earlier. The fact that they use averaged F tests for within-subjects factors is discussed in footnote e. Even by this less stringent criterion, however, neither the Factor B nor the interaction effects are multivariately significant, for "FACTB", $F(4, 32) = 1.56, p = .208$, and for the interaction, $F(8, 32) = 1.47, p = .207$. Note that the preceding F values were according to Hotelling's criterion; by Roy's criterion, p values are closer to .05 (.06–.09). However, footnote c indicates that Roy's provides a "lower-bound significance level" (i.e., an underestimate). Next comes the univariate tests, for each of the two dependent variables separately, tested both when sphericity is assumed and by each of the correction methods. Most analysts would not even examine these tests, because the multivariate tests were not close to significance by either the doubly multivariate or the averaged tests approach. If you were to do so, the results disclose that neither dependent variable is significant for either effect, the closest being the interaction effect on "DEP1", where the p value is as low as .116 (cf. boxes 10 and 12).

Similar to MANOVA, GLM does not provide the multivariate approach tests of within-subjects factors on each dependent variable separately within this run. To get them, run a separate analysis entering only one of the dependent variables. Doing so on "DEP2", in an analysis not shown here, would yield a significant interaction by Roy's criterion, $F(2, 9) = 3.929, p = .059$. The printout next gives individual dependent results for the between-subjects factor, "FACTA". These would be defensible to examine and interpret, because the multivariate test main effect reviewed earlier was significant. The printout reveals that there was a significant "FACTA" main effect on both "DEP1", $F(2, 9) = 8.95, p = .007$, and "DEP2", $F(2, 9) = 6.55, p = .018$ (cf. box 2). Finally, all the marginal and cell means (which cannot all be obtained in MANOVA) are provided to help identify where the differences reside.

13
GLM and UNIANOVA Syntax

Although PAC versions of analyses have been described at the end of most previous chapters, it was noted in each case that many of the more complicated analyses (e.g., simple effects, interaction contrasts) were not available from the PAC menus and that syntax was necessary. For between-subjects designs, instead of using the program MANOVA, the PAC version of SPSS produces syntax for a procedure called UNIANOVA (univariate analysis of variance). For within-subjects designs, PAC produces syntax for a very similar procedure called GLM (general linear model). Although the syntax for both is fairly similar to MANOVA, there are some important differences that are detailed in this chapter. In writing this book, it was assumed that most users will probably prefer to use UNIANOVA and GLM entirely for their PAC capabilities and, for the more complicated analyses requiring syntax, would use MANOVA. Some users, however, may wish to stick to GLM or UNIANOVA throughout, clicking where possible, writing syntax otherwise. This chapter is intended for those users wishing to understand the GLM and UNIANOVA syntax necessary for these more complicated analyses. The chapter begins with the simplest syntax.

ONE-FACTOR BETWEEN-SUBJECTS ANOVA

Basic Commands

If you followed the click sequence described in chapter 3 in Figs. 3.15, 3.16, and 3.19 and then clicked Paste, the syntax produced would be as follows:

```
1.  UNIANOVA
2.      dv BY facta
3.      /METHOD=SSTYPE(3)
4.      /INTERCEPT=INCLUDE
5.      /EMMEANS=TABLES(facta)
6.      /PRINT=ETASQ OPOWER
7.      /CRITERIA=ALPHA(.05)
8.      /DESIGN=facta.
```

After eliminating the preceding commands that are defaults, and thus unnecessary (i.e., lines 3, 4, 7, and 8), you would be left with the shorter program in Fig. 13.1. In line 1, it can be seen that the main command of "UNIANOVA" is almost identical to that for "MANOVA" (i.e., after the command name, specify the name of the dependent variable, then the keyword "BY", then the

1.	UNIANOVA dv BY facta
2d.	/EMMEANS=TABLES(facta)
3d.	/PRINT=ETASQ OPOWER.

FIG. 13.1.   Syntax commands to conduct a one-factor between-subjects ANOVA using UNIANOVA.

name of the grouping or between-subjects variable), except that in UNIANOVA you do not specify the number of levels for the between-subjects factor(s). Line 2 produces the group means (similar to the "OMEANS" subcommand in MANOVA, but here they are called *estimated marginal* means) and in line 3, effect size and power are requested. For this basic analysis, it is easiest simply to use the PAC menu and click on the appropriate options, as discussed in chapter 3. The output produced is in Fig. 13.2.

Univariate Analysis of Variance

Between-Subjects Factors

		N
FACTA	1.00	5
	2.00	5
	3.00	5

Tests of Between-Subjects Effects

Dependent Variable: DV

Source	Type III Sum of Squares	df	Mean Square	F	Sig.	Eta Squared	Noncent. Parameter	Observed Power[a]
Corrected Model	124.133[b]	2	62.067	6.443	.013	.518	12.886	.812
Intercept	1092.267	1	1092.267	113.384	.000	.904	113.384	1.000
FACTA	124.133	2	62.067	6.443	.013	.518	12.886	.812
Error	115.600	12	9.633					
Total	1332.000	15						
Corrected Total	239.733	14						

a. Computed using alpha = .05

b. R Squared = .518 (Adjusted R Squared = .437)

Estimated Marginal Means

FACTA

Dependent Variable: DV

FACTA	Mean	Std. Error	95% Confidence Interval	
			Lower Bound	Upper Bound
1.00	6.400	1.388	3.376	9.424
2.00	12.600	1.388	9.576	15.624
3.00	6.600	1.388	3.576	9.624

FIG. 13.2.   Output for a one-factor between-subjects ANOVA in UNIANOVA.

In addition to the effect for Factor A (labeled "FACTA"), you also obtain the corrected model and intercept effects because the program is conducting the analysis under a general linear model framework and provides output similar to that obtained from a regression analysis. You can simply concentrate on whether your effect is significant; identical to what you found in chapter 3, the overall $F(2, 12)$ of 6.44 is statistically significant ($p = .013$). Notice that the "Tests of Between-Subjects Effects" table also contains the partial eta squared and the observed power (in response to line 3).

Additionally, the group means are printed out (in response to line 2) in a table labeled "Estimated Marginal Means".

Contrasts

An easy way to prepare to run a planned contrast (or any other analysis in this chapter using UNIANOVA or GLM syntax) is to begin in the PAC menu, selecting all of the variables and options you want and then hitting Paste to paste the desired syntax into a new syntax window. You can then just start typing your additional syntax after the last line (remember to delete the period and place it after the last line you type in).

There are two different ways to obtain contrasts in UNIANOVA. First, you can use the "CONTRAST" method: Any of the canned contrasts (e.g., "SIMPLE", "REPEATED", "HELMERT", "DIFFERENCE", "POLYNOMIAL") are available from PAC (see Fig. 3.18). The syntax these clicks produce for contrasts is otherwise identical to that described in previous chapters (e.g., 'CONTRAST(facta)=HELMERT'). However, you should note that, in this method, you will not be provided with F tests for individual contrasts if you run more than one contrast at a time. For example, if you ran a set of "SIMPLE" contrasts on Factor A, you would get the "Contrast Results (K Matrix)" (see Fig. 13.3) for each contrast, including the significance level of each, but the F test provided below that (in a table labeled "Test Results" in Fig. 13.3) would be for the entire set of contrasts, rather than each individual one. Thus, you would know whether the individual contrast was significant, but would not be given an F value for that contrast. Instead, the F value would need to be manually computed (as described later) from the results provided.

Contrast Results (K Matrix)

FACTA Simple Contrast[a]		Dependent Variable DV
Level 1 vs. Level 3	Contrast Estimate	-.200
	Hypothesized Value	0
	Difference (Estimate - Hypothesized)	-.200
	Std. Error	1.963
	Sig.	.921
	95% Confidence Interval for Difference Lower Bound	-4.477
	Upper Bound	4.077
Level 2 vs. Level 3	Contrast Estimate	6.000
	Hypothesized Value	0
	Difference (Estimate - Hypothesized)	6.000
	Std. Error	1.963
	Sig.	.010
	95% Confidence Interval for Difference Lower Bound	1.723
	Upper Bound	10.277

a. Reference category = 3

Test Results

Dependent Variable: DV

Source	Sum of Squares	df	Mean Square	F	Sig.
Contrast	124.133	2	62.067	6.443	.013
Error	115.600	12	9.633		

FIG. 13.3. Output for a set of SIMPLE contrasts in UNIANOVA.

Alternatively, you could specify user-defined contrasts using the keyword "SPECIAL". The "SPECIAL" contrast is not available from PAC, as noted in chapter 3, and requires writing syntax. Unlike in MANOVA however, you can simply specify the contrast you are interested in and it is not necessary to include the contrast of all ones or $k-1$ contrasts. In order to obtain the F test for each contrast, however, you must specify each one on its own "CONTRAST" subcommand.

The second method of specifying contrasts in which you *would* obtain the F values for each contrast is to use the "LMATRIX" subcommand, which is also not available from PAC. "LMATRIX" is the name of the matrix of contrast weights in UNIANOVA. The specification is, for example:

/LMATRIX 'a2 vs. a3' facta 0 1 –1

After the subcommand "LMATRIX", you can optionally specify a label for the contrast that will be included on the printout by enclosing it in single or double quotation marks. After the label, specify the name of the factor that the contrasts are on, followed by the weights for that specific contrast. Like in the "SPECIAL" method for UNIANOVA, in the "LMATRIX" method, it is not necessary to include the contrast of all ones or $k-1$ contrasts. Figure 13.4 shows the output for the following set of two "LMATRIX" subcommands if they had been included after the "UNIANOVA" command in line 1 of Fig. 13.1:

/LMATRIX 'a1 + a2 vs. a3' facta 1 1 –2
/LMATRIX 'a1 vs. a2' facta 1 –1 0

Custom Hypothesis Tests Index

1	Contrast Coefficients (L' Matrix)	LMATRIX Subcommand 1: a1 + a2 vs. a3
	Transformation Coefficients (M Matrix)	Identity Matrix
	Contrast Results (K Matrix)	Zero Matrix
2	Contrast Coefficients (L' Matrix)	LMATRIX Subcommand 2: a1 vs. a2
	Transformation Coefficients (M Matrix)	Identity Matrix
	Contrast Results (K Matrix)	Zero Matrix

Custom Hypothesis Tests #1

Contrast Results (K Matrix)[a]

		Dependent Variable
Contrast		DV
L1	Contrast Estimate	5.800
	Hypothesized Value	0
	Difference (Estimate - Hypothesized)	5.800
	Std. Error	3.400
	Sig.	.114
	95% Confidence Interval for Difference Lower Bound	-1.608
	Upper Bound	13.208

a. Based on the user-specified contrast coefficients (L') matrix: a1 + a2 vs. a3

FIG. 13.4. *(Continues)*

Test Results

Dependent Variable: DV

Source	Sum of Squares	df	Mean Square	F	Sig.
Contrast	28.033	1	28.033	2.910	.114
Error	115.600	12	9.633		

Custom Hypothesis Tests #2

Contrast Results (K Matrix)ᵃ

			Dependent Variable
Contrast			DV
L1	Contrast Estimate		-6.200
	Hypothesized Value		0
	Difference (Estimate - Hypothesized)		-6.200
	Std. Error		1.963
	Sig.		.008
	95% Confidence Interval for Difference	Lower Bound	-10.477
		Upper Bound	-1.923

a. Based on the user-specified contrast coefficients (L') matrix: a1 vs. a2

Test Results

Dependent Variable: DV

Source	Sum of Squares	df	Mean Square	F	Sig.
Contrast	96.100	1	96.100	9.976	.008
Error	115.600	12	9.633		

FIG. 13.4. Output for main effect contrasts using the LMATRIX subcommand in UNIANOVA.

The first table (labeled "Custom Hypothesis Tests Index") reviews the contrasts requested. Next come the results for each contrast specified, labeled as "Custom Hypothesis Test # . . .". For each, you will first see a table labeled "Contrast Results (K Matrix)" then one labeled "Test Results". The latter provides the F test and you can see that the results obtained are identical to those from chapter 3. The former table gives an analogous result, but in a different way. In the top row it gives the "Contrast Estimate", which is identical to the $\hat{\Psi}$ described in chapter 3, the sum of each group mean multiplied by its appropriate contrast weight. Because the weights in Contrast 1 were 1 1 −2 and the group means were 6.4, 12.6, and 6.6, respectively, the contrast estimate is 1(6.4) + (1)(12.6) + (−2)(6.6) = 5.8. Note that the "Sig" is the same as the "Sig" of the F test in the subsequent table (in this case, .114). To manually calculate the F value from the "Contrast Results Table", divide the "Contrast Estimate" by the "Std. Error", and square the result (in this case, $[5.8/3.4]^2 = 2.91$). Because you are calculating an F value, you ignore the sign. Finally, the table also includes the 95% confidence interval around the contrast estimate, in this example, from −1.608 to 13.208 (the same as in Fig. 3.5).

An interesting feature of the "LMATRIX" subcommand is that it permits fractional weights, thus:

```
/LMATRIX 'a1 vs. a2+a3' facta 1/2 1/2 −1
```

is permissible and gives the same general result as:

```
/LMATRIX 'a1 + a2 vs. a3' facta 1 1 −2
```

except that the "Contrast Estimate" and the "Std Error" in the first is half that of the second and the confidence limits are similarly adjusted.

Post Hoc Tests

Post hoc tests are also available in UNIANOVA and were described in chapter 3 (see Fig. 3.17). It was noted there that post hoc test results were far more easily obtained with PAC GLM or UNIANOVA than with syntax-driven MANOVA. The syntax produced by PAC requesting SNK and Tukey tests, for example, is:

```
/POSTHOC = facta (SNK TUKEY )
```

The "Homogeneous Subsets" output this subcommand produces was described in Fig. 3.19.

TWO-FACTOR BETWEEN-SUBJECTS ANOVA

Similar to adding between-subjects factors in MANOVA, specifying two factors in PAC and requesting all the means (then eliminating the default syntax) would produce the UNIANOVA syntax seen in Fig. 13.5 for the variables from chapter 4.

```
1.    UNIANOVA shots  BY facta factb

2d.   /EMMEANS=TABLES(facta)

3d.   /EMMEANS=TABLES(factb)

4d.   /EMMEANS=TABLES(facta*factb).
```

FIG. 13.5.   Syntax commands to conduct a two-factor between-subjects ANOVA in UNIANOVA.

Note that three separate "EMMEANS" subcommands are necessary, one for each main effect, as well as one for the interaction effect. This differs from the otherwise similar "OMEANS" subcommand (see line 2 in Fig. 4.2).

Unequal N

By default, GLM and UNIANOVA produce Type 3 tests of significance (i.e., the same results that MANOVA provides with "METHOD=UNIQUE", its default). To obtain an alternative result, use the "METHOD" subcommand, for example, "METHOD = SSTYPE(2)". In addition, the means "EMMEANS" produces are unweighted.

Main Effect Contrasts and Post Hocs

To obtain main effect contrasts using the "CONTRAST" method using one of the canned contrasts, PAC would produce syntax similar to that discussed in chapter 4, for example, 'CONTRAST(factb)=DIFFERENCE'. "SPECIAL" contrasts are available in GLM and UNIANOVA for multifactor designs as well, but only from syntax. If you only want a contrast on one factor, you simply ignore the other (SPSS will assume the effects for the unnamed factor are zero). However, using the "CONTRAST" method, the "Sig" values are printed out, but F values are not provided in the printout and must be manually computed as described earlier for the one-factor designs (the exception here is if you specify one contrast at a time using the keyword "SPECIAL").

The "LMATRIX" subcommand is an alternative to the "CONTRAST" method and is the only way to obtain interaction contrasts. However, the "LMATRIX" subcommand in multifactor designs has the disadvantage of being more complicated. The syntax for the main effect contrasts for Factor A from chapter 4 (Fig. 4.11) using the alternative "LMATRIX" method is in Fig. 13.6.

5. /LMATRIX 'a1 vs. a3' facta 1 0 -1

6.   facta*factb 1/3 1/3 1/3 0 0 0 -1/3 -1/3 -1/3

7. /LMATRIX 'a1+a3 vs. a2' facta -1/2 1 -1/2

8.   facta*factb -1/6 -1/6 -1/6 1/3 1/3 1/3 -1/6 -1/6 -1/6

FIG. 13.6.   LMATRIX specifications to obtain main effect contrasts on Factor A in a two-factor between-subjects ANOVA.

It is important to note that, for the contrasts that were specified using the "LMATRIX" subcommand, you need to specify the contrast of interest on that factor and you must also specify weights that identify that contrast in the interaction effect. Thus, in line 5 you are telling SPSS that you want to test a1 versus a3, and identifying the weights that will do that, namely, 'facta 1 0 –1'. For reasons that will become clear, it is suggested that you always write the contrast weights so that one side's weights add up to +1 and the other side's to –1. On line 6 you are telling SPSS the same thing, but now identifying the contrast within the interaction effect. The easiest way to determine the correct weights is to list all possible combinations across a sheet of paper. In a 3×3 design, there are nine possible combinations:

a1b1   a1b2   a1b3   a2b1   a2b2   a2b3   a3b1   a3b2   a3b3

The cell identifiers should be combined with the factor listed first on the "UNIANOVA" command changing most slowly (thus Factor A changes most slowly here, i.e., the first three combinations are all for a1 and b1 changes to b2 for the second combination). After you have listed out the cell identifiers, you should copy the weights that identified the contrast on Factor A over to the interaction. Specifically, here you want all a1s to get a 1, all a2s to get a 0, and all a3s to get a –1. Thus, your weights so far would read:

a1b1	a1b2	a1b3	a2b1	a2b2	a2b3	a3b1	a3b2	a3b3
1	1	1	0	0	0	–1	–1	–1

As a last step, convert the whole numbers to fractions by determining how many cells there are with the same algebraic sign and dividing 1 or –1 by that number. Here there are three +1s, thus, each becomes a 1/3 and there are three –1s, thus, each becomes a –1/3, obtaining the weights in line 6. You must do this last step or the preceding contrast will not be estimated. You can use whole numbers, but whatever number your main effect adds up to must be the number that the interaction adds up to; so, for example, 'facta 3 –6 3 facta*factb 1 1 1 –2 –2 –2 1 1 1' would work, as both add up to 6 (+6 and –6), but 'facta 1 –2 1 facta*factb 1 1 1 –2 –2 –2 1 1 1' would not work, thus, the suggestion to simply use the +1/–1 convention.

To obtain the weights for line 8, you would follow the same steps described earlier. The contrast in line 7 is testing a1 + a3 versus a2, thus, your weights (using the +1/–1 rule) are –1/2 1 –1/2. To obtain line 8, again list out the cell identifiers and determine where you want 1s versus –1s. Here you want all a1s and a3s to have –1s and all a2s to have 1s.

a1b1	a1b2	a1b3	a2b1	a2b2	a2b3	a3b1	a3b2	a3b3
–1	–1	–1	1	1	1	–1	–1	–1

To determine how to turn these into fractions, note that there are six –1s, thus, each –1 becomes a –1/6 and there are three +1s, thus, each +1 becomes a 1/3, producing line 8. The results seen in Fig. 13.7 give the same Fs and significance values as their counterparts in chapter 4 (i.e., Fig. 4.12).

Custom Hypothesis Tests Index

1	Contrast Coefficients (L' Matrix)	LMATRIX Subcommand 1: a1 vs. a3
	Transformation Coefficients (M Matrix)	Identity Matrix
	Contrast Results (K Matrix)	Zero Matrix
2	Contrast Coefficients (L' Matrix)	LMATRIX Subcommand 2: a1+a3 vs. a2
	Transformation Coefficients (M Matrix)	Identity Matrix
	Contrast Results (K Matrix)	Zero Matrix

Custom Hypothesis Tests #1

Contrast Results (K Matrix)[a]

Contrast		Dependent Variable SCORE
L1	Contrast Estimate	-3.889
	Hypothesized Value	0
	Difference (Estimate - Hypothesized)	-3.889
	Std. Error	1.548
	Sig.	.022
	95% Confidence Interval for Difference Lower Bound	-7.140
	Upper Bound	-.638

a. Based on the user-specified contrast coefficients (L') matrix: a1 vs. a3

Test Results

Dependent Variable: SCORE

Source	Sum of Squares	df	Mean Square	F	Sig.
Contrast	68.056	1	68.056	6.314	.022
Error	194.000	18	10.778		

Custom Hypothesis Tests #2

Contrast Results (K Matrix)[a]

Contrast		Dependent Variable SCORE
L1	Contrast Estimate	1.833
	Hypothesized Value	0
	Difference (Estimate - Hypothesized)	1.833
	Std. Error	1.340
	Sig.	.188
	95% Confidence Interval for Difference Lower Bound	-.982
	Upper Bound	4.649

a. Based on the user-specified contrast coefficients (L') matrix: a1+a3 vs. a2

Test Results

Dependent Variable: SCORE

Source	Sum of Squares	df	Mean Square	F	Sig.
Contrast	20.167	1	20.167	1.871	.188
Error	194.000	18	10.778		

FIG. 13.7. Output for main effect contrasts in a two-factor between-subjects ANOVA using the LMATRIX subcommand.

Post hoc contrasts on main effects (i.e., on marginal means) in two-factor designs are easily accomplished by using the "POSTHOC" subcommand, described earlier. PAC also conducts these tests without syntax.

Simple Effects

Obtaining simple effects in GLM and UNIANOVA is considerably more complex than in MANOVA (because the keyword "WITHIN" is not allowed in GLM) and involves writing a series of contrasts using the "LMATRIX" subcommand. To demonstrate how to do this, the 3 × 2 example from chapter 4 will be used. In this example, the simple effects of Factor A at the two levels of Factor B were obtained. The syntax in Fig. 13.8 will produce the same simple effects results as in Fig. 4.14.

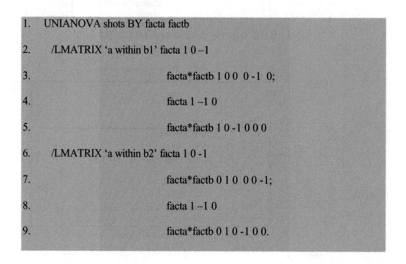

1.	UNIANOVA shots BY facta factb
2.	/LMATRIX 'a within b1' facta 1 0 –1
3.	facta*factb 1 0 0 0 -1 0;
4.	facta 1 –1 0
5.	facta*factb 1 0 -1 0 0 0
6.	/LMATRIX 'a within b2' facta 1 0 -1
7.	facta*factb 0 1 0 0 0 -1;
8.	facta 1 –1 0
9.	facta*factb 0 1 0 -1 0 0.

FIG. 13.8. Syntax commands to produce the simple effects of Factor A at both levels of Factor B in UNIANOVA.

Lines 2 through 5 test the simple effect of Factor A at the first level of Factor B and lines 6 through 9 test the simple effect of Factor A at the second level of Factor B. To test the simple effects, first write $k - 1$ contrasts for the factor that the simple effect is on, here, Factor A. For a simple effect, these $k - 1$ contrasts are tested at a specific level of the other factor. The set of contrasts does not have to be orthogonal. In the preceding example, $k - 1 = 2$; the two contrasts are, respectively, 1 0 –1 (lines 2 and 6) and 1 –1 0 (lines 4 and 8). As before, you must specify the contrast weights both on that factor (line 2) and on the interaction (cells; line 3). To determine the weights for the interaction (which is how you tell SPSS at which level to test the simple effect), write all the cell identifiers across a piece of paper and then match the overall contrast to each cell identifier. Here the first contrast on Factor A is 1 0 –1 and you want it to be at the first level of Factor B, so all of the b2s would get 0s:

a1b1	a1b2	a2b1	a2b2	a3b1	a3b2
	0		0		0

You can then simply copy the contrast weights into the blank spaces for the b1s:

a1b1	a1b2	a2b1	a2b2	a3b1	a3b2
1	0	0	0	–1	0

Put a semicolon after the first contrast to let SPSS know that it should test the contrasts before and after the semicolon as a set. The second contrast on Factor A is $1 - 1\ 0$ and is also tested at the first level of Factor B, thus, all the b2s again get 0s and for the b1s simply copy the weights over as seen in line 5:

a1b1	a1b2	a2b1	a2b2	a3b1	a3b2
1	0	−1	0	0	0

In lines 6 through 9, you are testing the simple effect of Factor A at the second level of Factor B, using the same contrasts on Factor A. Thus, all of the b1s are 0s and the b2s are copies of the contrast on Factor A. Abbreviated output is in Fig. 13.9.

Custom Hypothesis Tests #1

Test Results

Dependent Variable: SHOTS

Source	Sum of Squares	df	Mean Square	F	Sig.
Contrast	26.133	2	13.067	10.182	.001
Error	30.800	24	1.283		

Custom Hypothesis Tests #2

Test Results

Dependent Variable: SHOTS

Source	Sum of Squares	df	Mean Square	F	Sig.
Contrast	14.533	2	7.267	5.662	.010
Error	30.800	24	1.283		

FIG. 13.9.   Output for the simple effects of Factor A at both levels of Factor B in UNIANOVA.

It should be noted that the Fs and "Sig."s are identical to those obtained in Fig. 4.15. In this case, the two "Contrast Results (K Matrix)" tables should be ignored, because they contain the results of the two arbitrary contrasts (L1: 1 0 −1 and L2: 1 −1 0) that together comprise the simple effect. They would be examined more closely if simple comparison results were desired, as described in the next section.

Another way to obtain the simple effects is through the use of the "COMPARE" keyword on the "EMMEANS" subcommand. With this subcommand, you can test all pairwise differences on one factor at each level of the other, as well as obtain an F test for the set of contrasts at each level of the other factor (i.e., the simple effect). The syntax to do so is as follows:

```
/EMMEANS TABLES(facta*factb) COMPARE(facta)
```

You would obtain the output seen in Fig. 13.10.

Univariate Tests

Dependent Variable: SHOTS

FACTB		Sum of Squares	df	Mean Square	F	Sig.
1.00	Contrast	26.133	2	13.067	10.182	.001
	Error	30.800	24	1.283		
2.00	Contrast	14.533	2	7.267	5.662	.010
	Error	30.800	24	1.283		

Each F tests the simple effects of FACTA within each level combination of the other effects shown. These tests are based on the linearly independent pairwise comparisons among the estimated marginal means.

FIG. 13.10.   Output for the simple effects of Factor A at both levels of Factor B using the EMMEANS/ COMPARE method.

Simple Comparisons

Once you understand how to program the weights for simple effects, programming the weights for simple comparisons is identical, except for the fact that, instead of testing a set of contrasts, you will test a specific contrast. For example, in chapter 4 you tested the Control group versus the Imagine group for the varsity players (a1 vs. a2 at b1). The results were in Fig. 4.19. To test this in GLM or UNIANOVA, again use "LMATRIX". Specifically, all of the b2s would get 0s and you would then simply copy the contrast on Factor A into the b1 slots. The syntax to test this simple comparison in "UNIANOVA" follows. Interestingly, for simple comparisons and interaction contrasts, the contrasts do not have to follow the 1 versus −1 rule:

```
/LMATRIX 'a1 vs. a2 within b1' facta 1 −1 0
                           facta*factb 1 0 −1 0 0 0
```

If your contrast of interest was a pairwise comparison, you could use the "EMMEANS" subcommand as detailed earlier. Note, however, that you would not obtain the actual *F*-test values and would have to compute them by hand as shown earlier.

Interaction Contrasts

In chapter 4, you investigated whether the contrast of Control versus Imagine acted differently for (i.e., interacted with) the two types of players (see Fig. 4.21). In GLM and UNIANOVA this must again be explored with "LMATRIX", available only through syntax. The appropriate syntax is as follows:

```
/LMATRIX 'interaction contrast: a1 vs a2 by b' facta*factb 1 −1 −1 1 0 0
```

For an interaction contrast, you only need to specify weights for the interaction cells and not for the main effects. In order to obtain the weights, once again you would write the cell identifiers across the top of a piece of paper. Then write in the contrast weights from the contrast on Factor A (1 −1 0) at the first level of Factor B:

a1b1	a1b2	a2b1	a2b2	a3b1	a3b2
1		−1		0	

Then, using the same sequence of numbers, switch the signs for the second level of Factor B (switching the signs tells SPSS to test the contrast at b1 vs. b2), putting in −1 1 0:

a1b1	a1b2	a2b1	a2b2	a3b1	a3b2
1	−1	−1	1	0	0

You could also put the factors in a table and cross-multiply the weights as follows:

		1	-1	0
		a1	a2	a3
1	b1	1 × 1 = 1	-1 × 1 = -1	0 × 1 = 0
-1	b2	1 × -1 = -1	-1 × -1 = 1	0 × -1 = 0

You would specify the weights for the contrast on Factor A and cross-multiply those with the weights for Factor B (here Factor B only has two levels, thus, 1 −1 is the only possible contrast). You then copy the weights from the table into the "LMATRIX" syntax column by column, thus obtaining '1 −1 −1 1 0 0'. You can use the cross-products method for any of the analyses discussed earlier, putting in all 0s if there are no contrasts on a factor.

If both factors have more than two levels, things are more complex, but follow the same rules described previously. Again, for an interaction contrast, you will only be writing the weights for the interaction means. You first decide which contrast on Factor A is interacting with which contrast on Factor B. In chapter 4 you looked at a1 versus a2 by b1 versus b3 (see Fig. 4.22), thus the Factor A weights are 1 −1 0 and the Factor B weights are 1 0 −1. To obtain the interaction weights, write the cell identifiers across your paper. You are going to look at a contrast on Factor A at Level 1 versus Level 3 of Factor B, thus all b2s would get 0s:

a1b1	a1b2	a1b3	a2b1	a2b2	a2b3	a3b1	a3b2	a3b3
	0			0			0	

Next you would put in the Factor A weights at b1, thus putting in 1 −1 0 across the b1s:

a1b1	a1b2	a1b3	a2b1	a2b2	a2b3	a3b1	a3b2	a3b3
1	0		−1	0		0	0	

Finally, keep the numbers in the same sequence but reverse the signs when you put them in the b3 slots, so −1 1 0 will go in:

a1b1	a1b2	a1b3	a2b1	a2b2	a2b3	a3b1	a3b2	a3b3
1	0	−1	−1	0	1	0	0	0

Alternatively, using the cross-products method:

		1	−1	0
		a1	a2	a3
1	b1	1 × 1 = 1	−1 × 1 = −1	0 × 1 = 0
0	b2	1 × 0 = 0	−1 × 0 = 0	0 × 0 = 0
−1	b3	1 × −1 = −1	−1 × −1 = 1	0 × −1 = 0

Your weights would thus be '1 0 −1 −1 0 1 0 0 0'.

THREE OR MORE FACTOR ANOVA

It is recommended that MANOVA syntax rather than GLM or UNIANOVA syntax be used for all analyses not available in PAC (e.g., those requiring "SPECIAL" contrasts or "LMATRIX", such as simple effects, simple comparisons, simple simple comparisons, interaction contrasts, and simple interaction contrasts) for three or more factor designs. In principle, the "LMATRIX" methods suggested here may be extended to these complex analyses, but determining the weights becomes cumbersome and mistakes are easily made. In contrast, these types of analyses are quite simple to perform in MANOVA and the reader is referred to chapter 5.

ONE-FACTOR WITHIN-SUBJECTS ANOVA

Basic Commands

For within-subjects designs, PAC switches from the UNIANOVA to the GLM procedure. The syntax, however, is quite similar (in fact, in all previous examples in this chapter, identical results would be obtained by substituting "GLM" for "UNIANOVA"). However, "UNIANOVA" requires just one dependent variable to be named before the "BY" keyword on the main command, whereas "GLM" allows multiple dependent variables.

The PAC sequence described in Figs. 6.10 through 6.14 in chapter 6, when default commands and a certain keyword described later are deleted, would produce the basic syntax commands found in Fig. 13.11. Lines 1 and 2 are almost identical to the setup for a within-subjects analysis from chapter 6 (the primary difference being that you do not need to enclose the number of levels of the factor in parentheses). Lines 3 and 4 provide the means, power, and effect size, which are requested the same way as in "UNIANOVA" (see Fig. 13.1). It should be noted that, if you had pasted the syntax after setting this analysis up in PAC windows, line 2 would read 'WSFACTOR = facta 3 POLYNO-MIAL' because SPSS PAC automatically generates a trend analysis in GLM (see chap. 6) and will generate the trend analysis output whether or not you request it. The output of interest for the syntax in Fig. 13.11 has already been explained in chapter 6, in Figs. 6.15 and 6.16.

```
1.    GLM a1 a2 a3

2.      /WSFACTOR=facta 3

3d.     /EMMEANS=TABLES(facta)

4d.     /PRINT=ETASQ OPOWER.
```

FIG. 13.11.   Syntax for a one-factor within-subjects ANOVA in GLM.

Planned Contrasts

You can request any contrast by adding its keyword at the end of line 2 (e.g., "WSFACTOR=facta 3 SIMPLE"). If you are specifying "SPECIAL" contrasts, the contrasts do not have to be orthogonal, as they did for MANOVA contrasts. For example, to obtain the nonorthogonal contrasts from chapter 6 (Fig. 6.5), you would modify line 2, thus:

```
/WSFACTOR=facta 3 SPECIAL(1 1 1, 1 –2 1, 0 1 –1).
```

Note that for within-subjects factors you need the contrast of all ones and $k - 1$ contrasts. The output from this contrast is in Fig 13.12.

Tests of Within-Subjects Contrasts

Measure: MEASURE_1

Source	FACTA	Type III Sum of Squares	df	Mean Square	F	Sig.
FACTA	L1	259.200	1	259.200	5.268	.083
	L2	204.800	1	204.800	16.000	.016
Error(FACTA)	L1	196.800	4	49.200		
	L2	51.200	4	12.800		

FIG. 13.12.   GLM output from a SPECIAL contrast in a one-factor within-subjects ANOVA.

You can see that the obtained Fs are identical to those from Fig. 6.6. Note that GLM labels the contrasts as "L1", "L2", and so on, corresponding to which contrast you specified first, second, and so on.

Although the "TRANSFORM" subcommand from MANOVA does not function in GLM, and the "CONTRAST" and "LMATRIX" subcommands cannot be used for within-subjects factors, an alternative that, analogous to "LMATRIX", allows you to test only the contrasts desired, rather than exactly $k - 1$ of them, involves the "MMATRIX" subcommand. For the preceding contrasts, the syntax would be:

```
/MMATRIX 'a1+a3 v a2' ALL 1 –2 1;
'a2 v a3' ALL 0 1 –1.
```

The keyword "ALL" refers to all of the dependent variables named on the "GLM" command, in this instance, 'a1', 'a2', and 'a3' (an alternative to using the keyword "ALL" is to list each level of the factor involved in the contrast followed by its weight, here, 'a1 1 a2 −2 a3 1'). Results are found in Fig. 13.13.

Contrast Results (K Matrix)

Contrast[a]		Transformed Variable	
		a1+a3 v a2	a2 v a3
L1	Contrast Estimate	7.200	-6.400
	Hypothesized Value	0	0
	Difference (Estimate - Hypothesized)	7.200	-6.400
	Std. Error	3.137	1.600
	Sig.	.083	.016
	95% Confidence Interval for Difference Lower Bound	-1.509	-10.842
	Upper Bound	15.909	-1.958

a. Estimable Function for Intercept

Univariate Test Results

Source	Transformed Variable	Sum of Squares	df	Mean Square	F	Sig.
Contrast	a1+a3 v a2	259.200	1	259.200	5.268	.083
	a2 v a3	204.800	1	204.800	16.000	.016
Error	a1+a3 v a2	196.800	4	49.200		
	a2 v a3	51.200	4	12.800		

FIG. 13.13. Output from a SPECIAL contrast in a one-factor within-subjects ANOVA using the MMATRIX subcommand.

Post Hoc Tests

As was explained in chapter 6, PAC methods are not available for post hoc tests for within-subjects factors, precluding one of the real advantages of GLM over MANOVA. However, you can obtain all pairwise comparisons with either no adjustment or a Bonferroni or Sidak adjustment through the use of the "COMPARE" and "ADJUST" keywords on the "EMMEANS" subcommand as follows:

```
/EMMEANS TABLES(facta) COMPARE(facta) ADJUST(BONFERRONI)
```

Other post hoc tests must be conducted as planned contrasts, then corrections to significance levels must be applied manually by the researcher to the printout produced, as described in detail in chapter 3.

TWO OR MORE FACTOR WITHIN-SUBJECTS ANOVA

Adding in more within-subjects factors is done in almost exactly the same way as it is in MANOVA. The syntax to read in and analyze the data from Fig. 7.1 is in Fig. 13.14. You can see that lines 1 and 2 are almost identical to lines 4 and 5 in Fig. 7.2. The advantage of GLM over MANOVA for multiple-factor within-subjects designs is that it will generate the marginal means (lines 3 and 4). The overall output is similar to one-factor output, except now there would be tests for each effect, as well as the interaction. The output from this analysis is in Fig. 13.15.

```
1.    GLM a1b1 a1b2 a1b3 a1b4 a2b1 a2b2 a2b3 a2b4

2.    /WSFACTORS=facta 2 factb 4

3d.   /EMMEANS=TABLES(facta)

4d.   /EMMEANS=TABLES(factb)

5d.   /EMMEANS=TABLES(facta*factb)

6d.   /PRINT=ETASQ OPOWER.
```

FIG. 13.14.   Syntax commands to conduct a two-factor within-subjects ANOVA in GLM.

Tests of Within-Subjects Effects

Measure: MEASURE_1

Source		Type III Sum of Squares	df	Mean Square	F	Sig.	Eta Squared	Noncent. Parameter	Observed Power[a]
FACTA	Sphericity Assumed	34.031	1	34.031	30.533	.012	.911	30.533	.942
	Greenhouse-Geisser	34.031	1.000	34.031	30.533	.012	.911	30.533	.942
	Huynh-Feldt	34.031	1.000	34.031	30.533	.012	.911	30.533	.942
	Lower-bound	34.031	1.000	34.031	30.533	.012	.911	30.533	.942
Error(FACTA)	Sphericity Assumed	3.344	3	1.115					
	Greenhouse-Geisser	3.344	3.000	1.115					
	Huynh-Feldt	3.344	3.000	1.115					
	Lower-bound	3.344	3.000	1.115					
FACTB	Sphericity Assumed	127.844	3	42.615	33.997	.000	.919	101.992	1.000
	Greenhouse-Geisser	127.844	1.136	112.525	33.997	.007	.919	38.626	.980
	Huynh-Feldt	127.844	1.365	93.644	33.997	.003	.919	46.413	.994
	Lower-bound	127.844	1.000	127.844	33.997	.010	.919	33.997	.959
Error(FACTB)	Sphericity Assumed	11.281	9	1.253					
	Greenhouse-Geisser	11.281	3.408	3.310					
	Huynh-Feldt	11.281	4.096	2.754					
	Lower-bound	11.281	3.000	3.760					
FACTA * FACTB	Sphericity Assumed	3.094	3	1.031	3.062	.084	.505	9.186	.518
	Greenhouse-Geisser	3.094	1.690	1.831	3.062	.136	.505	5.173	.343
	Huynh-Feldt	3.094	3.000	1.031	3.062	.084	.505	9.186	.518
	Lower-bound	3.094	1.000	3.094	3.062	.178	.505	3.062	.235
Error(FACTA*FACTB)	Sphericity Assumed	3.031	9	.337					
	Greenhouse-Geisser	3.031	5.069	.598					
	Huynh-Feldt	3.031	9.000	.337					
	Lower-bound	3.031	3.000	1.010					

a. Computed using alpha = .050

FIG. 13.15.   GLM output from a two-factor within-subjects ANOVA.

The results of the sphericity test will determine which *F* value you look at (see chap. 6). The marginal and cell means output that results from the "EMMEANS" subcommands (lines 3–5) was presented in Fig. 7.19.

Main Effect and Interaction Contrasts

To specify a main effect contrast, simply place the contrast keyword after that factor name on the "WSFACTORS" subcommand. For example, to conduct the contrasts on Factor B from Fig. 7.4, you would change line 2 of Fig. 13.14 to be:

```
/WSFACTORS=facta 2 factb 4 SPECIAL (1 1 1 1, 3 –1 –1 –1, 0 –1 –1 2,
    0 1 –1 0)
```

In the output in Fig. 13.16 you can see that the obtained *F*s are identical to those from Fig. 7.5. (Remember that SPSS automatically generates the polynomial contrast, which is why the contrast on

Tests of Within-Subjects Contrasts

Measure: MEASURE_1

Source	FACTA	FACTB	Type III Sum of Squares	df	Mean Square	F	Sig.
FACTA	Linear		136.125	1	136.125	30.533	.012
Error(FACTA)	Linear		13.375	3	4.458		
FACTB		L1	946.125	1	946.125	26.434	.014
		L2	220.500	1	220.500	101.769	.002
		L3	24.500	1	24.500	29.400	.012
Error(FACTB)		L1	107.375	3	35.792		
		L2	6.500	3	2.167		
		L3	2.500	3	.833		
FACTA * FACTB	Linear	L1	21.125	1	21.125	14.486	.032
		L2	8.000	1	8.000	1.846	.267
		L3	2.010E-14	1	2.010E-14	.000	1.000
Error(FACTA*FACTB)	Linear	L1	4.375	3	1.458		
		L2	13.000	3	4.333		
		L3	1.000	3	.333		

FIG. 13.16.   GLM output for the contrast from Fig. 7.4.

"FACTA" is always labeled "Linear". Interaction contrasts are automatically produced in this way as well.)

As another example, consider a 3×3 design, with an interaction contrast desired as in Fig. 7.7 (Conditions 1 vs. 3 on Factor A by Conditions 2 vs. 3 on Factor B). All you have to do is specify the two contrasts as desired (e.g., 'WSFACTOR=facta 3 SIMPLE factb 3 REPEATED') and the interaction contrasts will automatically be generated as seen in Fig. 13.17, with the value pertaining to the desired interaction shaded.

Tests of Within-Subjects Contrasts

Measure: MEASURE_1

Source	FACTA	FACTB	Type III Sum of Squares	df	Mean Square	F	Sig.
FACTA	Level 1 vs. Level 3		78.028	1	78.028	19.372	.022
	Level 2 vs. Level 3		11.111	1	11.111	6.000	.092
Error(FACTA)	Level 1 vs. Level 3		12.083	3	4.028		
	Level 2 vs. Level 3		5.556	3	1.852		
FACTB		Level 1 vs. Level 2	7.111	1	7.111	32.000	.011
		Level 2 vs. Level 3	9.000	1	9.000	3.738	.149
Error(FACTB)		Level 1 vs. Level 2	.667	3	.222		
		Level 2 vs. Level 3	7.222	3	2.407		
FACTA * FACTB	Level 1 vs. Level 3	Level 1 vs. Level 2	1.000	1	1.000	.086	.789
		Level 2 vs. Level 3	225.000	1	225.000	16.463	.027
	Level 2 vs. Level 3	Level 1 vs. Level 2	64.000	1	64.000	19.200	.022
		Level 2 vs. Level 3	380.250	1	380.250	19.417	.022
Error(FACTA*FACTB)	Level 1 vs. Level 3	Level 1 vs. Level 2	35.000	3	11.667		
		Level 2 vs. Level 3	41.000	3	13.667		
	Level 2 vs. Level 3	Level 1 vs. Level 2	10.000	3	3.333		
		Level 2 vs. Level 3	58.750	3	19.583		

FIG. 13.17.   GLM output for an interaction contrast in a two-factor within-subjects ANOVA.

Simple Effects and Simple Comparisons

In order to conduct these types of analyses, a relatively easy and direct method is to select the subset of data that would be involved in the specific comparison of interest. For example, if you wished to test the simple effect of Factor B at the levels of Factor A, you would run two separate ANOVAs, one on a data set that had only the first level of Factor A and the other on a data set that had only the second level of Factor A. Thus, for the simple effects of Factor B at the first level of Factor A, you simply leave off all the a2s from the "GLM" command as follows:

```
GLM a1b1 a1b2 a1b3 a1b4
  /WSFACTOR=factb 4.
```

To obtain the simple effect of Factor B at the second level of Factor A, you would do the opposite and leave off the a1s as follows:

```
GLM a2b1 a2b2 a2b3 a2b4
  /WSFACTOR=factb 4.
```

If you ran these two sets of syntax, you would get the output in Fig. 13.18 (only the F test of interest has been included) and you can see that the Fs are identical to those from Fig. 7.10.

Tests of Within-Subjects Effects

Measure: MEASURE_1

Source		Type III Sum of Squares	df	Mean Square	F	Sig.
FACTB	Sphericity Assumed	46.688	3	15.563	17.372	.000
	Greenhouse-Geisser	46.688	1.667	28.014	17.372	.006
	Huynh-Feldt	46.688	3.000	15.563	17.372	.000
	Lower-bound	46.688	1.000	46.688	17.372	.025
Error(FACTB)	Sphericity Assumed	8.063	9	.896		
	Greenhouse-Geisser	8.063	5.000	1.613		
	Huynh-Feldt	8.063	9.000	.896		
	Lower-bound	8.063	3.000	2.688		

Tests of Within-Subjects Effects

Measure: MEASURE_1

Source		Type III Sum of Squares	df	Mean Square	F	Sig.
FACTB	Sphericity Assumed	84.250	3	28.083	40.440	.000
	Greenhouse-Geisser	84.250	1.181	71.309	40.440	.004
	Huynh-Feldt	84.250	1.499	56.206	40.440	.002
	Lower-bound	84.250	1.000	84.250	40.440	.008
Error(FACTB)	Sphericity Assumed	6.250	9	.694		
	Greenhouse-Geisser	6.250	3.544	1.763		
	Huynh-Feldt	6.250	4.497	1.390		
	Lower-bound	6.250	3.000	2.083		

FIG. 13.18. GLM output from two separate ANOVAs to obtain the simple effects of Factor B at levels of Factor A.

The following syntax yields the same simple comparison result of Fig. 7.11:

```
GLM a1b1 a1b2 a1b3 a1b4
  /WSFACTOR=factb 4 SPECIAL(1 1 1 1, –1 0 0 1, 0 1 –1 0, 1 –1 –1 1).
GLM a2b1 a2b2 a2b3 a2b4
  /WSFACTOR=factb 4 SPECIAL (1 1 1 1, –1 0 0 1, 0 1 –1 0, 1 –1 –1 1).
```

The output is in Fig. 13.19 and the F values of interest have been shaded; you can see they match the values in Fig. 7.12.

Tests of Within-Subjects Contrasts

Measure: MEASURE_1

Source	FACTB	Type III Sum of Squares	df	Mean Square	F	Sig.
FACTB	L1	81.000	1	81.000	22.091	.018
	L2	12.250	1	12.250	49.000	.006
	L3	.250	1	.250	.086	.789
Error(FACTB)	L1	11.000	3	3.667		
	L2	.750	3	.250		
	L3	8.750	3	2.917		

Tests of Within-Subjects Contrasts

Measure: MEASURE_1

Source	FACTB	Type III Sum of Squares	df	Mean Square	F	Sig.
FACTB	L1	156.250	1	156.250	69.444	.004
	L2	12.250	1	12.250	13.364	.035
	L3	.000	1	.000	.000	1.000
Error(FACTB)	L1	6.750	3	2.250		
	L2	2.750	3	.917		
	L3	6.000	3	2.000		

FIG. 13.19.   GLM output for two simple comparisons in a two-factor within-subjects ANOVA.

MIXED DESIGNS

PAC produces GLM syntax for mixed designs. To add a between-subjects factor, you would simply add in the between-subjects factor after the keyword "BY", as shown in Fig. 13.20.

```
1.    GLM b1 b2 b3 b4 BY facta

2.    /WSFACTOR=factb

3d.   /EMMEANS=TABLES(facta)

4d.   /EMMEANS=TABLES(factb)

5d.   /EMMEANS=TABLES(facta*factb)

6d.   /PRINT=ETASQ OPOWER.
```

FIG. 13.20.   Syntax commands to conduct a mixed ANOVA using GLM.

The output for a mixed design is similar to that for a within-subjects design. The "Within-Subjects Effects" portion will contain the tests for both the within-subjects factor and the interaction; at the end of that portion will be the test(s) of the between-subjects factor(s).

More Complex Analyses

For main effect contrasts, you would simply request them as described in earlier sections when there was only one type of factor in the design. You can also obtain the simple effects of the between-subjects factor through the use of the "COMPARE" keyword on the "EMMEANS" subcommand. You can obtain the multivariate, but not univariate, tests for the simple effects of the within-subjects factor in the same way (thus, it is suggested that MANOVA be used in that case). You can only obtain simple comparisons if they are pairwise and the tests will not provide the Fs. For interaction contrasts, you would use a combination of "LMATRIX" and "MMATRIX" subcommands. For example, the syntax in Fig. 13.21 would run the 'facta(2) BY factb(1)' interaction contrast from Fig. 8.10.

```
1.    GLM  b1 b2 b3 b4 BY facta

2.    /WSFACTORS=factb 4

3.    /MMATRIX 'b1 v b4' ALL 1 0 0 -1

4.    /LMATRIX 'a1+ a2 vs a3' facta  0 1 -1.
```

FIG. 13.21.   Syntax commands to conduct an interaction contrast in a mixed ANOVA in GLM.

The contrast on the between-subjects factor is set up in the same way as in a between-subjects design, namely, using the "LMATRIX" subcommand (line 4). The contrast on the within-subjects factor is set up using the "MMATRIX" subcommand, as described earlier (see line 3). The output of interest would be at the bottom under the "Custom Hypothesis Tests" section and you can see that the F obtained is identical to the F from Fig. 8.11 (see Fig. 13.22).

Custom Hypothesis Tests #1

Test Results

Transformed Variable: b1 v b4

Source	Sum of Squares	df	Mean Square	F	Sig.
Contrast	25200.125	1	25200.125	109.898	.000
Error	2063.750	9	229.306		

FIG. 13.22.   GLM output for an interaction contrast in a mixed ANOVA.

It is recommended for all other more complex designs (e.g., ANCOVA, random factors) that MANOVA syntax rather than UNIANOVA or GLM be used. Although it would be easy to obtain the basic syntax that GLM or UNIANOVA is using (by clicking on the Paste button), programming many of the more complex analyses is cumbersome and mistakes could easily be made.

References

American Psychological Association. (2001). *Publication manual of the American Psychological Association* (5th ed.). Washington, DC: Author.

Box, G. E. P. (1954). Some theorems on quadratic forms applied in the study of analysis of variance problems, II. Effect of inequality of variances and correlations between errors in two-way classification. *Annals of Mathematical Statistics, 25*, 484–498.

Braver, S. L., & Sheets, V. L. (1993). Monotonic hypotheses in multiple group designs: A Monte Carlo study. *Psychological Bulletin, 113*, 379–395.

Bryant, J. L., & Paulson, A. S. (1976). An extension of Tukey's method of multiple comparisons to experimental designs with random concomitant variables. *Biometrika, 63*, 631–638.

Cohen, J. (1988). *Statistical power analysis* (2nd ed.). Hillsdale, NJ: Lawrence Erlbaum Associates.

Geisser, S., & Greenhouse, S. W. (1958). An extension of Box's results on the use of the F distribution in multivariate analysis. *Annals of Mathematical Statistics, 29*, 885–891.

Harris, R. J. (2001). *A primer of multivariate statistics* (3rd ed.). Mahwah, NJ: Lawrence Erlbaum Associates.

Huitema, B. E. (1980). *The analysis of covariance and alternatives.* New York: Wiley.

Huynh, H., & Feldt, L. S. (1976). Estimation of the Box correction factor for degrees of freedom from sample data in the randomized block and split-plot designs. *Journal of Educational Statistics, 1*, 69–82.

Keppel, G. (1973). *Design and analysis: A researcher's handbook.* Englewood Cliffs, NJ: Prentice-Hall.

Keppel, G. (1982). *Design and analysis: A researcher's handbook* (2nd ed.). Englewood Cliffs, NJ: Prentice-Hall.

Keppel, G. (1991). *Design and analysis: A researcher's handbook* (3rd ed.). Englewood Cliffs, NJ: Prentice-Hall.

Kesselman, H. J., Rogan, J. C., Mendoza, J. L., & Breen, L. J. (1980). Testing the validity conditions of repeated measures F tests. *Psychological Bulletin, 87*, 479–481.

Kirk, R. E. (1982). *Experimental design: Procedures for the behavioral sciences* (2nd ed.). Monterey, CA: Brooks/Cole.

Levine, G. (1991). *A guide to SPSS for analysis of variance.* Hillsdale, NJ: Lawrence Erlbaum Associates.

Myers, J. L. (1979). *Fundamentals of experimental design* (3rd ed.). Boston: Allyn & Bacon.

Rencher, A. C. (1995). *Methods of multivariate analysis.* New York: Wiley & Sons.

SPSS Inc. (2001). *Statistical package for the social sciences* (version 11). Chicago: SPSS Inc.

Stevens, J. P. (1999). *Intermediate statistics: A modern approach* (2nd ed.). Mahwah, NJ: Lawrence Erlbaum Associates.

Stevens, J. P. (2002). *Applied multivariate statistics for the social sciences* (4th ed.). Mahwah, NJ: Lawrence Erlbaum Associates.

Tabachnick, B. G., & Fidell, L. S. (2000). *Using multivariate statistics* (4th ed.). Needham Heights, MA: Allyn & Bacon.

Tabachnick, B. G., & Fidell, L. S. (2001). *Computer-assisted research design and analysis.* Needham Heights, MA: Allyn & Bacon.

Winer, B. J. (1971). *Statistical principles in experimental design* (2nd ed.). New York: McGraw-Hill.

Winer, B. J., Brown, D. R., & Michels, K. M. (1991). *Statistical principles in experimental design* (3rd ed.). New York: McGraw-Hill.

APPENDIX A
F_T Values to Use for Tukey or Student-Newman-Keuls (SNK) Tests

df_{error}	α_{FW}	Number of Groups																		
		2	3	4	5	6	7	8	9	10	11	12	13	14	15	16	17	18	19	20
5	.05	6.62	10.58	13.62	16.07	18.18	20.03	21.65	23.12	24.43	25.70	26.79	27.90	28.88	29.80	30.65	31.44	32.24	32.97	33.70
	.01	16.25	24.36	30.42	35.45	39.69	43.43	46.75	49.70	52.43	54.92	57.25	59.30	61.38	63.17	64.98	66.70	68.21	69.74	71.16
6	.05	5.99	9.42	12.01	14.05	15.85	17.41	18.73	19.97	21.06	22.11	23.05	23.94	24.71	25.49	26.21	26.94	27.60	28.20	28.80
	.01	13.73	20.03	24.71	28.58	31.76	34.61	37.07	39.34	41.41	43.25	44.94	46.56	48.12	49.50	50.90	52.12	53.25	54.39	55.55
7	.05	5.58	8.65	10.95	12.80	14.36	15.74	16.94	18.00	18.97	19.85	20.67	21.45	22.18	22.85	23.46	24.08	24.64	25.21	25.70
	.01	12.25	17.52	21.39	24.57	27.16	29.49	31.52	33.37	35.03	36.55	37.93	39.25	40.50	41.59	42.69	43.71	44.75	45.60	46.56
8	.05	5.31	8.16	10.26	11.96	13.36	14.58	15.68	16.65	17.52	18.30	19.10	19.78	20.42	21.00	21.58	22.11	22.65	23.12	23.60
	.01	11.28	15.90	19.22	21.91	24.22	26.21	27.90	29.49	30.89	32.24	33.46	34.53	35.62	36.55	37.50	38.37	39.16	39.96	40.77
9	.05	5.12	7.80	9.72	11.33	12.60	13.73	14.74	15.62	16.47	17.23	17.88	18.54	19.16	19.72	20.22	20.74	21.19	21.65	22.04
	.01	10.58	14.74	17.76	20.16	22.18	23.87	25.42	26.86	28.05	29.26	30.26	31.28	32.24	33.05	33.87	34.69	35.36	36.04	36.72
10	.05	4.96	7.53	9.37	10.81	12.05	13.11	14.05	14.91	15.68	16.36	16.99	17.58	18.18	18.67	19.16	19.66	20.10	20.48	20.93
	.01	10.04	13.89	16.65	18.85	20.67	22.24	23.60	24.85	25.99	27.08	28.05	28.88	29.72	30.50	31.28	31.92	32.64	33.21	33.87
11	.05	4.84	7.30	9.07	10.44	11.62	12.65	13.52	14.31	15.07	15.74	16.30	16.88	17.41	17.88	18.36	18.79	19.22	19.66	20.03
	.01	9.64	13.26	15.79	17.82	19.53	21.00	22.24	23.39	24.43	25.42	26.28	27.08	27.83	28.58	29.26	29.88	30.50	31.05	31.60
12	.05	4.74	7.11	8.82	10.17	11.28	12.25	13.11	13.89	14.53	15.18	15.74	16.30	16.82	17.29	17.70	18.12	18.54	18.91	19.28
	.01	9.33	12.75	15.13	17.05	18.61	19.97	21.19	22.24	23.19	24.08	24.92	25.70	26.35	27.08	27.68	28.28	28.80	29.34	29.88
13	.05	4.68	6.96	8.61	9.90	11.00	11.91	12.75	13.47	14.15	14.74	15.29	15.85	16.30	16.76	17.17	17.58	17.94	18.30	18.67
	.01	9.07	12.30	14.58	16.42	17.88	19.16	20.29	21.32	22.24	23.05	23.81	24.57	25.21	25.85	26.43	27.01	27.53	27.98	28.50
14	.05	4.59	6.85	8.45	9.72	10.76	11.66	12.45	13.16	13.78	14.36	14.91	15.40	15.90	16.30	16.76	17.11	17.46	17.82	18.18
	.01	8.86	11.96	14.15	15.85	17.29	18.48	19.59	20.54	21.39	22.18	22.92	23.60	24.22	24.85	25.42	25.92	26.43	26.86	27.31
15	.05	4.53	6.73	8.32	9.55	10.53	11.42	12.20	12.90	13.52	14.10	14.58	15.07	15.51	15.96	16.36	16.70	17.11	17.41	17.76
	.01	8.69	11.71	13.78	15.46	16.82	17.94	18.97	19.91	20.74	21.45	22.18	22.85	23.39	24.01	24.50	24.99	25.49	25.92	26.35

(Continued)

APPENDIX A
(Continued)

Number of Groups

df_{error}	α_{FW}	2	3	4	5	6	7	8	9	10	11	12	13	14	15	16	17	18	19	20
16	.05	4.50	6.66	8.20	9.37	10.40	11.23	12.01	12.65	13.26	13.83	14.31	14.80	15.24	15.62	16.02	16.42	16.76	17.05	17.41
	.01	8.53	11.47	13.47	15.07	16.36	17.52	18.48	19.34	20.16	20.87	21.52	22.18	22.71	23.26	23.81	24.29	24.71	25.13	25.56
17	.05	4.44	6.59	8.08	9.25	10.22	11.05	11.81	12.45	13.06	13.57	14.10	14.53	14.96	15.35	15.74	16.07	16.42	16.76	17.05
	.01	8.41	11.23	13.21	14.74	16.02	17.11	18.06	18.91	19.66	20.35	21.00	21.58	22.18	22.65	23.19	23.60	24.08	24.50	24.85
18	.05	4.41	6.52	8.00	9.16	10.08	10.90	11.62	12.30	12.85	13.36	13.89	14.31	14.74	15.13	15.51	15.85	16.19	16.47	16.76
	.01	8.28	11.05	12.95	14.47	15.68	16.76	17.64	18.48	19.22	19.91	20.54	21.13	21.65	22.11	22.65	23.05	23.46	23.87	24.29
19	.05	4.38	6.44	7.92	9.03	9.99	10.81	11.47	12.10	12.70	13.21	13.68	14.10	14.53	14.91	15.29	15.62	15.96	16.25	16.53
	.01	8.20	10.90	12.75	14.20	15.40	16.42	17.35	18.12	18.85	19.53	20.10	20.67	21.19	21.65	22.11	22.58	22.98	23.39	23.74
20	.05	4.35	6.41	7.84	8.95	9.90	10.67	11.38	12.01	12.55	13.06	13.52	13.94	14.36	14.74	15.07	15.40	15.74	16.02	16.30
	.01	8.08	10.76	12.60	13.99	15.18	16.19	17.05	17.82	18.54	19.16	19.72	20.29	20.80	21.26	21.71	22.11	22.51	22.92	23.26
24	.05	4.26	6.23	7.61	8.69	9.55	10.31	10.95	11.57	12.10	12.55	13.01	13.42	13.78	14.15	14.47	14.80	15.07	15.40	15.62
	.01	7.84	10.35	12.05	13.36	14.42	15.35	16.19	16.88	17.52	18.12	18.67	19.16	19.59	20.03	20.42	20.80	21.19	21.52	21.85
30	.05	4.18	6.09	7.41	8.41	9.25	9.95	10.58	11.14	11.62	12.10	12.50	12.90	13.26	13.57	13.89	14.20	14.47	14.74	14.96
	.01	7.57	9.90	11.52	12.75	13.73	14.58	15.35	15.96	16.59	17.11	17.58	18.06	18.48	18.85	19.22	19.59	19.91	20.22	20.54
40	.05	4.09	5.92	7.18	8.16	8.95	9.64	10.22	10.72	11.19	11.62	12.01	12.40	12.70	13.06	13.31	13.62	13.89	14.10	14.36
	.01	7.30	9.55	11.05	12.15	13.06	13.83	14.53	15.13	15.68	16.19	16.59	16.99	17.41	17.76	18.12	18.42	18.73	18.97	19.28
60	.05	4.00	5.78	6.99	7.92	8.65	9.29	9.86	10.35	10.81	11.19	11.57	11.91	12.20	12.50	12.80	13.06	13.26	13.52	13.73
	.01	7.07	9.16	10.53	11.62	12.45	13.16	13.78	14.36	14.85	15.29	15.68	16.07	16.42	16.70	17.05	17.35	17.58	17.82	18.06
120	.05	3.92	5.64	6.77	7.68	8.41	8.99	9.50	9.99	10.40	10.76	11.09	11.42	11.71	12.01	12.25	12.50	12.70	12.95	13.16
	.01	6.85	8.82	10.13	11.09	11.86	12.55	13.11	13.57	14.05	14.42	14.80	15.13	15.46	15.74	16.02	16.30	16.53	16.76	16.99
∞	.05	3.84	5.48	6.59	7.45	8.12	8.69	9.20	9.64	9.99	10.35	10.67	10.95	11.23	11.52	11.76	11.96	12.15	12.35	12.55
	.01	6.62	8.49	9.68	10.58	11.33	11.91	12.45	12.90	13.31	13.68	13.99	14.31	14.58	14.85	15.07	15.35	15.51	15.74	15.96

Note.   Number of groups compared for Tukey test or number of groups between two compared (inclusive) for SNK.

APPENDIX B
F_D Values to Use for Duncan's New Multiple Range Test at $\alpha = .05$

Number of Steps Between Ordered Means

df_{error}	2	3	4	5	6	7	8	9	10	12	14	16	18	20	50	100
5	6.62	6.99	7.18	7.33												
6	5.99	6.41	6.62	6.77												
7	5.61	6.02	6.27	6.41	6.48	6.52										
8	5.31	5.75	6.02	6.20	6.30	6.34										
9	5.12	5.58	5.81	6.02	6.13	6.20										
10	4.96	5.45	5.68	5.88	5.99	6.02	6.02	6.02	6.02	6.02	6.02	6.02	6.02	6.06	6.06	6.06
11	4.84	5.35	5.61	5.75	5.88	5.92	5.95	5.99	5.99	5.99	5.99	5.99	6.02	6.06	6.06	6.06
12	4.74	5.22	5.54	5.64	5.78	5.85	5.92	5.92	5.99	5.99	5.99	5.99	6.02	6.06	6.06	6.06
13	4.68	5.15	5.45	5.61	5.71	5.81	5.85	5.92	5.95	5.95	5.99	5.99	6.02	6.02	6.02	6.02
14	4.59	5.06	5.35	5.54	5.68	5.75	5.81	5.85	5.92	5.95	5.99	5.99	6.02	6.02	6.02	6.02
15	4.53	4.99	5.28	5.48	5.64	5.71	5.78	5.85	5.88	5.92	5.95	5.99	6.02	6.02	6.02	6.02
16	4.50	4.96	5.22	5.45	5.58	5.68	5.75	5.81	5.88	5.92	5.95	5.99	6.02	6.02	6.02	6.02
17	4.44	4.90	5.18	5.38	5.54	5.64	5.71	5.78	5.85	5.88	5.95	5.99	6.02	6.02	6.02	6.02
18	4.41	4.87	5.15	5.35	5.51	5.61	5.68	5.75	5.81	5.88	5.95	5.99	6.02	6.02	6.02	6.02
19	4.38	4.84	5.09	5.31	5.48	5.58	5.68	5.75	5.81	5.88	5.92	5.99	6.02	6.02	6.02	6.02
20	4.35	4.81	5.06	5.28	5.45	5.51	5.64	5.71	5.78	5.85	5.92	5.99	6.02	6.02	6.02	6.02
22	4.29	4.74	5.02	5.25	5.41	5.48	5.61	5.68	5.75	5.85	5.92	5.95	5.99	6.02	6.02	6.02
24	4.26	4.71	4.96	5.18	5.38	5.45	5.58	5.68	5.71	5.81	5.92	5.95	5.99	6.02	6.02	6.02
26	4.23	4.68	4.93	5.15	5.35	5.45	5.58	5.64	5.71	5.81	5.88	5.95	5.99	6.02	6.02	6.02
28	4.21	4.62	4.90	5.12	5.31	5.41	5.54	5.61	5.68	5.78	5.88	5.92	5.99	6.02	6.02	6.02
30	4.18	4.62	4.87	5.12	5.28	5.35	5.51	5.61	5.68	5.78	5.88	5.92	5.99	6.02	6.02	6.02
40	4.09	4.53	4.81	5.02	5.18	5.25	5.45	5.54	5.61	5.75	5.85	5.88	5.99	6.02	6.02	6.02
60	4.00	4.44	4.74	4.93	5.12	5.18	5.38	5.48	5.54	5.68	5.78	5.85	5.95	6.02	6.02	6.02
100	3.92	4.35	4.65	4.87	5.06	5.09	5.31	5.41	5.51	5.64	5.78	5.85	5.95	6.02	6.02	6.02
∞	3.84	4.26	4.56	4.77	4.96	5.09	5.22	5.31	5.41	5.58	5.71	5.81	5.92	6.02	6.02	6.02

Author Index

A

American Psychological Association, 23, 149

B

Box, G. E. P., 71
Braver, S. L., 36, 37
Breen, L. J., 70
Brown, D. R., 106, 128, 140
Bryant, J. L., 124

C

Cohen, J., 23, 24

F

Feldt, L. S., 70, 71, 72
Fidell, L. S., 45, 47, 48, 127, 131, 149

G

Geisser, S., 71
Greenhouse, S. W., 71

H

Harris, R. J., 149
Huitema, B. E., 124, 125
Huynh, H., 70, 71, 72

K

Keppel, G., 21, 24, 25, 27, 29, 30, 31, 32, 33, 35, 45, 46,
    47, 48, 51, 54, 64, 70, 71, 106, 124, 132, 133, 137,
    138
Kesselman, H. J., 70

Kirk, R. E., 31

L

Levine, G., ix, x

M

Mendoza, J. L., 70
Michels, K. M., 106, 128, 140
Myers, J. L., 71

P

Paulson, A. S., 124

R

Rencher, A. C., 70
Rogan, J. C., 70

S

Sheets, V. L., 36, 37
SPSS, ix
Stevens, J. P., 24, 59, 67, 70, 120, 140

T

Tabachnick, B. G., 45, 47, 48, 127, 131, 149

W

Winer, B. J., 31, 106, 128, 140

Subject Index